DAY BY DAY

Presented to Jamie (ᵇᵇ ᴥ ᵇᵇ)

By Angelina & ESTHER

On June 16ᵗʰ 2012

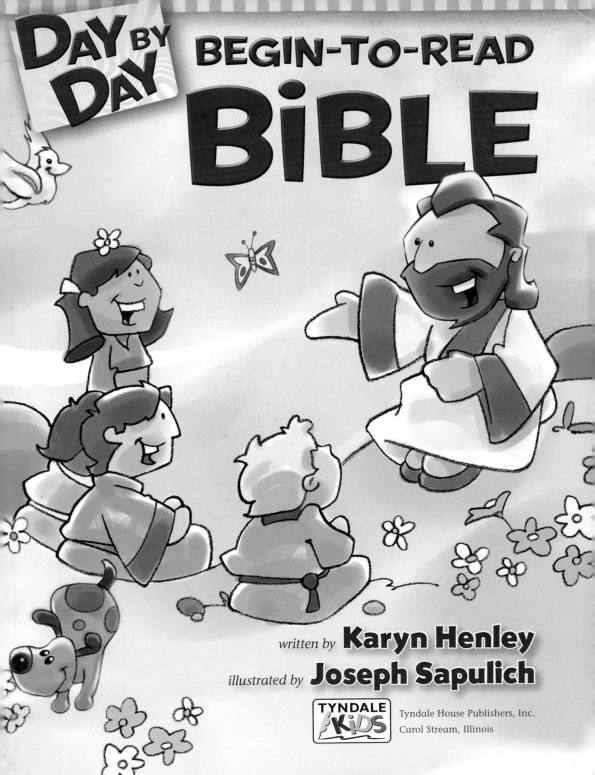

Day by Day
BEGIN-TO-READ
BIBLE

written by **Karyn Henley**

illustrated by **Joseph Sapulich**

TYNDALE KiDS

Tyndale House Publishers, Inc.
Carol Stream, Illinois

TYNDALE is a registered trademark of Tyndale House Publishers, Inc.

The Tyndale Kids logo is a trademark of Tyndale House Publishers, Inc.

Day by Day Begin-to-Read Bible

Copyright © 2007 by Karyn Henley. All rights reserved. Exclusively administered by Child Sensitive Communication, LLC. For permission to copy excerpts from this book, contact Tyndale House Publishers, Inc., 351 Executive Drive, Carol Stream, IL 60188.

Cover and interior illustrations copyright © 2007 by Joseph Sapulich. All rights reserved.

Designed by Luke Daab

Cover design by Julie Chen

Edited by Betty Free Swanberg

Adapted for beginning readers by Karyn Henley from her *Day by Day Kid's Bible*, published in 2002 by Tyndale House Publishers

---

Library of Congress Cataloging-in-Publication Data
Henley, Karyn.
   Day by day begin-to-read Bible / by Karyn Henley ; illustrations by Joseph Sapulich.
     p. cm. — (Tyndale kids)
Rev. ed. of: Day by day Kid's Bible
ISBN-13: 978-1-4143-0934-7 (hc)
ISBN-10: 1-4143-0934-1 (hc)
1. Bible stories, English. I. Sapulich, Joe. II. Henley, Karyn. Day by day kid's Bible. III. Title. IV. Series.
BS551.3.H47 2007
220.9'505—dc22
                                   2006009681

Printed in Thailand
13   12   11   10   09   08   07
7   6   5   4   3   2   1

Contents

Letter from Karyn Henley to Adult Friends   *x*
Letter from Karyn Henley to Young Friends   *xii*

Stories in the Order They Happened

(Complete list of stories in Bible-book order at the back)

Old Testament

Week 1: Genesis   *1*

Week 2: Genesis   *9*

Week 3: Genesis; Exodus   *17*

Week 4: Exodus   *25*

Week 5: Exodus; Numbers; Deuteronomy; Joshua   *33*

Week 6: Joshua; Judges; Ruth   *41*

Week 7: 1 Samuel   49

Week 8: 1 Samuel; Psalm 34   57

Week 9: 1 and 2 Samuel; 1 Chronicles;
Psalms 23; 46; 61; 77   65

Week 10: Psalms 95; 121; 1; 37; 50   73

Week 11: Psalms 84; 92; 8; 19; 24   81

Week 12: Psalms 33; 65; 93; 98; 100   89

Week 13: Psalms 104; 119; 139   97

Week 14: Psalms 150; 20; 32; 42; 131   105

Week 15: 1 Kings; 2 Chronicles   113

Week 16: Proverbs   121

Week 17: Proverbs   129

Week 18: Song of Songs; Ecclesiastes; 1 Kings;
2 Chronicles   137

Week 19: 1 Kings; 2 Chronicles   145

Week 20: 2 Kings   153

Week 21: 2 Chronicles; Obadiah; 2 Kings; Joel   161

Week 22: Jonah; Hosea; 2 Chronicles; Amos; Isaiah 169

Week 23: Isaiah; Micah 177

Week 24: 2 Kings; Isaiah 185

Week 25: Nahum; 2 Kings; 2 Chronicles; Zephaniah; Jeremiah 193

Week 26: Jeremiah; Habakkuk; Daniel; 2 Kings 201

Week 27: Lamentations; Ezekiel; Daniel 209

Week 28: Daniel; Job 217

Week 29: Job; Ezra; Haggai 225

Week 30: Zechariah; Psalm 147; Esther 233

Week 31: Malachi; Nehemiah 241

New Testament

Week 32: Matthew 1–2; Luke 1–2   *251*

Week 33: Matthew 3–4; Mark 1; Luke 3–4; John 1–2   *259*

Week 34: Matthew 9; Mark 2; Luke 5; John 4–5   *267*

Week 35: Matthew 5–6; 8; 12; Mark 3; Luke 6–7   *275*

Week 36: Matthew 8–9; 13; Mark 4–5; Luke 7–8; 13   *283*

Week 37: Matthew 9; 14; Mark 6–7; Luke 9; John 6   *291*

Week 38: Matthew 17; Mark 9; Luke 9; 17;
John 9–10   *299*

Week 39: Luke 10; 15; John 11   *307*

Week 40: Matthew 19; 21; 26; Mark 10–11; 14;
Luke 18–19; John 12   *315*

Week 41: Matthew 21; 25–26; Mark 12; 14;
Luke 21–22   *323*

Week 42: Matthew 26; Mark 14; Luke 22;
John 13–14; 18   *331*

Week 43: Matthew 27–28; Mark 15–16;
Luke 23–24; John 18–20   *339*

Week 44: Matthew 28; Mark 16; Luke 24;
John 20–21; Acts 1–3   *347*

Week 45: Acts 6–10   355

Week 46: Acts 12–14; 16; Galatians;
1 Thessalonians   363

Week 47: 1 Corinthians; Acts 19–20;
2 Corinthians; Romans   371

Week 48: Acts 23–27   379

Week 49: Acts 28; Colossians; Philemon   387

Week 50: Ephesians; Philippians; 1 Timothy;
Titus; James   395

Week 51: Jude; 1 Peter; Hebrews   403

Week 52: 1 John; Revelation   411

My Prayer   419
Complete List of Stories in Bible-Book Order   420
About the Author   429
About the Illustrator   431

Dear Adult Friends,

Young children, after seeing parents and older siblings read the Bible, look forward to reading the Bible on their own. So it's often a disappointment when they try to read but still can't. With the *Day by Day Begin-to-Read Bible*, early readers can journey on their own through the entire Bible in one year. They'll just need a little help with a few of the Bible names and terms.

The readings in this Bible are arranged in the order in which they happened historically. They parallel the order of the *Day by Day Kid's Bible*, which is written for the next reading level. This Begin-to-Read edition contains selections for five days a week. For each weekend, you will find a suggestion for passages that an adult or older sibling can read to the child from a traditional Bible or from the *Day by Day*

Kid's Bible. However, the weekend readings are not essential for your child's enjoyment and understanding of this overview of the Bible.

After reading each daily Begin-to-Read selection, your child can read the "I did it!" line and point to the star. It's not necessary to start the readings on January 1. Simply begin at the beginning, and let your child keep track of his or her progress.

May you and your child both be blessed by getting to know God better and growing to love him more as you read this Bible together.

By God's grace, to his glory,

Karyn

Hi Friend,

This Bible was made just for you.

Read it yourself to find out what God is like.

A grown-up can help with words you don't know.

You will read stories and songs.

You will read wise sayings and letters.

These are all from the Bible.

You can read one story a day.

At the end of the reading, the words
  by the star mean, "I read the story!"

Ready? Read and enjoy!

Love,

Karyn Henley

Old Testament

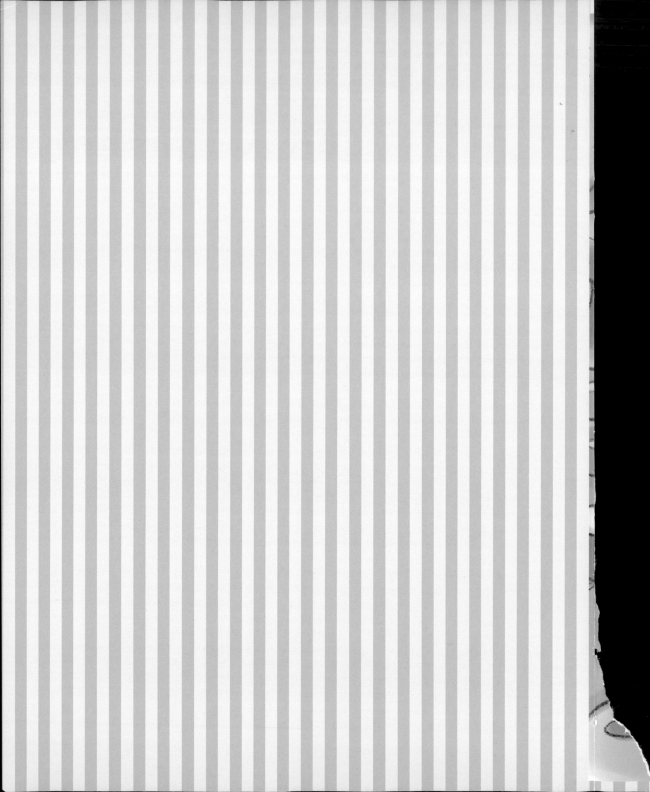

That Is Good!

Genesis 1:1–2:7

At first, there was no color. No shape.

All was dark and deep.

But God's Spirit moved softly over the water.

Then God said, "Light!" And light glowed.

"Sky!" said God. Sky rolled out wide.

"Water, move. Come up, land."

Up came mountains. Rivers flowed.

Seas and lakes and beaches formed.

"Now plants and trees!" said God.

Forests, grasses, and gardens grew.

"Let's have lamps in the sky!" said God.

The sun beamed, the moon and stars gleamed.

"Come, animals!" said God, and they came

creeping, jumping, swimming, flying.

"Now a man." Out of the dust,

God formed a man and breathed life into him.

"Good!" said God. "That is good!"

I did it! ☆

2

Adam's Helper

Genesis 2:15-22; 3:20

Adam took care of God's garden
   and picked names for the animals.
When Adam was hungry, he ate
   different kinds of fruit from the garden.
But God said, "Do not eat the fruit
   on the tree of knowing good and bad."
So Adam left that fruit alone.
Keeping a garden and naming animals
   were big jobs. Adam needed a helper.
The animals could not help.
So God made a woman to help Adam.
Adam named his new helper Eve.

I did it! ☆

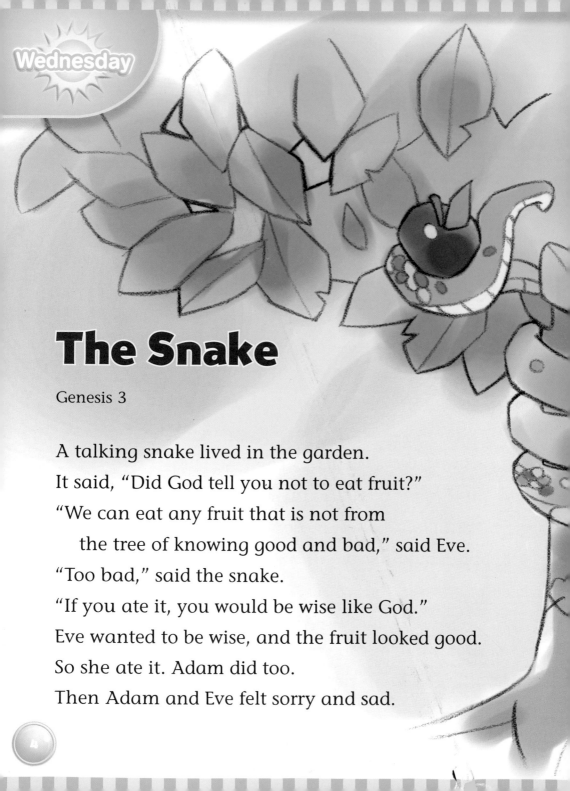

The Snake

Genesis 3

A talking snake lived in the garden.

It said, "Did God tell you not to eat fruit?"

"We can eat any fruit that is not from

the tree of knowing good and bad," said Eve.

"Too bad," said the snake.

"If you ate it, you would be wise like God."

Eve wanted to be wise, and the fruit looked good.

So she ate it. Adam did too.

Then Adam and Eve felt sorry and sad.

When God came to walk with them, they hid.

"Did you eat the fruit?" God asked.

Adam pointed to Eve. Eve pointed to the snake.

God pointed to the place that was outside
of the garden.

"You will have to leave the garden," he said.

I did it! ☆

A Big Boat

Genesis 6–8

After the time when Adam and Eve lived,
    people became mean and always did bad things.
Only Noah and his family kept loving God.
"I am going to start all over," said God.
"Noah, build a big, big boat."
Noah sawed and hammered and built a huge boat.
Then God brought animals: bee and flea,
    ox and fox, cat, bat, rat, dog, hog, frog.

Into the boat they went, big and small,
    short and tall, and last of all, Noah's family.
Rain drip-dropped, then rushed, then gushed.
Waves of water lifted the boat.
Off it floated for days and days until at last
    the sun came out and the water went down.
Out of the boat came animals big and small,
    short and tall, and last of all, Noah's family.
Noah said, "Thank you, God."

I did it! ☆

7

The Tower

Genesis 11:1-9

"High, high, high. Up to the sky.
We will build a tower," the people said.
"Everyone will say we are the best!"
But God said, "People want to rule the world.
They must not make a tower."
So he gave each of them a different language.
One said, "POH." Another said, "NWEE."
One said, "NAHK." Another said, "NEEK-tah."
They all meant "night."
But they could not understand each other.
So they all moved away to different places
    and never finished their tower.

I did it! ☆

Note to Parents: If you have the *Day by Day Kid's Bible*, read "Abram's Travels Begin" (page 9) and "Lot Chooses His Land" (page 10) to your child this weekend (Genesis 12–13).

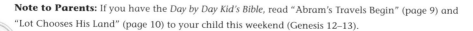

A Visit

Genesis 15:5-6; 18:1-15; 21:1-3

God talked to a man named Abraham.

"Count the stars if you can," God said.

"That's how many people will be
in your family someday."

Abraham trusted God to keep his promise.

One hot day Abraham saw three men
walking along.

He called, "Come and eat with me."

9

Abraham set out milk, meat, and bread.
One man said, "You and your wife, Sarah,
    will have a baby boy."
Sarah laughed. She thought she was too old.
"Is anything too hard for me?" asked God.
Some time later, Abraham and Sarah
    did have a baby boy. They named him Isaac.

I did it! ☆

Looking for a Wife

Genesis 24:1-27

Isaac grew up to be a fine young man.

He was ready to get married.

Abraham called a man who worked for him.

"Go find a good wife for my son," he said.

So the man rode his camels a long way.

One day, he stopped at a well and prayed.

"If a girl gives water to me and my camels,

   I will know she is the right one," he said.

Lots of girls came to the well.

But they did not share their water.

At last, a girl named Rebekah came.

She filled her jug with water.

Then she shared it with the man and his camels.

"Thank you, God," said the man.

"This is the girl I have been looking for."

I did it! ☆

12

Twins

Genesis 25:19-34

Rebekah married Abraham's son Isaac.

They had twin boys named Esau and Jacob.

Esau was born first.

He liked to be outdoors and became a good hunter.

Isaac liked to eat the meat Esau cooked.

So he loved Esau best.

But Jacob liked to stay home around the tents.

He learned how to cook good soup.

Even Esau liked the soup Jacob made.

Rebekah loved Jacob best.

I did it! ☆

A Trick

Genesis 27:1-41

Isaac grew old. He could not see.

He told Esau, "Go hunt for wild meat.

Cook it, and I will pray for you after I eat it."

Isaac would pray the blessing for the first born,

asking for good things to come to Esau.

But Rebekah wanted Jacob to get the blessing.

So she cooked goat meat to taste like wild meat.

She put goat skins on Jacob's hands

to make them feel hairy like Esau's.

Jacob took the meat to Isaac
  and said, "I am Esau."
"You sound like Jacob," said Isaac.
"But you feel like Esau."
Then Isaac prayed the blessing for the first born.
Some time later, Esau brought in his wild meat.
Then Isaac knew he had prayed for good things
  to come to Jacob and not Esau.
"Pray for me, too, Father!" Esau said.
So Isaac prayed, but it was not the blessing
  for the first born.
Esau was so angry, he wanted to kill Jacob.

I did it! ☆

The Ladder

Genesis 27:42-43; 28:10-16

Rebekah told Jacob how angry Esau was.

So Jacob was afraid Esau would kill him.

Jacob left to go to his uncle's house.

But night came before he got there.

So he had to sleep on the ground
with a rock for a pillow.

That night, God sent Jacob a dream.

Angels were going up and down a ladder.

God stood at the top.

He said, "I am with you, Jacob.

I will take care of you."

Jacob woke up. He said,
"God is here, and I didn't even know it!"

I did it! ☆

Note to Parents: If you have the *Day by Day Kid's Bible*, read "Jacob in the Land of the East" (page 25) and "Working for a Wife" (page 26) to your child this weekend (Genesis 29).

Going Home

Genesis 29:1–33:4

Jacob went to live with Uncle Laban.

He worked hard for his uncle for seven years,
    taking care of Laban's sheep.

Then he got married and had 12 sons.

One day, God told Jacob to go back home.

So Jacob and his big family packed up.

They left to go back to where Jacob grew up.

But Jacob was afraid Esau would still be mad.

So he sent gifts to Esau: goats and sheep,
    cows and bulls, camels and donkeys.

After that, he saw Esau coming with 400 men!

He was afraid they would fight his family.

Esau came closer. Then he hugged Jacob.

And Jacob knew everything would be all right.

I did it! ☆

Hard Times

Genesis 37; 39

One of Jacob's sons was Joseph.
Jacob loved Joseph and gave him a new coat.
That made Joseph's big brothers angry.
Joseph dreamed that his brothers
    were stars in the sky.
The stars all bowed to Joseph.

His big brothers got so angry at his dream
  that they threw Joseph into a dry well.
Then they sold him to some men
  who were going far away to Egypt.
In Egypt, Joseph worked for a captain.
But the captain got mad and sent Joseph to jail.
So Joseph helped take care of the jail.
Joseph did not understand why
  he was having such hard times.
But he knew God was taking care of him.

I did it! ☆

The King's Dream

Genesis 41:1-43

One night, the king of Egypt had a dream.
Seven thin cows ate up seven fat cows.
Seven thin plants ate up seven fat plants.
"What do my dreams mean?" asked the king.
His wise men did not know.
"Joseph can tell you," someone said.
"I cannot tell you," said Joseph. "But God can.
He wants you to know that your dreams mean
     food will grow for seven years.
Then for seven more years, no food will grow."
The king knew that God had helped Joseph
     become very wise.
He gave Joseph a gold necklace and fine clothes.
He made Joseph his best helper.

I did it! ☆

Joseph's Brothers

Genesis 41:46–47:12; 50:15-21

For seven years, Joseph saved food in barns.
So when no food grew and people were hungry,
  they could buy food in Egypt.
Even Joseph's brothers came to buy food there.
They bowed to Joseph
  without knowing who he was.
Joseph asked them about their family.
At last he said, "I am your brother Joseph."
His brothers were scared,
  because they had been mean to Joseph.

"Do not be afraid," said Joseph.
"You meant to hurt me,
   but God made it all work out for good."
Then all of Joseph's family moved to Egypt,
   and Joseph took care of them there.

I did it! ☆

22

The Princess and the Basket

Exodus 1:6–2:10

After Joseph's time,
   a mean king began to rule Egypt.
He said, "There are too many Jewish people.
Kill all the Jewish baby boys."
One mother hid her baby boy in a basket.
It floated among the plants at the river's edge.
The baby's sister watched nearby.

Soon the princess came to the river.

She found the basket with the baby inside.

She wanted the baby for herself.

But she let the baby's mother take care of him
until he was old enough to live in the palace.

The princess named the baby "Moses."

I did it! ☆

Note to Parents: If you have the *Day by Day Kid's Bible*, read "Running Away" (page 48) to your child this weekend (Exodus 2).

A Bush on Fire

Exodus 3:1-14

Moses grew up to be a leader.

At first he led only sheep out in the fields.

Then one day, he saw a bush on fire.

Moses watched, but the bush did not burn up.

Then Moses heard God say,

"Go to the king of Egypt.

Tell him to let my people go."

"But I cannot talk very well," said Moses.

"Don't worry," said God. "I will help you."

"What if people ask who sent me?" said Moses.

"Tell them you were sent by

THE ONE WHO ALWAYS IS," said God.

"That is my name."

I did it! ☆

The Stick

Exodus 4:1-5, 18-20, 29-31

Moses wondered, "What if the people
   don't believe what I say?"
"Throw down your walking stick," said God.
Moses threw down his walking stick.
It turned into a snake!
"Pick it up by its tail," said God.
Moses picked it up.

It turned back into a walking stick!

"Show that to the people," said God.

"Then they will listen."

So Moses went to Egypt.

He showed the stick and snake to the people,
and they believed that God had sent him.

I did it! ☆

Hay Bricks

Exodus 5:1–6:1

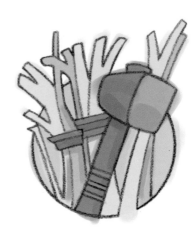

Moses told the king of Egypt
    to let God's people leave.
But the king just got angry.
"These people are my workers," said the king.
"They make bricks for my buildings.
You are trying to keep them from working."
Then the king made the people work harder.
"They will have to gather their own hay
    to make bricks," he said.
The people got angry with Moses.
"You made the king hate us!" they told him.
But God said to Moses,
    "Now watch what I can do.
I will make the king let my people go."

I did it! ☆

Wonders

Exodus 7:13–12:42

The king of Egypt would not let God's people go.
So God turned the water of Egypt into blood.
The king still would not let God's people go.
So God sent frogs all over the land.
But the king did not care.
So God sent tiny biting bugs,
    and then clouds of flies.

Animals got sick and died. People got sick.

But the king did not care.

God sent thunder and hail.

Grasshoppers ate up the plants.

Darkness covered the land so no one could see.

Still the king would not let God's people go.

One night, people all over Egypt began to cry,
    because someone in every house had died.

But no one died in the houses of God's people.

The king told Moses, "Take your people and go!"

That night, God had Moses take his people
    out of Egypt.

I did it! ☆

Across the Water

Exodus 14:5–15:21

The king of Egypt changed his mind
about letting God's people go.
He sent his army to bring them back.
God's people hurried to get away.
But they came to a big sea.
"What will we do now?" they cried.
"Don't worry," said Moses.
"Watch how God helps."

31

God told Moses to hold his walking stick
   over the sea.
When Moses did, the water moved out of the way.
The people walked across the sea on dry land.
Then the water flowed back across their path.
The king and his army could not follow.
God's people danced and sang and thanked God.

I did it! ☆

Note to Parents: If you have the *Day by Day Kid's Bible*, read "Making a Fuss for Food" (page 62) and "Water from a Rock" (page 64) to your child this weekend (Exodus 15–17).

A Thundering Cloud

Exodus 19:1-2, 16-20; 20:1-21; 24:1-3

God's people camped by a mountain.

The top of the mountain was covered in clouds.

Inside the cloud, thunder boomed
    and lightning blazed.

God called Moses to meet him on the mountain.

So Moses walked up into the cloud.

There God gave Moses rules for his people.

God said they should not worship any other gods.

They should not kill or steal or lie.

They should keep the worship day special, and
    treat fathers and mothers as important people.

Moses went back to the people
    and told them God's rules.

The people said, "We will do what God says."

I did it! ☆

A New Land

Numbers 13:1–14:35

God led his people to a new land.
But before they went into the land,
    they sent 12 men to see what it was like.
The men brought back grapes and figs.
"It is land with lots of milk and honey,"
    the 12 men said.
"But we cannot take the land," said 10 of them.
"The strong, tall people who live there will kill us."
"God will help us take the land,"
    said two of the men.
But the people were afraid and did not trust God.
God said, "You do not think I can help you.
So you will not get to live in this good land.
Instead, you will travel for 40 more years."

I did it! ☆

A Talking Donkey

Numbers 22:1-6, 21–24:9

God's people camped near the land of Moab.

The king of Moab was afraid of them.

He sent a letter to a man named Balaam.

"Come and pray for bad things to happen
    to God's people," the letter said.

So Balaam rode his donkey to go see the king.

On the way, his donkey kept stopping.

Every time the donkey stopped, Balaam beat it.

But the donkey was stopping
    because it saw an angel in the road.
At last, God made the donkey say,
    "Why are you beating me?"
Then Balaam saw the angel too.
"Pray for good things to happen
    to God's people," said the angel.
And that is just what
    Balaam did.

I did it! ☆

Moses' Song

Deuteronomy 31:19-22; 32:1-14, 18-20, 36, 43

God told Moses to write this song
   and teach it to the people.
Then they would not forget God.
They would not forget what he had done.

Listen, sky. Listen, land.

My teaching is as wonderful
    as rain on new grass.

God is like a Rock for us.

Everything he does is right.

He keeps his promises.

Remember the old days.

God gave his people milk, wheat, and grapes.

But they forgot God.

So God turned his face away from them.

But God will be kind to people who follow him.

God will save his land and his people.

I did it! ☆

A Wall Falls

Joshua 2; 3:17; 6

Joshua became the new leader of God's people.
He asked two of his men to go into the city
    where the enemy lived.
The two men came to Rahab's house.
"We must hide," said the men.
So Rahab hid them on top of her flat roof.
"Thank you," said the men. "You helped us."
Rahab told them, "Now you can help me.
Please save me and my family."
"Hang a red cord from your window,"
    said the men. "We will see it and save you."

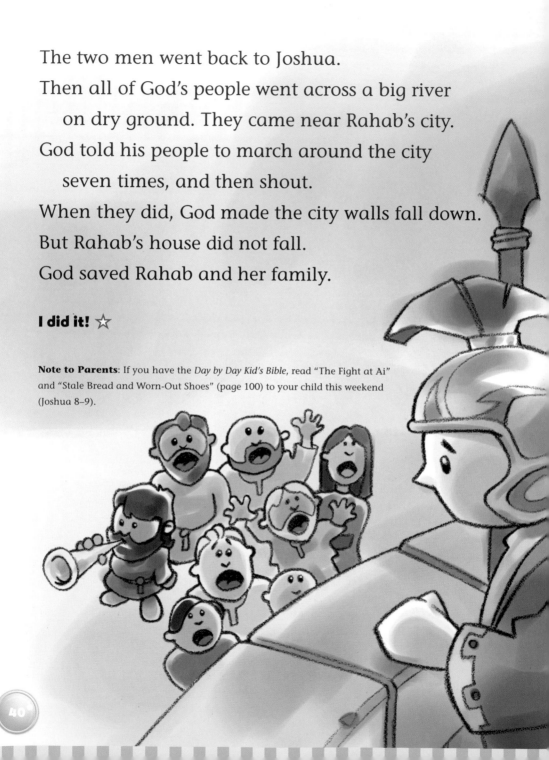

The two men went back to Joshua.

Then all of God's people went across a big river
on dry ground. They came near Rahab's city.

God told his people to march around the city
seven times, and then shout.

When they did, God made the city walls fall down.

But Rahab's house did not fall.

God saved Rahab and her family.

I did it! ☆

Note to Parents: If you have the *Day by Day Kid's Bible*, read "The Fight at Ai"
and "Stale Bread and Worn-Out Shoes" (page 100) to your child this weekend
(Joshua 8–9).

The Sun Stands Still

Joshua 10:1-15

The people from the land of Gibeon
    were friendly to God's people.
But that made kings of other lands angry.
The kings got their armies
    and went to fight Gibeon.
"Help!" the people of Gibeon cried to Joshua.
He was the leader of God's people.

God told Joshua, "Do not be afraid.
    I will help you."
So Joshua led God's people
    to a fight with the kings' armies.
God helped by
    making the kings' armies get mixed up.
He made big hail stones fall on them.
Then God made the sun and moon stand still
    until his people could win the fight.

I did it! ☆

Fire and Horns

Judges 6:1-16; 7

God's people stopped following God.

So God let the enemy take over.

Then God's people cried to him, "Help us!"

God chose Gideon to be their leader.

But God let Gideon have only a small army.

Gideon led his small army out to fight at night.

Each man hid a burning stick inside a jar.

And each man took a horn.

They stood around the enemy, hiding their lights.

All of a sudden, they broke the jars.

They held their lights high,
    blew their horns, and shouted.

All the men from the big enemy army ran away.

They were scared. So God's people won.

I did it! ☆

Lots of Leaders

Judges 3:12–4:5; 10:3-16; 12:7-15

God's people turned away from him
  again and again.
Each time they did,
  the enemy army would take over.
The people would cry to God for help.
Then God would send a leader called a judge
  to help them. One leader was left handed.
He killed a fat king and saved God's people.
Another leader fought with a stick
  that had been made for leading oxen.

One leader was a woman
who sat under a palm tree.
Another leader had 30 sons who rode 30 donkeys.
One leader had 30 sons and 30 daughters!
Another leader had 40 sons and 30 grandsons,
and they rode 70 donkeys!
God always helped his people
when they called to him.

I did it! ☆

45

Ruth

Book of Ruth

Once there were two women, Ruth and Naomi.

They were very sad,

because their husbands had died.

"I am going back to my old home," said Naomi.

"I will go with you," said Ruth.

They traveled a long way to Naomi's old home.

When they got there, Ruth had to work.

She got a job picking barley out of a field.

The farmer that the field belonged to

was a kind man named Boaz.

Boaz and Ruth fell in love and got married.

Then they had a baby boy named Obed.

Naomi helped take care of the baby.

Now Naomi and Ruth were happy again.

God had turned their sadness into joy.

I did it! ☆

Samson

Judges 13; 16

One time, God chose Samson to lead his people.
God made Samson strong
   and said he should never cut his hair.
Now the enemy wanted to get rid of Samson.
So they asked a lady to learn how to catch him.
Samson told her, "Tie me with bow strings."
But he broke the bow strings. Easy.
He said, "Tie me with a new rope."
But he broke the rope. Easy.

47

He said, "Thread my hair like yarn
   into the loom you make cloth on."
But he pulled away. Easy.
At last Samson said, "Cut my hair."
The lady did. Now Samson was not strong.
The enemy caught him.
But Samson's hair grew back. He got strong again.
One day, the enemies were making fun of him.
So he pushed on the posts that held up their roof.
Their house fell.
God helped Samson win at last.

I did it! ☆

Note to Parents: If you have the *Day by Day Kid's Bible*, read "A Sad Prayer and a Happy Answer" (page 121) to your child this weekend (1 Samuel 1–2).

Samuel

1 Samuel 3:1-20

Samuel helped in the worship tent
when he was a boy.
One night while he was in bed,
he heard someone say, "Samuel."
He ran to Eli, the priest. "Here I am," he said.
"I did not call you," said Eli. "Go back to bed."
Samuel went back to bed. He heard, "Samuel."
He ran to Eli. "Here I am."

"I did not call you," said Eli. "Go back to bed."
Samuel went back to bed. He heard, "Samuel."
He ran to Eli. "Here I am."
Eli told him that the next time
    he should say, "I hear you, God."
Samuel went back to bed. He heard, "Samuel."
"I hear you, God," said Samuel.
Then God talked to Samuel,
    and Samuel told Eli what God said.

I did it! ☆

Fighting with Thunder

1 Samuel 3:19-21; 7:2-13

Samuel grew up. He became a prophet of God.
One day, the enemy army came
    to fight God's people.
The enemy won, and God's people cried.
"Stop praying to idols. They are fake gods,"
    said Samuel.
"Follow the true God. He will help you."
So the people put away their idols
    and prayed to God.
One day, the enemy army came to fight again.
God's people were scared.
"We need God!" they said.

So Samuel prayed to God.
Then God spoke in a voice
    that sounded like thunder.
God's voice scared the enemy army,
    and they ran away.
So Samuel set up a stone.
He called it the Help Stone.
"God has helped us this far," he said.

I did it! ☆

Lost Donkeys

1 Samuel 9:1–10:1

Saul was a tall young man.

One day, his father's donkeys ran away.

Saul looked and looked but did not find them.

So he went to ask Samuel about it.

God told Samuel, "Saul will be the king

    for my people."

Samuel told Saul,

    "Do not worry about the donkeys.

Your father found them.

God wants you to know that you will be king."

Then he took Saul to his house for dinner,

    and Saul spent the night there.

I did it! ☆

A King behind the Bags

1 Samuel 10:17-24; 13:1; 14:47-48; 15:10-23

When it was time for Saul to become king, he hid.

No one could find him.

God told Samuel that Saul was hiding
   behind bags.

That's where Samuel found Saul.

Samuel told the people, "Here is your king!"

Saul stood up. He was taller than everyone else.

"Long live our king!" the people shouted.

At first Saul was a good king.

But then he stopped obeying God.

So God had to give Samuel bad news for Saul:

God would choose a new king.

I did it! ☆

54

Choosing a New King

1 Samuel 16:1-13

A man named Jesse had eight sons.
God told Samuel that one of them
   would be the new king.
Samuel saw Jesse's oldest son and said,
   "This must be the one God chose to be king."
But God said, "Do not choose by his looks.

I see what is in people's hearts."

Seven of Jesse's sons came to see Samuel,

   but God said not to choose any of them.

"One more son is with the sheep," said Jesse.

"Go and get him," said Samuel.

The last son came. His name was David.

"David is the one who will be king," said God.

I did it! ☆

Note to Parents: If you have the *Day by Day Kid's Bible*, read this weekend about Jonathan and his father, Saul, when Saul was still the king. Read "Jonathan Climbs up a Cliff" and "Honey on a Stick" (page 134) to your child (1 Samuel 14).

David and the Giant

1 Samuel 17:1-51

David knew God wanted him to be king someday.

But it was not yet time. David was still a boy.

One day David went to take food

    to his brothers who were in the army.

He saw that a giant

    was making the whole army feel scared.

"I will fight that giant," said David.

He picked up five small rocks.

"Ha!" said the giant.

"I will feed you to the birds."

"You come to fight with a sword," called David.

"But I come in the name of the Lord."

David threw his first rock at the giant.

It hit the giant's head, and the giant fell.

When the enemy army saw that, they ran away.

I did it! ☆

A Friend and a Spear

1 Samuel 18:1-9; 19:8-24

King Saul's son Jonathan was David's best friend.
Jonathan gave David his robe and his long shirt.
He also gave David his belt, his sword,
    and his bow for shooting arrows.

King Saul gave David a job leading the army.
David was so good at his job,
    people sang about it.
But King Saul was angry,
    because people liked David best.
One day when David played his harp for the king,
    Saul threw his spear at David to kill him.
So David ran away. But King Saul chased him.

I did it! ☆

The Arrow

1 Samuel 20

David asked Jonathan,

"Why does Saul want to kill me?"

"My father will not kill you," said Jonathan.

"I am not going to dinner with him," said David.

"I will go," said Jonathan.

"If he is angry, I will tell you.

I will shoot an arrow.

If it lands close by, you can come back.

If it lands far away,

you must run from my father."

So David hid in a field,
  and Jonathan went to dinner.
Later, Jonathan took a boy to the field.
Jonathan shot an arrow and called to the boy,
  "Go get the arrow. It landed far away."
David knew this was a sign
  that the king was angry.
He hugged Jonathan, said good-bye, and left.

I did it! ☆

62

David Hides

1 Samuel 24

David had to hide,
   because King Saul wanted to kill him.
Lots of strong men went with David to help him.
One day David and his men hid in a cave.
King Saul and his men were nearby.
King Saul needed a restroom,
   so he went into the cave.
He did not see David and his men inside.
David's men said, "Now you can kill the king!"
"No," said David. "That would be wrong."
David knew God would make him king
   at the right time.

I did it! ☆

Taste and See

by David, written when he was running from Saul

Psalm 34:4, 8-10

I called to God, and he heard me.

God saved me from all my troubles.

Taste and see. God is good.

Good things come to people who trust him.

People who love him have all they need.

Lions might get hungry and weak.

But people who look to God

    have every good thing they need.

I did it! ☆

Note to Parents: If you have the *Day by Day Kid's Bible*, read "The Man Whose Name Means 'Fool' " (page 151) and "In Saul's Camp at Night" (page 153) to your child this weekend (1 Samuel 25–26).

David Becomes King

1 Samuel 31:1-6; 2 Samuel 2:1-4; 1 Chronicles 12:23-40

The enemy army came to fight God's people,
and the enemy began to win.
They killed three sons of King Saul one day.
The king died that day too.
So God's people chose David to be their king,
just as God had said they would.
People brought donkeys and oxen to David.
They brought him bags of food,
and cakes made of figs and raisins.
Everyone was very happy.
David lived in Jerusalem.
The people called it David's City.
David became great, because God was with him.

I did it! ☆

My Shepherd *by David*

Psalm 23

The Lord is my shepherd.

I am like a sheep that has everything it needs.

God takes me to green fields so I can rest.

He brings me to peaceful water.

He makes me strong again.

He leads me in the way that is right.

Sometimes I feel like I am
    in a valley of dark shadows.
But I will not be afraid,
    because you are with me, God.
You make me feel safe.
You set a table for me
    even when my enemies are near.
You make me feel special.
My life is full. I have more than I need.
Your love and goodness will always be with me.
And I will be with God forever.

I did it! ☆

Be Still *by Korah's family*

Psalm 46

God is like a safe place.

He is strong. He helps when there is trouble.

So we will not be afraid
　　even if the earth shakes.

Even if mountains fall into the sea.

Even if oceans roar and make huge waves.

"Be still and know that I am God.
All people will call me great."
God has all the power, and he is with us.

I did it! ☆

A High Rock *by David*

Psalm 61

Hear me call to you, God.
Please listen to me pray.
I call to you from the ends of the earth.
I call out when I am tired.
You are like a rock that is higher than I am.
You are like a strong tower where I can be safe.
I want to live with you forever.
I want to be safe under your wings.

I will always sing songs of praise
    to your name.
Every day I will do my part
    to keep my promises to you.

I did it! ☆

God Who Does Wonders *by Asaph*

Psalm 77:13-19

Your ways are best, God.

You are the God who does wonders.

When the water saw you, it splashed.

Clouds spilled their rain.

Your thunder was loud in the wind.

Your lightning lit up the world.

The earth shook.

You made a path through the sea.

But no one saw your footprints.

I did it! ☆

Note to Parents: If you have the *Day by Day Kid's Bible*, read "A Whole Heart" and "Under His Wings" (page 188) to your child this weekend (Psalms 86; 91).

The Deep Earth in His Hand

Psalm 95:1-7

Come! Let's sing with joy to God!

He is the great King above all gods.

He holds the deep earth in his hands.

The mountain peaks belong to him.

The sea is his, because he made it.

His own hands made the dry land.

So let's bow down to show God our Maker

    how wonderful we think he is.

He is our God, and we are his people.

We are like sheep that he loves and leads.

I did it! ☆

My Eyes Look Up

Psalm 121

My eyes look up to the hills.

Where does my help come from?

My help comes from God.

He made heaven and earth.

God will not let you trip and fall.

He watches over you and never sleeps.

God is the shade at your right hand.

The sun will not hurt you during the day.

The moon will not hurt you at night.

God will keep you safe.

He will watch over you when you go out
and when you come in.

He will watch over you now
and forever.

I did it! ☆

A Tree by the Water

Psalm 1

Good things come to people
   who are happy to follow God's way.
Day and night they think about what God says.
They are like trees growing by the river.
They give fruit at the right time.
Their leaves never dry up.

Everything they do turns out good.

It is not that way for sinful people.

They are like dust that the wind blows away.

God watches over people who do what is right.

But the path of sinful people goes nowhere.

I did it! ☆

Like the Sun at Noon *by David*

Psalm 37:1-9

Do not worry because of sinful people.

Do not wish to be like people who do wrong.

They will dry up like grass and die like plants.

Trust in God, and do what is good.

Live and enjoy being safe.

Choose to always follow God.

Trust him, and he will help you.

He will make your goodness glow like sunshine.

Be with God, and be still.

Be quiet and wait for him.

Keep away from anger, and don't worry.

People who trust God will get all he has for them.

I did it! ☆

Every Animal *by Asaph*

Psalm 50:7-15

"Hear me, my people, and I will speak to you.

I am your God.

Every forest animal is mine.

I own the cows on the hills.

I know every bird in the mountains.

The animals in the fields are mine.

If I were hungry, I would not tell you.

The world and everything in it is mine.

Give thanks to me. Keep your promises to me.

Call on me when you are in trouble,

and I will save you.

Then everyone will see how great I am."

I did it! ☆

Note to Parents: If you have the *Day by Day Kid's Bible*, read "Riches" (page 194) and "My Feet Almost Tripped" (page 195) to your child this weekend (Psalms 49; 73).

Even the Sparrow *by Korah's family*

Psalm 84:1-3, 10

The place where you live is beautiful, God.

I want to be with you.

You are the living God.

Even the sparrow has a home with you.

The swallow has a nest there too.

She can raise her baby birds

    at a safe place near you.

One day with you in your house is better

    than a thousand days anywhere else.

I did it! ☆

Morning and Night

Psalm 92:1-2, 12-15

It is good to praise you, God.
It is good to make music to your name, Most High.
In the morning, it is good to talk about your love.
At night, it is good to remember
how you keep promises.
People who do what is right
will grow like palm trees.

They will grow as tall as cedar trees.
They will grow in God's palace
and stay fresh and green.
They will say, "God is right.
There is no sin in him."

I did it! ☆

Children and Babies Praise *by David*

Psalm 8

Lord, our Lord, your name is great!

Your greatness is higher than the sky.

You planned for children and babies to praise you.

I see the sky you made with your hands.

I see the moon and stars you put in place.

Then I wonder why you even think about people.

I wonder why you care about us.

But you made us
important to you.
You put people
in charge of
everything you made:
sheep and cows,
wild animals, birds in
the sky, fish in the sea.
Lord, our Lord, your name is great!

I did it! ☆

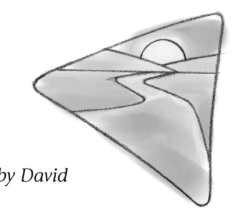

God's Way *by David*

Psalm 19:1-4, 7-11, 14

The sky shows how great God is.

It tells his greatness every day.

It shows his greatness every night.

No matter what language people speak,

   they can understand what the sky says.

God's way is best and keeps us strong.

His rules are better than gold.

They are sweeter than honey.

Good comes to people who obey them.

I want everything I say and think

   to make you happy, God.

I did it! ☆

The Great King *by David*

Psalm 24:1-4, 7-10

The earth and everything in it belong to God.

He made the land and set it on the sea.

Who can live with God?

Only people who don't keep thinking about sin.

Only people who put God first.

Lift up your heads, you gates.

Open up, you doors.

Then the Great King can come in.

Who is this Great King?

God, strong and full of power.

He is the Great King.

I did it! ☆

Note to Parents: If you have the *Day by Day Kid's Bible*, read "Tell about God" and "Who Is Strong?" (page 202) to your child this weekend (Psalms 29; 33:12-22).

A New Song

Psalm 33:3, 5-9, 11

Sing a new song to God.

The earth is full of his love.

The sky was made by his word.

The stars were made by breath

from his mouth.

He brings the sea waves together.

He keeps the deep water in store houses.

All the earth should be filled

with wonder for God.

All people should know how special he is.

He said one word, and the world was made.

The plans of his heart always come true.

I did it! ☆

The Hills Look Glad *by David*

Psalm 65:9-13

God, you take care of the land.
You water it and make it ready to grow crops.
Your rivers flow full of water.
You soak the fields and make them flat.
You send light rain so the dirt becomes soft.

You make good crops grow
    so we have plenty of food.
Carts spill over with more food than we need.
The hills look glad, and sheep fill the fields.
Crops of grain cover the valleys.
        The fields and valleys
            all shout and sing for joy.

I did it! ☆

91

The Thunder of the Water

Psalm 93:1-4

God, you are King!

Greatness is like a robe you wear.

You became King long ago.

You have lived forever.

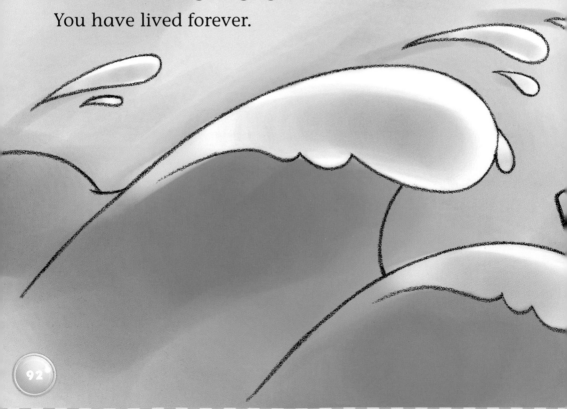

The ocean lifts up its voice.

The seas lift up their pounding waves.

But you are stronger than the thunder of the water.

You are stronger than the waves of the sea.

I did it! ☆

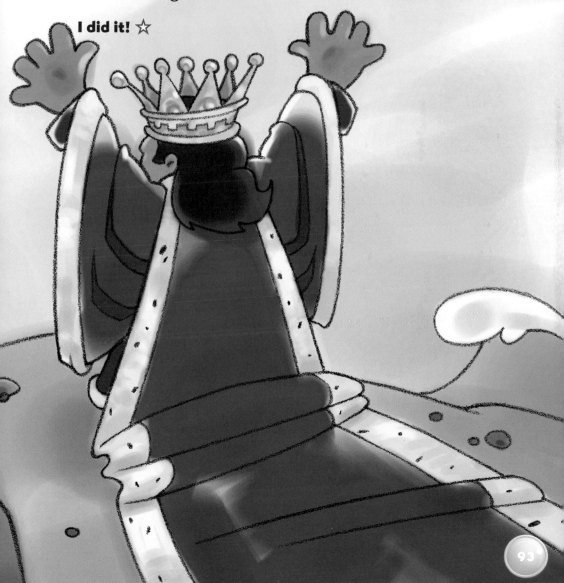

Make Music!

Psalm 98:4-9

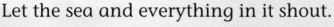

Shout to God with joy.

Sing glad songs with music.

Make music to God with harps and horns.

Shout with joy before God, the King!

Let the sea and everything in it shout.

Let the world and everyone in it sing.
Let rivers clap their hands.
Let mountains sing with joy.
Let them all sing to God.

I did it! ☆

His Sheep

Psalm 100:3-5

Know that the Lord is God.

He made us. We are his people.

We are like sheep in his field.

So go through God's gates giving thanks.

Go into his palace with praise.

Give thanks to him.

Shout for his name, because God is good.

His love has no end.

He always keeps his promises.

I did it! ☆

Note to Parents: If you have the *Day by Day Kid's Bible*, read "As High As the Sky" (page 206) and "Sunrise to Sunset" (page 208) to your child this weekend (Psalm 103; 113).

Wings of Wind

Psalm 104:1-4

My soul will shout for God!

The Lord my God is very great.

He wraps himself in light.

He rolls out the sky like a tent.

He puts his upstairs rooms in the rain clouds.

He rides the clouds.

He sails on wings of wind.

Winds carry his messages.

Flames of fire serve him.

I did it! ☆

Tuesday

The Earth and the Deep, Wide Sea

Psalm 104:10-12, 14, 17-19, 24-25, 33, 35

God makes springs of water
flow into rivers where wild donkeys drink.
Birds make nests nearby and sing in the trees.
God grows grass for cows,
and he grows plants for people.

98

The stork makes its home in the pine trees.

Wild goats live in the high mountains.

Badgers hide in the rocks.

The moon shows the seasons.

The sun knows when to go down.

You have made so many things, God!

The earth and the deep, wide sea

    are full of living things, big and small.

I will sing to God all my life.

    Shout for God, my soul! Praise God!

I did it! ☆

Sweet Words

Psalm 119:103, 105, 110-111

Your words taste so sweet, Lord.

They are sweeter than honey in my mouth.

Your word is like a lamp

    that shows my feet where to go.

It is like a light for my path.

I will not leave your ways.

Your rules will always be a gift for me.

Your ways fill my heart with joy.

I did it! ☆

You Know Me *by David*

Psalm 139:1-10

God, you know me.

You know when I sit down and when I get up.

You know what I am thinking.

You know when I go out and when I lie down.

You know all my ways.

Even before I say a word,

    you know everything I will say, God.

You go behind me and in front of me.
You put your hand on me.
I do not understand this, but it is wonderful.
Where can I go to get away from your Spirit?
If I go up into space, you are there.
If I go deep into the earth, you are there.
I could fly on the morning's wings.
I could land far beyond the sea.
But even there, your hand will lead me.
Your right hand will hold on to me.

I did it! ☆

In the Secret Place *by David*

Psalm 139:13-18

You made every part of me, God.

You put me together inside my mother.

I praise you, because the way you made me
is wonderful.

My body was not hidden from you
when you made me in the secret place.

You saw my body before it had a shape.

You planned all my days. You wrote them in
your book, even before I had lived one of them.

103

What you think about is so important to me, God!

I can't count all the things you think.

If I could, I am sure

    the number of your thoughts would be

    more than all the bits of sand in the world.

I did it! ☆

Note to Parents: If you have the *Day by Day Kid's Bible*, read "You Made Me Bold" (page 212) and "Wonderful Love" (page 213) to your child this weekend (Psalms 138; 145).

Dancing

Psalm 150

Praise God in his mighty heavens.

Praise him for the powerful things he has done.

Praise him for how great he is.

Praise him with horns and harps.

Praise him with tambourines and dancing.

Praise him with flutes and ringing cymbals.

Let everything that lives praise God!

I did it! ☆

Chariots and Horses *by David*

Psalm 20:1-2, 4, 6-8

I pray that God will answer you
    when you are sad.
I pray that God will watch over you
    and send you help.
I pray that he will make your plans work out.
God answers his people from heaven.

He saves them with his great power.

Some people trust in horses.

Some people trust in chariots.

Those people will fall someday.

But we trust in God.

We will always stand strong.

I did it! ☆

Not like a Horse *by David*

Psalm 32:8-10

God says, "I will teach you how you should live.

I will watch over you.

Do not be like a horse or a mule.

Horses and mules don't understand.

They have to be led by a bit in their mouth.

They will not move

without a harness and long reins."

People who do bad things have many troubles.

But the people who trust God

will always have God's love to help them.

I did it! ☆

Like a Deer *by Korah's family*

Psalm 42:1-3, 7-8, 11

My soul is like a deer that is thirsty for water.
My soul is thirsty for the living God.
When can I meet with God?
My tears are all I have for food day and night.
Deep water roars down in a waterfall.
I feel like its waves have rolled over me.
But God sends his love every day.
At night he sends his song.

So why am I sad?

Why am I troubled inside?

I will trust God.

I will praise him,

   because he saves me.

I did it! ☆

Like a Well-Fed Baby *by David*

Psalm 131

My heart is not proud, God.

I do not worry about things

    that are too big for me to understand.

I do not worry about things

    that are too wonderful for me.

My soul is still and quiet

    like a well-fed baby with its mama.

I will put my hope in you, God, now and forever.

I did it! ☆

Note to Parents: If you have the *Day by Day Kid's Bible*, read "Do Not Trust Princes" (page 218) and "Clap!" (page 219) to your child this weekend (Psalms 146; 47).

Solomon's Wise Choice

1 Kings 2:10-12; 3:5-15

King David had a son named Solomon.

He became the king after David died.

One night, God came to Solomon in a dream.

"What do you want most of all?" asked God.

"I want to be wise," said Solomon.

"You did not ask for a long life," said God.

You did not ask for money or riches.

You did not ask for your enemies to die.

You asked to be wise.

So I will give you what you asked for.

You will be the wisest of all kings.

I will also make you rich and great."

I did it! ☆

A Wise King

1 Kings 3:16-27

One day two women came to King Solomon.
"This lady took my baby, because hers died,"
    said one woman.
"No," said the other woman.
"The dead baby is yours,
    and the living one is mine."
"Then cut the baby in two," said Solomon.
"You can each have half."
"Okay," said one woman.
"If I cannot have the baby,
    you will not have the baby either."
"No!" said the other. "Do not kill the baby.
She can have it."

Then wise Solomon knew who the mother was.

He gave the baby to the woman

who wanted it to live.

I did it! ☆

King Hiram Helps

1 Kings 5–6; 2 Chronicles 2:1–5:1

King Solomon planned to build a worship house.

King Hiram said he would help.

Hiram sent logs from different kinds of trees.

He sent workers to build with silver and gold.

He sent more workers to weave cloth.

They made it from red, purple, and blue yarn.

To pay Hiram, Solomon sent him
wheat and barley, oil and wine.

The builders worked long and hard.

They covered the main room with gold.

Even the nails were gold.

They made a gold altar, a gold table,
   and gold lamps.

For seven years,
   they worked on the worship house.

When they finished, it was beautiful.

I did it! ☆

Solomon Prays

1 Kings 8:1-24; 2 Chronicles 5:2–6:15

All God's people came to see
the new worship house.
There was music from horns,
cymbals, and harps.
The people sang, "God is good.
His love lasts forever."
All of a sudden,
a cloud filled the worship house.
God had come in his greatness.
Solomon bowed down
and held out his hands.
"There is no God like you," he said.
"You promised to love people
who follow you.
And you kept your promise."

 I did it! ☆

118

Riches for a Wise King

1 Kings 4:29-34; 10; 2 Chronicles 9

Solomon became very wise,
just as God had promised.
People from all around the world came to see him.
Solomon's ships brought him
gold and silver, apes and baboons.
Solomon wrote thousands of wise words and songs.
He wrote about big trees and little plants.
He taught about birds, fish, snakes,
and other animals.
The queen of Sheba came
to see how wise Solomon was.
She asked him many questions,
and he answered them all.
The queen said, "What I heard about you is true.
Praise God who has made such a wise king!"

I did it! ☆

Note to Parents: If you have the *Day by Day Kid's Bible*, read "Listen and Learn" and "What Is Wise Thinking?" (page 230) to your child this weekend (Proverbs 1; 8).

Listen *Wise Words from Solomon*

Proverbs 2:1-5; 3:21-24

My child, listen to what is wise.

Ask for help with what you need to know.

Then you will understand how to look up to God.

You will find out how to know God.

My child, always choose wisely.

Wise thinking will help you be safe.

Then you will not be afraid when you lie down,

and you will have a good night of sleep.

I did it! ☆

121

Love, Hate, and Caring
Wise Words from Solomon

Proverbs

Hate brings fussing.

But love covers all wrongs. *(10:12)*

Eating simple food where there is love

is better than eating a feast

where there is hate. *(15:17)*

Give food to your enemy if he is hungry.

Give water to your enemy if he is thirsty.

God will bring good things to you
   for doing this. *(25:21-22)*

People who do what is right
   take care of their animals. *(12:10)*

Worry makes a person feel bad.

Kind words make him feel better. *(12:25)*

I did it! ☆

Self-Control and Pride *Wise Words from Solomon*

Proverbs

If you find honey, then eat just enough.

If you have too much, you will get sick. *(25:16)*

Someone who cannot control himself

    is like a city with broken-down walls. *(25:28)*

A fool shows all his anger.

But a wise person controls himself. *(29:11)*

You heat silver in a pot.

You heat gold in a fire.

That is how you test them to see if they are good.

But we get tested

    when people say good things about us. *(27:21)*

I did it! ☆

The Words We Say

Wise Words from Solomon

Proverbs

Kind words are like honey.

They are sweet to the heart. *(16:24)*

Good words said at the right time

   are like gold apples on a silver plate. *(25:11)*

A kind word will take away anger.

But a mean word will bring anger. *(15:1)*

A fire goes out if there is no wood to burn.

Fussing stops when people stop saying bad things
    about each other. *(26:20)*

Starting a fight is like breaking a dam.

So stop before you get into a fight. *(17:14)*

I did it! ☆

Fighting and Hurting

Wise Words from Solomon

Proverbs

Rocks are heavy, and sand makes a big load.
But a fool who dares you to do wrong
   is the biggest load. *(27:3)*
Don't say, "I will get even with you
   for being mean to me."
Wait for God. He will take care of it. *(20:22)*

Eating a bite of dry bread in peace
 is better than eating a big dinner
 while you fuss. *(17:1)*
Fussing keeps friends apart
 like a gate with iron bars. *(18:19)*

I did it! ☆

Note to Parents: If you have the *Day by Day Kid's Bible*, read "Right and Wrong" (page 236) and "Plans of the Heart" (page 237) to your child this weekend (Selected Proverbs).

Being Rich and Poor

Wise Words from Solomon

Proverbs

Do not make yourself tired by trying to get rich.

Be wise. Control yourself.

Riches do not last.

They seem to grow wings.

They seem to fly away like birds. *(23:4-5)*

When you are full, you do not want honey.

But when you are hungry,

    even foods you do not like taste good. *(27:7)*

Being poor and doing what's right is better

    than being rich and doing what's wrong. *(28:6)*

People who hurry to get rich

    will get trouble instead. *(28:20)*

I did it! ☆

Working Hard or Being Lazy *Wise Words from Solomon*

Proverbs

Lazy people should watch ants
    and learn from them.
Ants do not have a king
    to tell them what to do.
But in the summer time, they store up
    their food for the winter. *(6:6-8)*

I passed a lazy man's field.
Weeds were everywhere.
The stone wall was broken down.
I learned something from that:
Lazy people who sleep all day
  grow poor. *(24:30-34)*

I did it! ☆

Friends *Wise Words from Solomon*

Proverbs

People who do right say helpful things
   to their friends. *(12:26)*

A friend loves you no matter what,
   and brothers and sisters help you
   through hard times. *(17:17)*

Sweet-smelling perfume makes you happy.

Friends make you happy too.

They tell you what is right. *(27:9)*

Do not forget your friends, and be glad
    to get help from a neighbor. *(27:10)*
Wise people see danger coming
    and go to a safe place.
But foolish people keep going
    and get into trouble. *(22:3)*

I did it! ☆

Happy and Sad

Wise Words from Solomon

Proverbs

When you are happy, your face shows it.

But a sad heart makes you look unhappy. *(15:13)*

A happy heart can make you feel well.

But a sad heart

makes your bones feel dried up. *(17:22)*

People who do wrong are trapped

by their own sin.

But people who do right

can sing and be happy. *(29:6)*

A smile gives people joy.

Good news gives people good health. *(15:30)*

I did it! ☆

A Wise Man Wonders

Wise Words from Agur

Proverbs 30:18-19, 24-28

There are four things I do not understand:

How an eagle flies in the sky.

How a snake crawls over a rock.

How a ship sails among the tall waves.

And how a man loves a woman.

Four things are small but wise:

Ants. They are not strong,

but they store up food in the summer.

Rock badgers. They are not strong,

but they make their homes among rocks.

Big grasshoppers. They do not have a king,

but they move together like an army.

Lizards. You can hold them in your hand,

but they can also climb into kings' palaces.

I did it! ☆

Note to Parents: If you have the *Day by Day Kid's Bible*, read "Early Morning Light" (page 231) and "Wise Words of King Lemuel" (page 256) to your child this weekend (Proverbs 4; 31:1-9).

Solomon's Song

Song of Songs 2:10-13; 8:6-7

The king said, "Get up, my beautiful one.

The winter is gone now.

It has stopped raining.

Flowers are growing all over the earth.

It is time to sing!

So come with me, my bride."

"Love is strong," said the king's bride.

"It is like a fire that burns.

Water can never put it out.

Rivers can never wash it away.

No one can buy it away from you."

I did it! ☆

A Time for Everything *Solomon's Thoughts*

Ecclesiastes 3:1-8, 11

There is a time for everything.

There is a season for everything people do.

There is a time to be born, and a time to die.

A time to plant, and a time to pull plants up.

A time to break, and a time to build.

A time to cry, and a time to laugh.

A time to throw stones, and a time to gather them.

A time to hug, and a time not to hug.

A time to hunt, and a time to give up the hunt.

A time to keep things,

and a time to throw things away.

A time to tear, and a time to mend.

A time to be quiet, and a time to talk.

A time to love, and a time to hate.

A time for war, and a time for peace.

God made everything beautiful in its own time.

I did it! ☆

Two Are Better Than One *Solomon's Thoughts*

Ecclesiastes 4:9-12

Two are better than one.

They can get more done together.

When one falls down, the other picks him up.

But it is sad if there is nobody to help.

Two can lie down together and stay warm.

But how can one stay warm by himself?

An enemy can win over one.

But two can fight back.

It is like tying three strings together.

Three together is hard to break.

I did it! ☆

A Torn Coat

1 Kings 11:29–12:20

Solomon grew old and died. He had a son
    named Rehoboam. (Say: ree-ho-BO-um.)
Rehoboam said, "I will be a mean king."
God did not want Rehoboam to be king
    of the whole country.
So God sent a prophet to a man named Jeroboam.
(The man's name sounds like this: jair-uh-BO-um.)
The prophet tore his own coat
    and gave 10 parts of it to Jeroboam.
"You'll be king of Israel in the north," he said.
"Israel will have 10 groups of God's people."
So now Solomon's son Rehoboam
    was king only of Judah in the south.
God's people had become two different nations.

I did it! ☆

Good King Asa

1 Kings 15:9-24; 2 Chronicles 14:1-7; 15:1-15

Many years passed.

Asa became king of God's people in Judah.

He was a good king.

He told the people to obey God.

King Asa built forts and towers and gates.

He took down all the idols, the fake gods.

143

He fixed God's worship house.

Then he called God's people together.

They shouted and blew horns.

The people were happy,

    because they had looked for God and found him.

I did it! ☆

Note to Parents: If you have the *Day by Day Kid's Bible*, read "Making a Deal" (page 277) and "Trouble in Israel" (page 278) to your child this weekend (1 Kings 15–16; 22; 2 Chronicles 16–17; Joshua 6).

No Rain, No Food

I Kings 16:29–17:16

Ahab was a mean king who ruled over Israel.
Elijah was a prophet who obeyed God.
One day, God sent Elijah to King Ahab.
Elijah told him, "Because you are a bad king,
    God will keep rain away from your land."
Then God told Elijah to hide from the king.
God told him to hide by a brook, where he
    would have water to drink. So Elijah did.

God had big, black birds bring Elijah food.

The brook dried up, and God told Elijah
to go to a town and ask a woman for food.

"I have only enough food for my family,"
she said.

"Don't be afraid," said Elijah.

"God says you will not run out of flour or oil."

So the woman made bread for Elijah.

And she did not run out of flour or oil.

She and her family were able to feed Elijah
for a long time.

I did it! ☆

Fire on the Mountain

1 Kings 18:15-39

King Ahab worshipped a fake god named Baal.

One day Elijah said,

"Let's see who the real God is."

People who prayed to Baal built an altar to him.

Elijah built an altar to God.

People who prayed to Baal asked him to send fire.

They called to Baal all day, but no fire came.

"Maybe Baal is busy," said Elijah.

"Maybe he is asleep or on a trip. Call louder."

The people called louder to Baal. No fire.

Elijah poured water onto his altar.

Then he prayed to God.

Fire came from heaven!
It burned the altar and the water, too!
All the people shouted, "The Lord is God!"

I did it! ☆

Afraid in the Desert

1 Kings 19:1-18

King Ahab's wife, Queen Jezebel, was angry
  about what happened on the mountain.
She wrote, "Elijah, I am going to kill you!"
Elijah ran away and hid in a mountain cave.
"Stand outside the cave. I am coming," said God.
A strong wind blew. God was not in the wind.
The earth shook. God was not in the shaking earth.
A fire came. God was not in the fire.

Then Elijah heard a soft, quiet voice.

"Why are you here, Elijah?" asked God.

"I am the only one who follows you," said Elijah.

"And Jezebel is going to kill me."

"There are 7,000 people who follow me," said God.

"Elisha is one of them. He will help you."

I did it! ☆

Elijah's Helper

1 Kings 19:19-21

Elijah found Elisha in a field.

He was leading oxen that were pulling a plow.

Elijah put his coat around Elisha's shoulders.

That meant he was choosing Elisha to help him.

Elisha left the plow.

"I have to kiss my mother and father good-bye,"
    he said. "Then I will come."

"All right," said Elijah.

So Elisha went back and told his family good-bye.

Then he went to help Elijah.

I did it! ☆

A Singing Army

2 Chronicles 19:1–20:30

Jehoshaphat was a good king who ruled Judah.

(His name sounds like this: juh-HOSH-uh-fat.)

A big army came to fight the people of Judah.

King Jehoshaphat asked all his people to pray.

God's Spirit came on one of the men.

He said, "God is telling you not to be afraid

   and not to give up.

Face the enemy. God will be with you."

So the king chose singers to lead his army.

As they marched, they sang,

"Give thanks to God. His love lasts forever."

Then God made the enemy fight each other.

Jehoshaphat's army won. They didn't have to fight!

I did it! ☆

Note to Parents: If you have the *Day by Day Kid's Bible*, divide "Orders from the King" (page 293) into two readings and read them to your child this weekend (2 Kings 1; 3:1-3).

Horses of Fire

2 Kings 2:1-14

Elijah and his helper, Elisha, walked to a river.

Elijah hit the water with his coat.

The water moved apart,

   and they crossed the river on dry ground.

"I am leaving soon," said Elijah.

"Is there something I can do for you first?"

"I want to be like you, but greater," said Elisha.

"That is hard," said Elijah.

"But if you see me go,

   you will have what you want."

All of a sudden, Elisha saw horses of fire.

They galloped past, pulling a chariot of fire.
Then a strong wind gathered Elijah up to heaven.
Elisha picked up Elijah's coat and hit the river.
The water moved apart, and he crossed the river.

I did it! ☆

Oil to Sell

2 Kings 4:1-7

One day a prophet died.

His wife went to Elisha, crying.

"My husband owed money to a man.

Now this man wants to take my sons.

He wants them to work for him to pay him back."

"Can you pay this man anything?" asked Elisha.

"All I have is a little oil," said the woman.

"Ask your neighbors for jars. Fill them with oil.

Sell the oil and pay the man," said Elisha.

The woman did not have much oil.

But she got a lot of jars and poured oil into them.

Her oil did not run out until every jar was full.

She sold the oil and paid the man.

Then her sons were safe.

I did it! ☆

A Room on the Roof Top

2 Kings 4:8-17

One day, a rich lady was talking to her husband.

"Elisha comes to our town a lot," she said.

"Let's make a room for him on our roof.

We can put a bed, table, chair, and lamp in it."

So they built the room on their roof.

The next time Elisha came, he stayed there.

He wanted to do something to thank the woman.

He knew she had no children. So he told her,

"This time next year, you will have a baby."

And that is just what happened.

I did it! ☆

Death in the Soup

2 Kings 4:38-41

Elisha met with a group of prophets.

They put a big pot on the fire to cook soup.

One man found a wild vine with fruit on it.

No one knew what the fruit was,

but they put it in the soup anyway.

When they started to eat it, they cried,

"There is death in this soup! It is poison!"

Elisha put some flour into the pot.

"You can eat it now," he said.

Then the soup was not poison anymore.

I did it! ☆

FLOUR

159

An Ax on the Water

2 Kings 6:1-7

Elisha went with his prophet friends
    to build a new meeting house.
They started cutting down trees at the river.
The sharp iron top of one man's ax fell off.
It fell into the river. "Oh no!" said the man.
"That is not my ax! It belongs to a friend."
He showed Elisha where the ax
    had fallen into the water.
Elisha cut a stick and threw it into the water
    at that spot.
Then the heavy ax top came back up.
"Pull it out," said Elisha. And the man did.

I did it! ☆

Note to Parents: If you have the *Day by Day Kid's Bible*, read "Water That Looked Red" (page 299) and "The King Whose Insides Came Out" (page 300) to your child this weekend (2 Kings 3; 2 Chronicles 21).

Obadiah

2 Chronicles 21:8-9; Obadiah 1:1, 3-4, 17

The nation of Edom came to fight God's people.

About that time, Obadiah the prophet spoke.

He told the people of Edom
 what God said about them.

"Edom, you are proud.

You live in the rocks high in the mountains.

You say nobody can bring you down.

You may fly like an eagle.

You may have your nest in the stars.

But I will bring you down from there.

And my people will be saved."

I did it! ☆

A Great Army

2 Kings 6:8-23

The army of Aram wanted to get rid of Elisha.
They camped in a circle
    around the city where he lived.
"What will we do?" cried Elisha's helper.
"Don't be scared," said Elisha.
"Our army is bigger than their army."
Elisha prayed, "God, let my helper see."

Then Elisha's helper saw an army in the hills.

It was an army of horses and chariots of fire.

Elisha prayed again:

"God, make the enemy army blind."

So God did. They could not see anything.

Elisha led them away from the city.

He took them back home where they had started.

Then Elisha prayed for the men to see again.

After that, they stopped fighting God's people.

I did it! ☆

Dipping into the River

2 Kings 5:1-15

Naaman was the leader of the army of Aram.

But he had a bad skin sickness.

Naaman's wife had a helper,
   a girl who followed God.

The girl said, "Elisha can make Naaman well."

So Naaman went to see Elisha.

"Dip in the Jordan River seven times,"
    said Elisha.

Naaman thought that was silly.

He got angry and left.

Naaman's helpers said, "It can't hurt to try it."

So Naaman went to the Jordan River and dipped
    one, two, three, four, five, six, seven times.

Then his skin was like new again.

"Now I know that God is the only God!"
    said Naaman.

I did it! ☆

The Boy King

2 Kings 11

A mean queen was killing the princes in Judah.
She did not want anyone else to rule.
But a lady saved the baby prince, Joash,
    and hid him in the worship house.
For seven years, the mean queen did not know
    that Prince Joash was living
    in the worship house.

All that time, there were many leaders
who did not like the mean queen.
So when Joash turned seven years old,
they put the crown on his head.
They shouted, "Long live the king!"
When the queen saw it, she yelled,
"You tricked me!"
The leaders took her away. After she died,
the people were glad that Joash was the king.

I did it! ☆

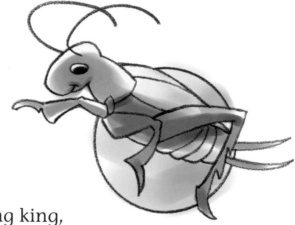

Joel

Joel 1:1-7, 10-12; 2:21-26

When Joash was a young king,
  the prophet Joel spoke.
"Listen, people. Tell your children this.
An army of big grasshoppers came and ate plants.
They tore down vines and fig trees.
Now the fields are dry. Wheat crops are gone.
Even palm trees and apple trees are dry.
Your joy has dried up too.
But do not be afraid.
Fields will turn green again. Trees will grow fruit.
God will send plenty of rain in the fall and spring.
He will give back what the grasshoppers ate.
Then you will eat and get full and praise God."

I did it! ☆

Note to Parents: If you have the *Day by Day Kid's Bible*, read "Turning Away" (page 315) and "Arrows" (page 317) to your child this weekend (2 Kings 12–13; 2 Chronicles 24).

A Big Fish

Jonah 1:1–3:3

God said, "Jonah, go to the city of Nineveh.
Tell the people there to stop doing bad things."
But Jonah ran the other way and got on a ship.
So God sent a storm with a strong wind.

Jonah knew the storm had come because of him.
He said, "Throw me out, and the storm will stop."
So the sailors threw Jonah into the sea.
The storm did stop. But Jonah sank down, down.
Then—gulp! A big fish swallowed him.
For three days and three nights,
   Jonah prayed inside the fish.
Then the fish spit Jonah out on the land.
Again God said, "Jonah, go to Nineveh."
This time, Jonah did!

I did it! ☆

Hosea

Hosea 1:2-3; 4:1, 16; 7:8; 10:4; 14:1, 5-8

A man named Hosea had a wife
   who would not stay with him.
God said, "My people are like her.
My people will not stay with me.
They do not care about me anymore.
They are like a cow
   that will not go where you lead.
So how can I take them to green fields?
They are like a pancake
   that is cooked on only one side.
They are like weeds in a good field.
Come back to me, my people.

Then you will bloom like a lily
and grow great like an olive tree.
And I will take care of you."

I did it! ☆

Forts and Towers

2 Chronicles 26:3-5, 9-10, 15

Uzziah was a good king.

He looked for ways to make God happy.

So God brought good things to him.

King Uzziah built towers and forts.

He dug wells and had lots of cows.

He loved to grow things.

King Uzziah also made machines to shoot arrows
and throw rocks.

He used the machines when enemy armies came.

God helped King Uzziah win over his enemies.

I did it! ☆

Amos

Amos 1:1; 2:6-7; 4:6-9; 7:17; 9:14-15

Amos took care of sheep. He listened to God
and told people what God told him.
God said, "My people do not obey me.
They worship idols, which are not real gods.
They treat poor people like dirt.
I let them go without food,
but they did not turn to me.
I kept rain from coming,
but they did not turn to me.

Grasshoppers ate their trees,

   but they did not turn to me.

So another nation will take my people away.

But someday I will bring them back home.

Then they will build cities and grow gardens.

They will drink wine and eat fruit.

And they will never be sent away again."

I did it! ☆

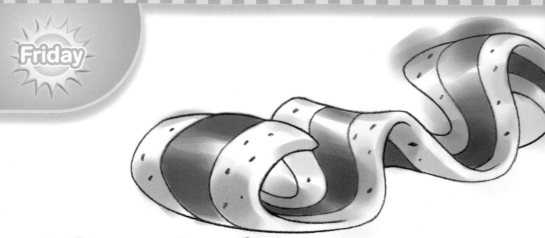

I Saw God

Isaiah 6:1-3, 8

Isaiah the prophet wrote:

The year King Uzziah died, I saw God.

He was sitting in heaven above everything.

His robe was so long it filled the worship house.

Beings from heaven flew above him.

They called, "God Who Has All Power

    is good and right and holy.

His greatness fills the whole earth."

Then I heard God say, "Who will I send?"

"I am here," I said. "Send me."

I did it! ☆

Note to Parents: If you have the *Day by Day Kid's Bible*, read "The Ox Knows" (page 333) and "Tunnels and Caves" (page 334) to your child this weekend (Isaiah 1–2).

176

Signs from God

Isaiah 8:11-18

Isaiah wrote:

God told me not to act like
 the rest of his people.
He told me not to be afraid of
 the things they are afraid of.
God has all power.
He is good and right and holy.
He will be a safe place.
Here I am.
Here are the children God gave me.
We show how great God is.

I did it! ☆

Prince of Peace

Isaiah 9:1-2, 6-7

"Someday people who are sad
  will be glad," wrote Isaiah.
"People walking in the dark
  will see a great light.
A child is born. A son is given to us.
He will rule, and people will call him
    Wonderful Leader, Powerful God,
    Father Forever, Prince of Peace.
He will be fair and right forever.
God planned this,
    and he will work hard to do it."

Who is this Prince of Peace? Read about him in John 14:27.

I did it! ☆

A Branch

Isaiah 11:1-5

The family of King David is like a tree.

It was cut down.

But a Branch will grow up from its roots.

This Branch will grow fruit.

A new King will come.

God's Spirit will stay upon him:

God's wise, understanding Spirit;

God's guiding, strong Spirit.

This King will be glad to treat God

as the most important one of all.

He will be fair to the poor.

And he will keep his promises.

Who is this Branch, this King? Read Luke 1:30-33.

I did it! ☆

Shout with Joy

Isaiah 35:4-10

Tell people who are afraid, "Be strong.
Do not be scared. God will come.
He will come and save you."
Then people who could not see will see.
People who could not hear will hear.
People who could not walk will jump.
People who could not talk will shout with joy.
Water will flow in the desert.
Hot sand will turn into pools of water.

A wide road will be there.
It will be called the Way of What Is Right.
It will be a road for people who follow God.
They will sing as they go to God's city.

I did it! ☆

Hope for God's People

Micah 1:1; 5:1-2, 4-5

God sent Micah to talk to his people.

Here is part of what Micah said.

"Bethlehem, you are a small town.

But a King will come from you.

He comes from long, long ago.

Like a shepherd, he will lead God's people.

He will lead in God's power and great name.

God's people will be safe.

All people will see how great God is.

This King will bring peace."

Who is this King that Micah told about? Read Matthew 2:1-2.

I did it! ☆

Note to Parents: If you have the *Day by Day Kid's Bible*, read "Trying to Scare God's People" (page 355) and "God Sends His Angel to Fight" (page 356) to your child this weekend (2 Kings 18–19; 2 Chronicles 32; Isaiah 36–37).

A Shadow Moves Backward

2 Kings 20:1-11

King Hezekiah got sick
   and knew he was soon going to die.
He cried and prayed, "Remember me, God.
I have always obeyed you."
God told Isaiah, "I heard King Hezekiah pray.
I will let him live 15 more years."
So Isaiah told Hezekiah he would live.
The king asked, "How will I know this is true?"
"Watch the shadow on the stairs," said Isaiah.
"Do you want it to move forward or backward?"

"It is easy for a shadow to move forward,"
said Hezekiah. "I want it to move backward."
That is just what happened.
And King Hezekiah got well.

I did it! ☆

Who Is like God?

Isaiah 40:12, 26-28

Who measured the water in his hand?

Who planned where to put the sky?

Who held the dust of the earth in a basket?

Who weighed the mountains and hills?

Look up at the sky.

God brings out each star, one by one.

He calls each star by its name.

Why do you say God does not see you?

Don't you know? God lasts forever.

No one will ever know

    how much God understands.

I did it! ☆

Trees Will Clap

Isaiah 55:8-13

"The sky is higher than the earth," says God.

"And my ways are higher than your ways.

My thoughts are higher than your thoughts.

Rain and snow come down from the sky.

They water the earth and make things grow.

Then the farmer will have seeds,

    and people will have bread.

My word is like that.

It will do what I want it to do.

You will go out with joy and peace.

Mountains and hills will sing.

The trees of the field will clap.

Everyone will see that God is the Lord."

I did it! ☆

Here I Am

Isaiah 58:7-11

God says,

"You should share food with hungry people.
You should give poor people a place to stay.
You should give clothes to people who need them.
You should take care of your own families.
Then you will be like light in the early morning.

My greatness will watch over you as you go.
You will pray, and I will answer.
You will call me, and I will say, 'Here I am.'
I will give you what you need."

I did it! ☆

The Wolf and the Lamb

Isaiah 65:17-25

God says, "Look!

I will make a new sky and a new earth.

There will be no crying.

My people will live a long time.

They will work and have all they need.

I will bring good things to their families.

I will answer before they ask.

I will hear while they are still talking.

The wolf and the lamb will eat together.

The lion will eat hay like the ox.

Nothing will hurt anyone anywhere

on my mountain."

I did it! ☆

Note to Parents: If you have the *Day by Day Kid's Bible*, read "Get Up and Shine!" and "God Chose Me" (page 372) to your child this weekend (Isaiah 60:1-3, 11, 19-22; 61:1-3).

A Safe Place

Nahum 1:1-7

God told Nahum the prophet to say this:

"God wants people to follow his way.

He does not get angry quickly.

But he will not let people get away with sin.

You can feel his power in the rushing wind.

You can see it in the storm.

Clouds are the dust from his feet.

God can dry up seas and rivers.

Mountains shake and hills melt.

Rocks break in front of him.

But God is good.

He is like a safe place in times of trouble."

I did it! ☆

King Josiah

2 Kings 22:1-13; 23:1-3; 2 Chronicles 34:33

Josiah was eight years old when he became king.

He followed God with all his heart.

Almost 20 years later, King Josiah sent workers
    to fix the worship house.

It was broken and old.

One day, a worker found a book.

It was the book of laws God had given Moses.

He took it to King Josiah and read it to him.

King Josiah was upset.

"Our families have not obeyed God," he said.

So he read the book of laws to all the people.

He told them to follow God.

And that is what they did
      as long as King Josiah lived.

I did it! ☆

Sing and Shout

Zephaniah 1:1-3; 3:14-18

While Josiah was king,
    God told the prophet Zephaniah what to say.
"If people do not follow God,
    he will sweep away animals.
He will sweep away birds from the air
    and fish from the sea.
They will have only trash left.
But God's people will be able to sing and shout.
God is with you, and you will not be afraid.
He will be happy with you and enjoy you.
He will love you, and you will rest quietly.
He will take away your sadness."

I did it! ☆

God Chooses Jeremiah

Jeremiah 1:4-8, 18-19

God talked to a man named Jeremiah.
God said, "I knew you before I made you
    inside your mother.
I chose you to teach my people."

197

"But I am not good at talking," said Jeremiah.

"Do not be afraid. I am with you," said God.

"I will take care of you.

I have made you like a fort.

You are like an iron post and a metal wall.

Kings and other leaders will fight you.

But they will not win, because I am with you.

I will save you."

I did it! ☆

A Family That Obeyed

Jeremiah 35:1-10, 12-15

God told Jeremiah, "Go to Recab's family.
Ask them to come to the worship house.
Give them some wine to drink."
Recab's family came to the worship house.
Jeremiah set out cups and wine.
"Have a drink," said Jeremiah.

"We do not drink wine," they said.

"Our father told us not to."

God said, "My people should learn this lesson.

The people in Recab's family obey him.

They do what he told them.

But I talk to my people over and over again.

And they still do not obey."

I did it! ☆

Note to Parents: If you have the *Day by Day Kid's Bible*, read "The Clay Jar" (page 385) and "The Stocks" (page 386) to your child this weekend (Jeremiah 19–20).

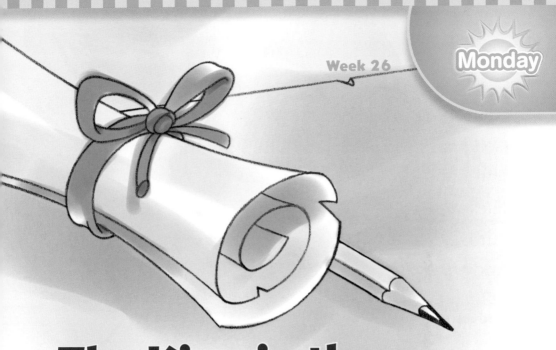

The King in the Winter House

Jeremiah 36

God told Jeremiah what to tell his people.

Jeremiah's helper, Baruch,

    wrote the words on a roll of paper.

Then he read the paper out loud to the people.

The leaders heard Baruch reading.

They took the roll of paper

    to the king in his winter house.

Fire was burning in a pot in front of the king.

His helper read God's words from the paper.

But the king got angry at what God had said.

He cut up the paper and threw it into the fire.

Then he ordered his men
   to get Jeremiah and Baruch.

But God had hidden them to keep them safe.

Still, Baruch had to write the words from God
   all over again.

 I did it! ☆

Wow!

Habakkuk 3:1-2, 4, 10-13, 17-19

Here is a prayer Habakkuk prayed:

"Wow, God! Your greatness
   is brighter than the morning sun.
The mountains saw you, and they shook.
The deep sea roared, waves jumped high,
   sun and moon stood still in the sky.
You walked over the earth.
You came out to save your people.
The fig tree may not have buds.
There may not be grapes on the vine.
There may not be sheep or cows in the pen.
But I will be glad in you, because you save me.
You make me strong."

I did it! ☆

Daniel and the King's Food

Daniel 1

The army of Babylon came to Judah.

They took some of God's people to Babylon.

They took Daniel and his friends.

The king of Babylon was looking for young men.

He wanted the strongest and wisest to help him.

So he sent all kinds of food to make them strong.

But Daniel knew that God would not be pleased
   if he and his friends ate the king's food.

So they asked for vegetables to eat.

They asked for water to drink.

"You will be sick and weak,"
   said the king's helper.

"Then the king will get mad at me."

"Let us try it for 10 days," said Daniel.

So the helper gave them
   only vegetables and water.

After 10 days, they were the strongest and wisest!

I did it! ☆

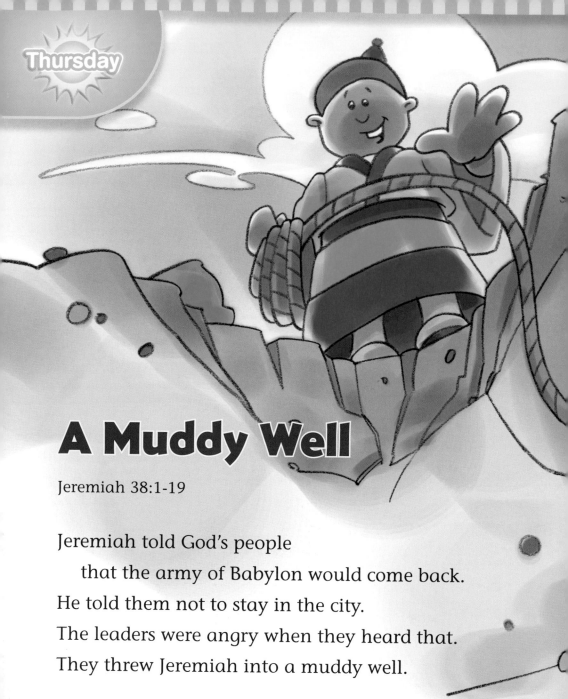

A Muddy Well

Jeremiah 38:1-19

Jeremiah told God's people
  that the army of Babylon would come back.
He told them not to stay in the city.
The leaders were angry when they heard that.
They threw Jeremiah into a muddy well.

But a leader from the palace heard about it.
He let ropes down into the well.
Jeremiah put the ropes under his arms.
And 30 men pulled him up out of the well.
The king asked Jeremiah to come see him.
Jeremiah said, "Let Babylon win.
Then you will live."
"I can't," said the king. "I am afraid."

I did it! ☆

207

A City on Fire

Jeremiah 39:1-2, 8; 40:1-6; 2 Kings 25:8-15

Just as Jeremiah had said,
    the army of Babylon came again.
They broke down the city walls.
They set God's worship house on fire.
They took dishes from the worship house.
They took everything made of gold and silver.
They burned down all the houses.
They took the people of Judah to Babylon.
Only the poorest people were left in Judah.
Jeremiah would have been taken away too.
But the captain of the army set Jeremiah free.
So Jeremiah got to stay in Judah.

I did it! ☆

Note to Parents: If you have the *Day by Day Kid's Bible*, read "Enemies Laugh" (page 424) and "The Wives and Their Idols" (page 427) to your child this weekend (Lamentations 2; Jeremiah 44:1-7, 15-30).

Great Love

Lamentations 1:1, 4; 3:21-26

Jeremiah wrote this sad poem:

The city is like a desert.

Once it was full of people.

Now no one comes through the gates.

But I remember one thing that gives me hope.

God has great love. So we are not lost.

God's care never ends.

His care is new every morning.

He keeps his promises.

I tell myself, "God is what I want.

So I will wait for him."

It is good to wait quietly for God to save you.

I did it! ☆

In the Cloud

Ezekiel 1:1-5, 26-28; 2:1-3

A man named Ezekiel
    was with God's people in Babylon.
Here is part of what he wrote:
One day, I saw pictures in my mind.
There was a big cloud with lightning inside it.
A bright light was all around it.
And fire was in the middle.
Four beings were in the fire.
Above them was
    something like a king's chair.
It was made of beautiful blue stones.
Someone who looked
    like a man sat on it.
He looked like a rainbow in the clouds.
That is what God's greatness looked like.

Then I heard a voice say, "I am sending you.
Tell my people what I say."

I did it! ☆

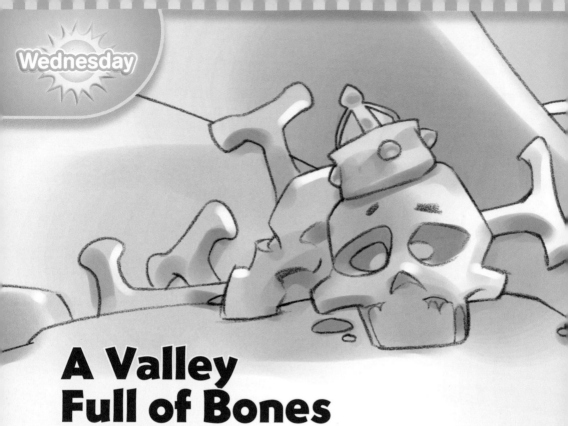

A Valley Full of Bones

Ezekiel 37:1-14

Ezekiel wrote:

God's Spirit took me to the middle of a valley.

The valley was full of dry bones.

"Ezekiel, can these bones live?" asked God.

"Only you know," I said.

"Talk to these bones," said God.

"Say, 'Dry bones, hear God's word!

212

You will get skin and breath, and you will live.' "
So that is what I told the bones, and they stood.
Breath went into them, and they came to life.
They made a big army.
God said, "I will put my Spirit into my people.
I'll do it just like I put breath into the dry bones."

I did it! ☆

A Big, Burning Oven

Daniel 3

The king of Babylon made a gold idol
   that was 90 feet high.
Everyone bowed down to worship it,
   but not Daniel's three friends.
The king told them, "If you do not bow down,
   I will throw you into the burning oven."
"Our God can save us," said Daniel's friends.
"Even if he does not, we will not bow down
   to your idol. It's not a real god."

So the king had them thrown into the huge oven.

The guards got burned, but not Daniel's friends.

Then the king saw another man in the fire.

"He looks like the son of a god!" said the king.

He called the three friends to come out.

They did not even smell like smoke.

The king said, "No other god can save like this!"

I did it! ☆

A King Eats Grass

Daniel 4

I, the king, was walking on my palace roof.

I said, "See how great I am?

I built Babylon by my own strong power."

A voice from heaven said,

"You cannot be king until you say God is great."

Right away, I lost my mind and left my people.

I ate grass like a cow.

My hair grew out like eagle feathers.

My nails grew out like bird claws.

After seven years, I looked up to heaven.

My right mind came back.

Now I praise God as the King of heaven.

He is the one who is great.

I did it! ☆

Note to Parents: If you have the *Day by Day Kid's Bible,* read "Four Big Animals" (page 451) and "A Ram and a Goat" (page 452) to your child this weekend (Daniel 7–8).

Words on a Wall

Daniel 5

The king's son became king of Babylon.

He had a dinner for his leaders.

They drank from cups that had been taken
    from God's worship house.

While they drank, they praised their idols.

All of a sudden a hand began writing on the wall.

The king was so scared, his legs shook.

He asked his magic men to read the words.

But they couldn't, so the king grew more afraid.

The queen said, "Call Daniel. He will read it."

When Daniel came, he said,

    "God sent the hand to write on the wall.

It says that you will not be king anymore."

That same night, another king took over Babylon.

I did it! ☆

Lions!

Daniel 6

The new king wanted Daniel to rule
 the other leaders.
That made the other leaders angry.
They knew Daniel prayed to God every day.
So they got the king to make a new law:
"Pray to the king or be thrown to the lions."
Then they said, "Daniel prays to God,
 not to the king!"
They threw Daniel into the lions' den.
But the king liked Daniel.
That night, he was too worried to sleep.
The next morning, he hurried to the lions' den.

"Daniel," he called. "Did your God save you?"
"God's angel closed the lions' mouths,"
   said Daniel.
The king let Daniel out and made a new law:
"All people must say Daniel's God is great."

I did it! ☆

Job in Trouble

Job 1:1–2:11; 11:14-15; 12:4, 7-10, 13-14; 13:15-16

Job was a very rich man.

He was also a good man who obeyed God.

But Job lost his riches and his children.

Then he got very sick.

Job's wife said, "Why do you still trust God?"

His friends said,

    "You must have done something wrong."

"No," said Job. "I have always followed God.

Ask animals. Ask birds. Let fish tell you.

God holds the life of every being in his hand.
Power is God's. He is the one who wins."
Job would not say anything bad about God.

I did it! ☆

God Talks

Job 38:1-4, 12, 22, 25, 29-30, 32, 35; 40:10-14

Job and his friends asked questions about God.

They tried to say how God did things, and why.

At last God said,

    "It's my turn to ask questions.

You answer me.

Where were you when I made the earth?

Did you show the sunrise where to start?

Have you gone to where the snow is stored?

Who makes a road for the rain to follow?

Who is the father of ice and frost?

Can you put the stars in their places?

Do you send out the lightning?

Can you do all these things?

If you can, I will say you can save yourself."

I did it!

Who?

Job 39:5, 9, 19, 26-27; 40:1-5

God asked Job and his friends,
   "Who lets the wild donkeys run free?
Will the wild ox serve you?
Do you make the horse strong?
Do you put a flowing mane on his neck?
Does the hawk fly because you are wise?
Does the eagle fly when you tell him to?
Do you tell him to build his nest up high?
Do you tell me what is right and wrong?"

"How can I answer you?" said Job.

"I will put my hand over my mouth."

I did it! ☆

Note to Parents: If you have the *Day by Day Kid's Bible*, read "Do I Have to Wait?" (page 444) and "Nobody Can Understand" (page 445) to your child this weekend (Job 32–33; 35–37).

The Elephant

Job 40:15-23

God told Job, "Look at the elephant.

I made him, just as I made you.

His legs are strong, and his belly has power.

His trunk swings like a cedar tree.

His bones are like metal bars.

He is one of the best of all I have made.

He lets me come near him.

All the wild animals play nearby.

But he hides under the water plants.

The river rushes past, but he is not scared.

He is safe,

    even if the water comes up to his mouth."

I did it! ☆

Too Wonderful for Me

Job 41:1-11; 42:1-6, 10, 12-13, 16

God asked Job, "Can you catch a crocodile
　　without getting hurt?
If you can't, how can you be sure
　　you are safe to stand
　　before me and question me?"
"I am sorry, God," said Job.
"I talked about things
　　I did not understand.
But now I know that
　　you can do all things."
Then God made Job well.
And God made him rich again.

After that, Job and his wife
   had seven more sons and three more daughters.
Job got more sheep and camels, oxen and donkeys.
And Job lived a long, long time.

I did it! ☆

Going Home

Ezra 1:1–6:12

The land of Babylon got a new name.

It was Persia.

And Persia got a new king.

His name was Cyrus.

God worked in King Cyrus's heart.

Cyrus told God's people, "Go back to Jerusalem.

Build God's worship house again."

Many people traveled back and began building.

But then another new king began to rule Persia.

Enemies wrote the new king a letter.

"These people are trouble makers," they wrote.

So the new king made God's people stop building.

At last Persia got still another king.

He told God's people

they could build the worship house.

I did it! ☆

Ezra's Trip

Ezra 7:6-26; 8:22-23, 31-32

Ezra was a teacher of God's people in Persia.

He wanted to move back to Jerusalem.

Then he could bring singers and servants
   for the worship house.

The king told Ezra to take wheat, wine, olive oil,
   salt, bulls, rams, lambs, gold, and silver.

Ezra knew there were robbers on the road.

They might steal everything the king gave them.
But Ezra had told the king
 that God takes care of people who obey him.
So he did not want to ask the king to send guards.
Instead, he and the people prayed for a safe trip.
And God kept robbers away.
Everyone got to Jerusalem safely.

I did it! ☆

Haggai

Haggai 1

The king of Persia had told God's people

    they could build the worship house again.

But they stopped to build their own houses.

God sent Haggai to tell them, "You plant.

But you grow only a few crops.

You eat, but there is never enough food.

You wear clothes, but you don't get warm.

Your money bags seem to have holes in them.

That is because my worship house

    is still a pile of sticks and stones.

Build my worship house.

Then I will know that you care about me."

So the people began to build

    the worship house again.

I did it! ☆

Note to Parents: If you have the *Day by Day Kid's Bible*, read "Shaking the Earth" and "A Man on a Red Horse" (page 464) to your child this weekend (Haggai 2:1-9; Zechariah 1).

City of Truth

Zechariah 8:1-5, 12-17, 20-23

God told the prophet Zechariah,

"I plan good things for you and all my people.

I will come back to Jerusalem.

It will be called the City of Truth.

Old people will sit safely beside the streets.

Boys and girls will play there.

Rain will come.

Seeds will grow, and vines will make fruit.

So do not be afraid.

Tell the truth and be fair.

Then people will look for me and pray to me."

I did it! ☆

What Makes God Happy

Psalm 147:4-5, 8, 10-11

There is no end to what God knows.

He counts the stars and calls each one by name.

He makes clouds cover the sky.

He brings rain to the earth.

He makes grass grow on the hills.

A horse may be strong,

    but that is not what makes God happy.

A man's legs may be strong,
   but that is not what makes God happy.
God is happy with people who love him.
He is happy when people trust his love
   and know that his love never ends.

I did it! ☆

Snow and Ice

Psalm 147:12-18, 20

Bow before God.

He gives your land peace.

He brings you fine wheat.

He lays out snow like wool.

He sends frost like dust that's left from a fire.

He throws down his hail like tiny rocks.

Who can stand against icy wind?

But God sends his word, and the ice melts.

He brings his light winds, and water flows.
Shout for God!

I did it! ☆

A New Queen

Esther 1:1–2:20

The king of Persia got mad at his queen.

He told her she could not be queen anymore.

Then he looked for a new queen.

Many women came to see him, hoping to be queen.

One of God's people was an older man.

He had a beautiful young cousin named Esther.

The king had a helper
   who took Esther to the palace.

When it was Esther's turn to see the king,
   he liked her most of all.

He made her the new queen.

But he did not know
   that she was one of God's people.

I did it! ☆

For Such a Time as This

Esther 3–4; 7:1-4; 8:3–9:5

When Esther was queen, she met Haman,
   a man who hated God's people.
Haman got the king to make a new law.
It said that on one day
   all God's people would be killed.

Esther was upset. Her cousin wrote her a note.

"Ask the king to change the law," he said.

Later he wrote, "Maybe you became queen
for such a time as this."

So Esther told the king
that she was one of God's people.

She asked him to make a new law
to save her people.

Then the king changed the law,
and God's people were saved.

I did it! ☆

Note to Parents:
If you have the *Day by Day Kid's Bible*, tell your child you are going to read more about Queen Esther and the new law she asked the king to write. Read "Fast Horses Carry the News" (page 482) and "The Holiday" (page 483) to your child this weekend (Esther 8–10).

240

Dance like a Calf

Malachi 3:1, 10-11; 4:2, 5-6

God sent Malachi with a message to his people:

"I'll send someone to get the way ready for me.

But first, bring your gifts and offerings to me.

Then I will open the gates of heaven.

I will let so many good things flow out,
   you will not have room for all of them.

I will keep bugs from eating your plants.

Your vines will always have good fruit.

You will dance like a calf let out of its pen.

Then I will send someone to you.

He will turn the fathers' hearts around
   so they will love their children.

He will turn the children's hearts around
   so they will love their fathers."

I did it! ☆

Broken Walls

Nehemiah 1:1–2:18

Nehemiah worked for the king of Persia.

He took the king's wine to him.

One day, Nehemiah looked upset.

"Why are you sad?" asked the king.

Nehemiah said, "Jerusalem is my people's city.

Its walls are broken into piles of stones."

"What do you want to do?" asked the king.

Nehemiah said a quick prayer. Then he said,

"Let me go build up the city and its walls."

The king was glad to send Nehemiah.

He also sent wood and guards on horses.

Nehemiah rode around Jerusalem's walls.

Then he told the people, "Let's start building."

And they did.

I did it! ☆

Tools and Swords

Nehemiah 4

Two men lived near Jerusalem.
They did not want God's people
   to build the city walls.
So they made fun of the people.
"They are not doing a good job," they said.

"A fox could jump on the wall and break it."

But the people kept working.

The two men and their friends got angry.

They said, "We will kill the people.

Then they will stop working."

But God's people held tools in one hand
and swords in the other.

And they kept working.

They started every day when the sky got light.

And they worked until
the stars came out at night.

I did it! ☆

Letters and Messages

Nehemiah 6:1-16

The men who did not want Nehemiah
   to build the wall sent a letter to him:
"We hear that you are going to fight the king.
You will be in trouble, so come meet with us."
But Nehemiah knew they wanted to hurt him.
He sent a message back: "You're making that up."
But the men sent more letters to scare Nehemiah.
They sent people to tell Nehemiah to give up.
But Nehemiah did not give up.
Soon the wall was finished.
When the men heard about it, they were afraid.
They saw that God had helped with the work.

I did it! ☆

Singers on the Wall

Nehemiah 12:27-43; 13:1, 12

Now the wall of Jerusalem was built up again.
So people came to sing and shout and thank God.
It was time to say that God was in charge
    of the city of Jerusalem.
Singers marched around the wall.
Some people played cymbals or horns.
Others played harps or lyres.
The happy sound could be heard far away.

Then Moses' Law Book was read out loud.

All the people could hear it.

Everyone brought God gifts of grain, wine, and oil.

They did it because God had made them
very happy.

The women and children shouted with joy.

I did it! ☆

Note to Parents: If you have the *Day by Day Kid's Bible*, read "An Angel at the Altar" (page 503) and "Naming the Baby" (page 505) to your child this weekend (Luke 1:5-25, 57-80).

New Testament

God's Son

Luke 1:26-38

One day, God sent an angel
    to a young woman named Mary.
"Hello," the angel said. "God is with you."
Mary was afraid. She wondered
    why an angel was talking to her.
But the angel said, "Do not be afraid.

God is happy with you.

He is going to give you a baby boy.

You should name him Jesus.

He will be God's Son."

"I want whatever God wants," said Mary.

"So let it happen the way God says."

I did it! ☆

Joseph's Dream

Matthew 1:18-25

Mary was supposed to marry Joseph.

But Joseph was not sure they should marry.

So God sent an angel to Joseph in a dream.

"Do not be afraid to let Mary be your wife," he said.

"She will have a baby by the power of the Spirit.

You will name the baby Jesus.

He will save his people from sin."

Joseph woke up from his dream.

Now he knew what to do.

He married Mary.

I did it! ☆

A Trip to Bethlehem

Luke 2:1-7

The king made a law
  that everyone should be counted.
People had to go back to the place
  where their families had lived long ago.
Joseph was from the family of King David.
So he and Mary went to Bethlehem to be counted.
But all the rooms at the inn were full.

They had to stay in a stable
with cows and donkeys.
That is where Mary's baby was born.
Mary and Joseph named him Jesus.
Mary put a warm blanket around the baby.
She made him a bed
in the animals' feed box.

I did it! ☆

In the Fields

Luke 2:8-17

The night when Jesus was born,
   shepherds were in the fields watching sheep.
Suddenly, God's greatness shone all around.
The shepherds were afraid.

But an angel came and said, "Do not be afraid.
I have good news. Jesus the Lord
    was born in Bethlehem today."
Then many angels came, praising God.
When they left, the shepherds ran into town.
They found baby Jesus
    in a feed box for animals.
Then they left to tell everyone
    what they had seen.

I did it! ☆

Wise Men

Matthew 2:1-13

Some time after Jesus was born,
   wise men from the East came to Jerusalem.
They asked, "Where is the child
   who was born to be King of the Jews?
We saw his star and want to worship him."
This upset King Herod.
He said, "Tell me when you find this baby.
Then I can worship him too."
But Herod really wanted to hurt Jesus instead.
The wise men followed the star to a house.
There they found Jesus with his mother.
They bowed down to Jesus and gave him gifts.
In a dream, God told them not to tell the king.
So they took a different road home.

I did it! ☆

Note to Parents: If you have the *Day by Day Kid's Bible*, read the last half of "Wise Men from the East" (starting with the last two paragraphs in the left column on page 509) and "In the Big City" (page 510) to your child this weekend (Matthew 2:13-23; Luke 2:39-52).

The Man Who Ate Honey

Matthew 3:1-4, 11; Mark 1:2-7; Luke 3:1-3, 15-16

Once there was a man named John.

He lived in the desert.

He wore clothes made of camel's hair.

He ate honey and grasshoppers called locusts.

Many people went to hear John teach.

John told them to be sorry for their sins.

He baptized people, dipping them in the river.

People wondered if John was the man
    that God had sent to save his people.

But John said, "Someone else will come.

He has more power than I have.

I am not even good enough to untie his shoes."

I did it! ☆

Jesus at the River

Matthew 3:13-17; Mark 1:9-11; Luke 3:21-22

One day Jesus asked John to baptize him.

"You should baptize me," said John.

"Instead, you want me to baptize you?"

"Yes," said Jesus. "It's the right thing to do."

So John dipped Jesus in the river.

When Jesus came out of the water,
   God's Spirit came down.
His Spirit came like a dove
   and landed on Jesus.
"This is my Son," said a voice from heaven.
"I love him. I am very happy with him."

I did it! ☆

Jesus in the Desert

Matthew 4:1-11; Mark 1:12-13; Luke 4:1-13

Jesus went to the desert.
For 40 days and nights, he had no food.
Satan said to him, "If you are God's Son,
    turn these rocks into bread."
Jesus told Satan, "God's Word says
    that people live on more than just bread.
They live by believing what God says."
Satan said, "If you are really God's Son,
    jump off the worship house.
God's angels will keep you safe."
"God says not to test him," said Jesus.
Satan said, "Worship me, and I will give you
    all the world's kingdoms."

Jesus told Satan, "Go away.
God's Word says to worship only God."
After that, Satan left, and angels came
    to take care of Jesus.

I did it! ☆

Meeting Jesus

John 1:35-47

One day, Andrew saw Jesus passing by,
    so he followed him.
"What do you want?" Jesus asked Andrew.
"I want to know where you are staying,"
    Andrew said.
"Come and see," said Jesus.
So Andrew went with Jesus and talked with him.

Then Andrew ran to his brother Peter.

"I met the Promised One," said Andrew.

He took Peter to meet Jesus.

Later, Jesus saw Philip and said, "Come with me."

Philip ran to find Nathanael.

"We found the man Moses wrote about!" he said.

Then Philip took Nathanael to meet Jesus.

I did it! ☆

A Wedding Party

John 2:1-10

Jesus and his mother were at a wedding party.

In the middle of the party, his mother told him,

    "They ran out of wine!"

Then she told the servants,

    "Do whatever Jesus says."

Six big stone jars stood nearby.

Jesus said, "Fill those jars with water."

So the servants filled them to the top.

"Now dip some out," said Jesus.

"Take it to the host of the party."

The servants obeyed, and the host drank.

The water had turned into wine!

"This is the best wine of all!" said the host.

I did it! ☆

Note to Parents: If you have the *Day by Day Kid's Bible*, read "The Money Tables" and "A Night Visit" (page 516) to your child this weekend (John 2:13-25; 3:1-21).

At the Well

John 4:3-15, 25-26

Jesus had been walking a long way.

He grew tired, so he stopped at a well to rest.

Soon a woman came to the well to get water.

"Would you give me a drink?" Jesus asked.

"Why do you ask me for a drink?" she said.

"You would ask ME for a drink

    if you knew who I was," said Jesus.

"I would give you water that brings life.

My water is like a spring that never runs dry.

Everyone who drinks it lives forever."

The woman wanted this water. She said,
"Someday the Promised One will come.
He will tell us all about these things."
"I am the Promised One," said Jesus.

I did it! ☆

A Sick Son

John 4:46-53

Once there was a man whose son was very sick.

The man went to find Jesus.

"Please come before my son dies," he said.

"Go back home. Your son will live," said Jesus.

The man believed Jesus and left to go home.

While he was on the way, his servants met him.

They told him that his son was alive.

"What time did he get better?" the man asked.

"At one o'clock yesterday afternoon," they said.

That's when Jesus had said, "He will live."

So the man and his family believed in Jesus.

I did it! ☆

Nets Full of Fish

Luke 5:1-11

Two boats bobbed up and down
  at the edge of the lake.
Jesus got into the boat that was Peter's.
"Take the boat into deep water," said Jesus.
"We can catch some fish."
"We fished all night," said Peter,
  "and we didn't catch anything.
But if you say so, I will let the nets down."

The men threw their nets into the water.

Right away, hundreds of fish swam into the nets.

The nets got so heavy that they began to break.

James and John brought the other boat to help.

After they pulled the nets in,

    Jesus told the men, "Follow me."

And they did.

I did it! ☆

A Hole in a Roof

Matthew 9:1-7; Mark 2:1-12; Luke 5:17-25

Four men had a friend who could not walk.
They carried him on his mat
    to a house where Jesus was.
Because so many people were there,
    the four men could not get in.
So they made a hole in the roof.
Then they lowered their friend into the room.
Jesus told the man, "Your sins are forgiven."
Some people wondered why Jesus said that.
"Only God can forgive sin," they said.

Jesus asked, "Is it easier to say,
'Your sins are forgiven'
or, 'Get up and walk'?"
Then he told the man,
"Get up, take your mat, and go home."
The man stood, picked up his mat, and walked!

I did it! ☆

At the Pool

John 5:1-10, 16-17

A man was by a pool near the Sheep Gate.

He had not been able to walk for 38 years.

He thought the bubbly pool might heal him.

Jesus asked him, "Do you want to get well?"

"Yes," he said. "But I can't get into the pool."

Jesus said, "Get up, take your mat, and walk."

Right away, the man took his mat and walked.

But the Jewish leaders saw him and got angry.

They had a rule: No working on the worship day.

No one could carry a mat, and no one could heal.

But Jesus said, "God works all the time,

even on the worship day.

So I do whatever I see God my Father doing."

I did it! ☆

Note to Parents: If you have the *Day by Day Kid's Bible*, read "A Party at Matthew's" (page 525) and "Father and Son" (page 526) to your child this weekend (Matthew 9:9-15; Mark 2:13-20; Luke 5:27-35; John 5:16-47).

Is It Right?

Matthew 12:9-14; Mark 3:1-6; Luke 6:6-11

One worship day, Jesus saw a man
   with a small, bent hand.
The leaders asked Jesus, "Is it right
   to make people well on the worship day?"
Jesus said, "Your sheep might fall into a pit
   on the worship day.
If it does, you pull it out.
A person is more important than a sheep."
He told the man, "Hold out your hand."
So the man held out his hand.
He could reach out all the way. He was well!
But the leaders got angry.
That's because it was against their rules
   to heal someone on the worship day.

I did it! ☆

Twelve Friends

Mark 3:13-19; Luke 6:12-19

One time Jesus prayed all night.

The next morning, he called his friends to him.

He picked 12 of them to be his special helpers:

    Peter and his brother Andrew,

    James and his brother John,

    Philip, Nathanael, and Matthew,

    Thomas, Simon, and another James,

    Thaddaeus, and Judas.

Lots of other people came to see Jesus.

Some came to listen to him teach.

Some came to be made well.

Everyone tried to touch him.

They knew that power came from him.

And he was healing everyone.

I did it! ☆

Jesus the Teacher

Matthew 5:1, 14-16, 43-45

Jesus sat on a hill with his followers.

"You are like a light to this world," he said.

"People do not put a lamp under a bowl.

Instead, they put it where it will shine.

So let your light shine where people can see it.

They will see the good things you do.

Then they will praise God your Father.

You have heard, 'Love your neighbor
   and hate your enemy.'
But I'm telling you to love your enemies.
Pray for people who hurt you.
Then you'll be children of your Father in heaven.
He makes the sun shine on all people,
   bad and good."

I did it! ☆

Birds and Flowers

Matthew 6:26-33

"See the birds?" said Jesus.

"They do not plant seeds or bring in crops.

They do not save food in barns.

God your Father feeds them.

You are more important than birds.

Look at the flowers.

They do not work or make their own clothes.

God dresses them.

So do not worry about food or clothes.

God knows you need these things.

Put God first in your life.

Then he will make sure you have all you need."

I did it! ☆

A Sick Servant

Matthew 8:5-13; Luke 7:1-10

A Roman army captain sent a message to Jesus:

"Come and make my servant well again."

Then the captain sent another message:

"I'm not good enough for you to come to my house.

Just say the word and my servant will be well.

Men obey me, so I know sickness will obey you."

Jesus was surprised.

"I have not seen such great faith before," he said.

Then he sent word to the captain.

"You believed I would heal your servant.

So I will do just what you believed."

At that very moment, the servant got well.

I did it! ☆

Note to Parents: If you have the *Day by Day Kid's Bible*, read "Getting a Son Back" (page 537) and "What Did You Come to See?" (page 538) to your child this weekend (Matthew 11:1-19; Luke 7:11-35).

Perfume

Luke 7:36-47

One day, Jesus went to dinner at the house
of a Jewish leader named Simon.
A woman who was crying came to Jesus there.
Her tears got Jesus' feet wet.
So she wiped his feet with her long hair.
Then she poured perfume on his feet.
Simon said, "If Jesus was smart,
he would know this is a sinful woman."
Jesus said, "Simon, you did not even
wash my feet with water.

But this woman washed my feet with perfume.
Her many sins have been forgiven.
People love a lot
    when they have been forgiven a lot."

I did it! ☆

Seeds and Dirt

Matthew 13:3-23; Mark 4:2-20; Luke 8:4-15

"Once a farmer planted seeds," said Jesus.

"Some seeds fell on the road. Birds ate them.

Some seeds fell on rocks and grew no roots.

Some seeds fell in weeds and got crowded out.

Some seeds fell on good dirt and grew strong.

The seeds are the news of God's kingdom.

Some people have hearts like the hard road.

They hear God's news but do not understand.

Some people's hearts are like rocks.

They forget God's news when trouble comes.

Worry is like weeds in a heart.

It pushes God away.

But some hearts are like good dirt.

God's love sinks in and grows and grows."

I did it! ☆

Seeds and Pearls

Matthew 13:31-32, 44-46; Mark 4:30-34; Luke 13:18-19

"God's kingdom is like a mustard seed,"
   said Jesus.
"It is the smallest seed of all.
But it grows into a big tree where birds nest.
God's kingdom is like hidden treasure
   that a man found when he was digging.

He sold everything he owned
  so he could buy the field he was digging in.
God's kingdom is like a man
  shopping for fine pearls.
One day he found the perfect pearl.
He sold everything he owned
  so he could buy that pearl."

I did it! ☆

The Storm

Matthew 8:23-27; Mark 4:35-41; Luke 8:22-25

The sun began to go down.

"Let's cross the lake," Jesus told his friends.

So they got into a boat.

And they left all the people

   who had been following them.

Soon Jesus fell asleep on a pillow.

But a storm blew in. Waves slapped the boat.

"Jesus!" called his friends. "Wake up!

We're going to die in all this water!"

Jesus sat up and spoke to the wind and waves.

"Be quiet. Be still," he said.

Then the wind died down. All was still.

Jesus' friends said, "Who is Jesus?

Even the wind and waves obey him!"

I did it! ☆

A Sick Girl

Matthew 9:18-26; Mark 5:21-43; Luke 8:40-56

A leader named Jairus came to see Jesus.

"My little girl is very sick," said Jairus.

"Please come to my house and make her well."

So Jesus went with Jairus.

On the way, some men came up to them.

The men told Jairus, "Your little girl has died."

Jesus told Jairus, "Do not be afraid. Just believe."

At the house, Jesus went to the girl's room.

He held her hand and said, "Little girl, get up."

The girl got up and walked! She was alive!

I did it! ☆

Note to Parents: If you have the *Day by Day Kid's Bible*, read "Sheep with No Shepherd" (page 553) and "Like Sheep Going Where Wolves Are" (page 554) to your child this weekend (Matthew 9:35-38; 10:1-6, 40-42; 13:53-58; Mark 6:1-11; Luke 9:1-5).

Two Men Who Could Not See

Matthew 9:27-33

Once there were two men who could not see.

They followed Jesus, calling, "Heal us! Heal us!"

"Do you believe I can heal you?" asked Jesus.

"Yes, Lord," they said.

Then Jesus touched their eyes.

All of a sudden, they could see.

They hurried away and told everybody about it.

So then a man who could not talk came to Jesus.

Jesus made him well too.

People were surprised.

They said, "We never saw such a thing before."

I did it! ☆

Bread for Everyone

Matthew 14:13-21; Mark 6:30-44; Luke 9:10-17; John 6:1-13

A big crowd listened to Jesus all day.

At supper time, Jesus' friends came to him.

They said, "Send the people to town
   so they can eat."

"You get food for them," said Jesus.

"We do not have enough money," said Philip.

But a boy gave Jesus five rolls and two fish.

Jesus told all the people to sit on the grass.
Then he thanked God for the food.
And he told his friends
   to hand the rolls and fish to the people.
When they did, they found that there was
   more than enough food for everyone!
All the people ate as much as they wanted.

I did it! ☆

On Top of the Water

Matthew 14:22-33; Mark 6:45-51; John 6:15-21

One night, Jesus went up on a hill to pray.

His friends were crossing the lake in a boat.

But the wind was strong.

High waves tossed the boat up and down.

Jesus could see that his friends were in trouble.

So he went to them, walking on the water.

They thought he was a ghost.

But Jesus called,

    "Don't be afraid. It's just me."

"Then let me come to you," called Peter.

"Come on," said Jesus.

So Peter began to walk to Jesus on the water.

But then he saw the waves and got scared.

He began to sink. "Save me!" he cried.

Jesus lifted Peter up,

   and they climbed into the boat.

Jesus' friends said, "You really are God's Son!"

I did it! ☆

Bread from Heaven

John 6:28-40

One day some people asked Jesus,
    "What does God want us to do?"
"God wants you to believe in me," said Jesus.
"Then show us a miracle like God did long ago,"
    they said.
"God sent his people bread from heaven,"
Jesus told them. "I am the Bread of Life.
Come to me,
    and your heart will never be hungry.
Believe in me,
    and your spirit will never be thirsty.
I can feed your spirit like food feeds your body.
And you can know God now and forever."

I did it! ☆

Making People Well

Mark 7:31-37

Once there was a man who could not hear.

He could hardly talk.

Some people asked Jesus to make him well.

So Jesus put his fingers into the man's ears.

He touched the man's tongue.

"Open up," he said.

Right away, the man's ears opened.

He started talking clearly too.

Jesus told the people not to tell anyone.

But the more Jesus said, "Don't tell,"
the more people told.

"Jesus does everything right," they said.

I did it! ☆

Note to Parents: If you have the *Day by Day Kid's Bible*, read "Seven Rolls" (page 562) and "Keys" (page 563) to your child this weekend (Matthew 15:32–16:4, 13-20; Mark 8:1-12, 22-30; Luke 9:18-21).

As White as Light

Matthew 17:1-8; Mark 9:2-8; Luke 9:28-36

One day Jesus went up on a high mountain.

He went with three special friends,

    Peter, James, and John.

All of a sudden, Jesus' clothes

    became as white as light.

His face began to shine as bright as the sun.

Moses and Elijah showed up and talked with him.

Then a bright cloud came, and a voice said,

    "This is my Son. I love him.

    I am happy with him. Listen to him."

Peter, James, and John were too afraid to look.

Jesus came over and said, "Do not be afraid."

When they looked up, they saw only Jesus.

I did it! ☆

Fishing for Money

Matthew 17:24-27

Some tax men came to Peter and asked,
"Does Jesus pay the worship-house tax?"
"Yes," said Peter. "He does."
Then Peter went to Jesus.
But before Peter could say anything,
Jesus said, "Who pays taxes to the king?
Is it the king's family or other people?"
"Other people," said Peter.
"Then the king's family does not pay,"
said Jesus.

"But we don't want to make these men mad.
So go fishing and look in the mouth
of the first fish you catch.
You will find money inside to pay our taxes."

I did it! ☆

The Shepherd

John 10:1-5, 10-11, 14-18

"Sheep listen for their shepherd's voice,"
  said Jesus.
"The shepherd calls them by their names.
They follow him, because they know his voice.
I am the Good Shepherd.

I know my people. They are my sheep.
I came so they can have a good, full life.
I will even die to save them.
Nobody will be able
   to take my life away from me.
But I choose to give my life to save my people."

I did it! ☆

Seeing

John 9:1-7

One day, Jesus and his friends saw a blind man.

Jesus' friends asked, "Why can't this man see?

Did he sin? Did his mother and father sin?"

"It's not because of anyone's sin," said Jesus.

"It happened so God can show his power.

And I must do God's powerful work.

While I am here, I am the Light of the World."

Then Jesus spit on the dirt and made some mud.

He put it on the man's eyes.

"Go wash the mud off in the pool," said Jesus.

So the man went to the pool and washed.

When he came back, he could see!

I did it! ☆

Ten Men and One Thank-You

Luke 17:11-19

One day, Jesus saw 10 men
   who had a very bad skin sickness.
They called to Jesus, "Help us!"
"Go to the priest," called Jesus.
"Let him look at your skin."
So the men left to go to the priest.
On the way, they saw that their skin was well.

One of the men ran back to Jesus.

He bowed down at Jesus' feet and thanked him.

"Didn't 10 men get well?" asked Jesus.

"Where are the other nine?"

Then Jesus told the man, "You can get up and go.

You are well because you believed in me."

I did it! ☆

Note to Parents: If you have the *Day by Day Kid's Bible*, read "Writing on the Ground" (page 572) and "Seventy-Two Men" (page 577) to your child this weekend (Matthew 11:25-30; Luke 10:1-11, 16-21; John 8:2-11).

The Neighbor

Luke 10:25-37

Once a man told Jesus that he knew
   he should love God and his neighbor.
"But who is my neighbor?" asked the man.
To answer him, Jesus told this story:
"A man was walking down a road one day.
Robbers jumped out and hit him.
They took what he had and left him by the road.
There was man who worked at the worship house.
He came down the road, saw the hurt man,
   and passed by.
There was a man who knew all the rules
   God gave Moses.
He came down the road, saw the hurt man,
   and passed by.

Then a man from another land saw the hurt man.
He stopped and took care of the man.
Which man was a neighbor?" asked Jesus.
"The one who was kind," said the man
    who had heard the story Jesus told.
"Right," said Jesus. "So go and be kind."

I did it! ☆

Taking Time

Luke 10:38-42

Jesus had friends named Mary and Martha.

When he went to their house,

Mary sat and listened to Jesus talk.

But Martha was busy getting everything ready.

At last, Martha went to Jesus.

"Mary left me with all the work," she said.

"Tell her to help me."

"Martha, Martha," said Jesus.

"You are upset and worried.

Only one thing is important right now,

and that is what Mary is doing.

She is taking time to be with me."

I did it! ☆

Lost and Found

Luke 15:3-10

"Once there was a shepherd," said Jesus.
"He had one hundred sheep.
One of his sheep got lost.
So he looked and looked until he found it.
He told all his friends how happy he was."
Then Jesus said, "Once there was a woman
who had 10 silver coins.
When she lost one, she cleaned house.
Then she looked and looked until she found it.
She told all her friends how happy she was."
Jesus said, "Angels in heaven get happy too.
They are happy when God finds
one person who will follow him."

I did it! ☆

Pig Food

Luke 15:11-24

A man had two sons.

The younger son asked for his part

of the family's money.

Then he left home and lived a wild life.

Soon his money was gone.

He had no food and no house.

So he got a job feeding pigs.

He was so hungry, he wanted to eat the pig food.

He said, "People who work for my father
    are better off than I am. I'm going home."
When his father saw him coming,
    he ran and hugged his son.
"Father, I have sinned," said the son.
"Just let me work for you like a servant."
"No!" said his father. "We'll have a party!"
The man told his servants,
    "My son was lost, but now he is found!"

I did it! ☆

Out of the Grave

John 11

Mary and Martha's brother, Lazarus, was sick.
By the time Jesus got to their house,
    Lazarus had died.
His body had been in the grave four days.
A big stone covered the opening of the grave.
Jesus cried when he saw how sad everyone was.
He asked some men to move the stone away.
And he prayed, thanking God for hearing him.

Then Jesus called, "Lazarus, come out!"
And Lazarus came out. He was alive!
Many people saw it and believed in Jesus.
But their leaders were afraid that everyone
would start following Jesus instead of them.
So they began making plans to get rid of him.

I did it! ☆

Note to Parents: If you have the *Day by Day Kid's Bible*, read "The Judge" and "The Proud Prayer" (page 587) to your child this weekend (Luke 18:1-14).

Let the Children Come

Matthew 19:13-15; Mark 10:13-16; Luke 18:15-17

People began bringing children to Jesus.
They wanted Jesus to pray for their children.
But Jesus' friends would not let
 the boys and girls come.

"Do not bother Jesus," they said.

When Jesus saw this, he was upset.

He said, "Let the little children come to me.

Do not stop them.

God's kingdom belongs to people
who are like these children."

Then he picked the children up
and prayed for them.

He asked God to bring them good things.

I did it! ☆

Up in a Tree

Luke 19:1-10

Zacchaeus was in a crowd of people.

Everyone was waiting to see Jesus.

But Zacchaeus was a very short man.

He could not see around all the people.

So he ran ahead and climbed up into a tree.

When Jesus got to the tree, he stopped.

"Zacchaeus!" called Jesus. "Come down.

I need to stay at your house today."

Zacchaeus came down.

He was glad to take Jesus to his house.

Zacchaeus told Jesus that he
would start sharing and helping others.

Jesus was glad. "That is why I came," he said.

I did it! ☆

By the Side of the Road

Mark 10:46-52; Luke 18:35-43

Bartimaeus could not see. He was blind.

One day he heard that Jesus was coming.

So he shouted, "Jesus! Be kind to me!"

People got mad and told him to be quiet.

But Bartimaeus shouted louder.

Jesus heard him and called him to come.

Bartimaeus threw his coat off and jumped up.

"What do you want?" asked Jesus.

"I want to see!" said Bartimaeus.

"All right," said Jesus.

"You are well because you believe in me."

Right away, Bartimaeus could see.

He followed Jesus, praising God.

I did it! ☆

A Jar of Perfume

Matthew 26:6-13; Mark 14:1-9; John 12:1-8

Jesus went to a dinner party.

Martha served the food.

Lazarus ate at the table with Jesus.

But Mary carried a jar of perfume to Jesus
and poured it on his feet.

Then she wiped his feet with her hair.

Judas, one of Jesus' helpers, said,
"Why didn't Mary sell this perfume?

She could have given the money to poor people."

But Judas did not care about poor people.

He wanted the money for himself.

"Leave Mary alone," said Jesus.

"She is showing her love for me before I die."

I did it! ☆

A Colt

Matthew 21:1-9; Mark 11:1-10; Luke 19:28-40; John 12:12-15

Jesus sent two of his friends to town.

He sent them to get a baby donkey for him to ride.

So they brought the donkey's colt to Jesus
  and put their coats on its back.

Then Jesus rode the colt into Jerusalem.

People heard that Jesus was coming.

So they got big palm branches
  and ran to meet him.

They called, "Hosanna!

    Shout for the King of God's people!"

Some Jewish leaders were in the crowd.

They told Jesus,

    "Make your followers be quiet!"

Jesus said, "If the people are quiet,

    the stones will shout!"

I did it! ☆

Note to Parents: If you have the *Day by Day Kid's Bible*, read "A Fig Tree and a Hiding Place for Robbers" (page 597) and "A Seed" (page 598) to your child this weekend (Matthew 21:10-16; Mark 11:11-18; Luke 19:45-48; John 12:17-36).

Two Sons and a Grape Garden

Matthew 21:28-32

Jesus told this story to the Jewish leaders.

"There was once a man who had two sons.

He told his first son, 'Go work in the garden.'

But the first son said, 'No.'

Later he changed his mind and he did go.

The man told his other son,

   'Go work in the garden.'

'Yes, sir,' said the son. 'I will.'

But he did not go," said Jesus.

"Which one did what his father wanted?"

"The first one," said the leaders.

Jesus said, "You are like the second son.

You say you will obey God, but you don't."

I did it! ☆

The Most Money

Mark 12:41-44; Luke 21:1-4

One day, Jesus sat in the worship house.
He watched people put money
   into the offering box.
Lots of rich people came by
   and put in lots of money.
Then a poor woman walked up.
She dropped in two small pennies.

"Look!" said Jesus.

"This woman put in more than anyone else.

She even put in more than the rich people did.

They gave only part of their riches.

This poor woman gave all

the money she had."

I did it!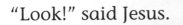

Ten Lamps

Matthew 25:1-13

Jesus told a story about 10 young people.

They were going to a wedding party.

They all brought lamps with them.

Five brought extra oil to keep their lamps lit.

But five did not bring extra oil.

They all fell asleep waiting for the party.

At last, in the middle of the night,

    someone called, "Here comes the groom!"

The young people woke up.

But five of them had run out of oil.

They went to get more oil to light their lamps.

But the party started without them.

"So watch," said Jesus. "Be ready.

You do not know when I will come."

I did it! ☆

Ready for You

Matthew 25:31-45

Jesus said, "Someday I will come back.
Then I will say to some people, 'Come!
My Father's kingdom has been ready for you
      since the world was made.
I was hungry, thirsty, and sick,
      and you took care of me.'
'When did we do this?' they will ask.
'When you helped other people,' I will say.

To some people, I will say, 'Go away.
I was hungry, thirsty, and sick,
    and you did not take care of me.'
'When did that happen?' they will ask.
'When you did not help others,' I will say."

I did it! ☆

Thirty Silver Coins

Matthew 26:3-5, 14-16; Mark 14:1-2, 10-11; Luke 22:1-6

The Jewish leaders wanted to get rid of Jesus.

Judas was one of Jesus' friends.

But he went to the Jewish leaders.

He told them he could show them
where Jesus was.

"What will you pay me to do that?" he asked.
The leaders counted out 30 silver coins.
Judas took the money.
Then he waited and watched for a time
    when no crowds were around.

I did it! ☆

Note to Parents: If you have the *Day by Day Kid's Bible*, read "Tricks" and "More Tricks" (page 601) to your child this weekend (Matthew 22:15-46; Mark 12:13-25; Luke 20:20-44).

The Room Upstairs

Matthew 26:17-20, 26-29; Mark 14:12-17, 22-25; Luke 22:7-20

Jesus sent Peter and John into the city.
He sent them to find a room
  where he and his friends could eat.
They found a house with a big room upstairs.
When dinner was ready,
  Jesus and his 12 helpers sat at the table.
Jesus picked up the bread and thanked God.

Then he shared it with his friends.

"Eat this to remember me," he said.

After dinner, Jesus picked up a cup of wine.

"Drink this to remember me," he said.

He knew it was time for him to leave the world.

Jesus loved his friends very much.

Soon he would show them
    how much he loved them.

I did it! ☆

Clean Feet

John 13:3-15

Jesus took a long cloth and a big bowl of water.
Then he began washing his helpers' dusty feet.
He dried their feet with the cloth.
"I cannot let you wash my feet," said Peter.
"That means you will not be part
   of what I am doing," Jesus said.
"Then wash my feet and my hands.
Wash my head, too!" said Peter.
Jesus said, "The rest of your body is clean."

After Jesus washed his helpers' feet,

he asked, "Do you understand what I did?
You call me Teacher and Lord.
Your Teacher and Lord just washed your feet.
I am showing you the way to treat others."

I did it! ☆

God's Spirit of Truth

John 13:33-35; 14:16-17, 26-27

Jesus said, "I will be here just a little longer.

Here is a new rule for you.

Love each other like I love you.

Everyone will know you are my friends

   if you love each other.

I will ask my Father to give you a Helper.

He is God's Spirit of truth.

He will be with you forever.

He lives with you, and he will be in you.

He will help you and teach you.

He will remind you about what I have told you.

I am also giving you my peace.

So do not worry, and do not be afraid."

I did it! ☆

Praying in the Garden

Matthew 26:36-40; Mark 14:32-37; Luke 22:39-45; John 18:1

Jesus and his friends went
    to a garden of olive trees.
"Sit here while I go and pray," said Jesus.
He was starting to feel very sad.
He walked a little way from his friends.
Then he got down on his knees and prayed.
"Father, if you will, don't let me die this way.
But do whatever you think is best.
I will do whatever you want me to do."
An angel came and helped Jesus be strong.
Then Jesus went back to his friends.

I did it! ☆

Judas and the Guards

Matthew 26:47-57; Mark 14:43-53; Luke 22:47-54; John 18:2-14

Judas led guards to the garden.

He told them, "The man I kiss will be Jesus."

Jesus saw Judas and the guards coming.

"Teacher!" said Judas. Then he kissed Jesus.

The guards started to take Jesus.

But Peter pulled out a sword.

He swung it at the servant of the high priest.

And he cut off the man's right ear.

"Put your sword away," said Jesus.

He touched the servant's ear and healed it.

Then the guards tied Jesus up

and took him to the Jewish leaders.

I did it! ☆

Note to Parents: If you have the *Day by Day Kid's Bible*, read "The Rooster Crows" (page 616) and "The Son of God" (page 617) to your child this weekend (Matthew 26:57-75; 27:1, 3-10; Mark 14:53-72; 15:1; Luke 22:54-71; John 18:12-27).

Skull Hill

Matthew 27:11-26, 33, 50; Mark 15:1-15, 22, 24, 37;
Luke 23:1-5, 13-25, 33-34, 46; John 18:28–19:18, 30

The Jewish leaders took Jesus to Pilate,

   the Roman leader.

Pilate was the boss of Jerusalem.

"Jesus tells us he is God's Son," the men said.

"Our rules say he must die for telling us that."

Pilate tried to set Jesus free.

But people shouted louder and louder.

They said that they wanted Jesus to die.

In the end, Pilate let them take Jesus
   to a place called Skull Hill.
There they hung him on a cross.
Jesus said, "Father, forgive them.
They do not know what they are doing."
And there on the cross, Jesus died.

I did it! ☆

The Grave

Matthew 27:57-66; Mark 15:42-46;
Luke 23:50-54; John 19:38-42

Joseph, a Jewish leader, went to see Pilate
    the evening that Jesus died.
Joseph believed in Jesus.
He asked Pilate if he could have Jesus' body.
Pilate said he could.
So Joseph put Jesus' body in a new grave.
A big stone was rolled in front of the opening.
Some Jewish leaders told Pilate,
    "Jesus said he would come back to life.
We do not want his friends to take his body.
They might say Jesus is alive again."
So Pilate sent guards to the grave.
They stood there to make sure no one opened it.

I did it! ☆

An Angel

Matthew 28:1-4

On Sunday after Jesus died,
   the sun was just coming up.
The earth shook, and an angel
   showed up at Jesus' grave.

The angel looked like lightning.
His clothes were as white as snow.
He rolled away the stone
   that was in front of the grave.
Then he sat on the stone.
The guards saw the angel
   and were so afraid that they shook.
The men fell down as if they were dead.

I did it! ☆

Joy Again

Mark 16:1-8; John 20:1-16

Mary and some friends walked to Jesus' grave.
They had some spices to put on Jesus' body.
"Who will roll the stone away?" they asked.
But the stone had already been rolled away.
When they looked inside, an angel was there.
"Do not be afraid," he said. "Jesus is alive!"
When Peter and John heard about this,
    they ran to the grave to see
    for themselves.

It was true. Jesus' body was not there.

So Peter and John left. But Mary stayed.

She was crying.

She heard a man ask, "Why are you crying?"

When she turned around, she saw Jesus!

He really was alive!

I did it! ☆

345

On the Road

Mark 16:12-13; Luke 24:13-35

Two of Jesus' friends walked home,
    talking about how Jesus had died.
Jesus came up and walked with them.
But they did not know it was Jesus.
He walked with them all the way to their house.
They asked Jesus to stay and eat with them.
So he did. When Jesus held the bread
    and thanked God, they knew who he was.
But all of a sudden, Jesus was gone.
Right away, the two friends walked back
    to Jerusalem.
They went to tell Jesus' other friends
    what had happened.

I did it! ☆

Note to Parents: If you have the *Day by Day Kid's Bible*, read about more things that happened on the morning after Jesus came back to life. Read "Running to the Grave" and "The Guards' Story" (page 626) to your child this weekend (John 20:2-18; Matthew 28:11-15).

In a Locked Room

Mark 16:14; Luke 24:33-43; John 20:19-28

Jesus' friends were together in a locked room.

All of a sudden, there was Jesus!

His friends thought he was a ghost.

"Look at my hands and feet," said Jesus.

"A ghost does not have skin and bones

  like I have."

347

Then Jesus ate some fish.

Jesus' friends were surprised and glad.

But Thomas was not there that night.

He did not believe Jesus had really come.

A week later, Jesus came to his friends again.

This time, Thomas was with them.

Jesus showed Thomas his hands and feet.

"My Lord and my God!" said Thomas.

He believed. **I did it!** ☆

Going Fishing

John 21:1-17

"I am going fishing," said Peter.
Some other friends of Jesus'
   sailed with him out on the lake.
All night they fished, but they caught nothing.
When the sun came up,
   someone on shore called to them.
"Try looking for fish in the water
   on the other side of the boat."
So they did, and they caught lots of fish.

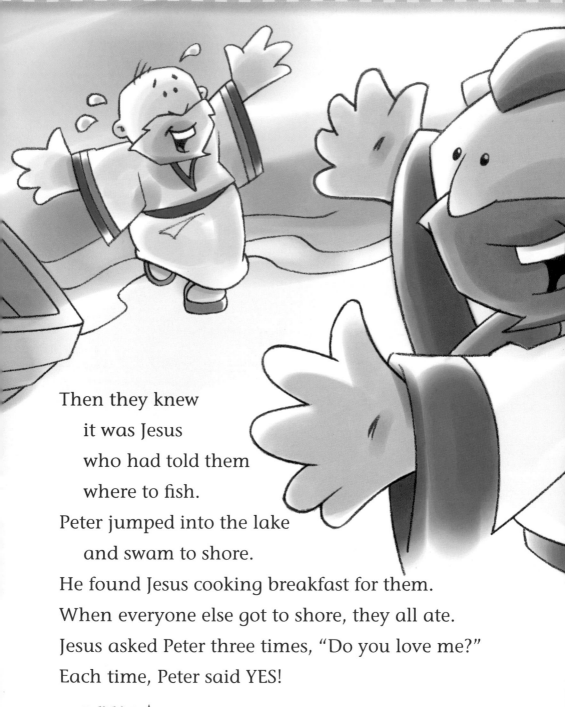

Then they knew
   it was Jesus
   who had told them
   where to fish.
Peter jumped into the lake
   and swam to shore.
He found Jesus cooking breakfast for them.
When everyone else got to shore, they all ate.
Jesus asked Peter three times, "Do you love me?"
Each time, Peter said YES!

I did it! ☆

Into the Clouds

Matthew 28:18-20; Mark 16:15, 19; Luke 24:46-52; Acts 1:8-12

"I rule over heaven and earth," said Jesus.
"So go and make followers for me in all lands.
Teach people everything I have told you.
I will always be with you,
    even to the end of time.
And I'll send you the gift my Father promised."
Then Jesus went up off the ground.

His friends watched until a cloud hid him.

Then they saw two men dressed all in white.

The men asked, "Why are you looking up?

Jesus has gone into heaven.

He will come back someday

the way you saw him go."

Then Jesus' friends were full of joy.

I did it! ☆

Wind, Fire, and Different Languages

Acts 2:1-40

One day Jesus' friends were together in the city.

The sound of a strong wind filled the house.

Something that looked like fire sat on them.

Then God's Holy Spirit filled them.

And they began talking in different languages.

Jewish people from every country were there.

When all of them heard their own language,

   they came together and listened to Peter.

He said, "God sent Jesus, and you killed him.

But God brought him back to life.

So change your ways,

   and be baptized in Jesus' name.

He will forgive you.

And he will give you the gift of God's Holy Spirit."

I did it! ☆

A Lame Man

Acts 3:1-26

One day, Peter and John went
    to the worship house to pray.
A lame man sitting at the gate
    asked them for money.
"I have no money to give you," said Peter.
"But I have something else.
In Jesus' name, get up and walk."
Right away, the man's feet got strong.
He stood and walked and jumped!
The people who saw him were surprised.
So Peter began telling them about Jesus.

I did it! ☆

Note to Parents: If you have the *Day by Day Kid's Bible*, read "Plain Men and Proud
Leaders" (page 636) and "A Locked Jail" (page 637) to your child this weekend
(Acts 4:1-24, 29-37; 5:1–6:1).

Stephen Sees Jesus

Acts 6:8-14; 7:51-60

Stephen was a man full of God's kind love.

But Jewish leaders said

   that Stephen was against God.

"What about you?" said Stephen.

"You killed Jesus."

The leaders were very angry.

But Stephen looked up to heaven.

"I see heaven. It's open!" he said.

"Jesus is standing right beside God!"

At first, the leaders covered their ears.

Then they took Stephen out of the city

   and began throwing rocks at him.

They killed him.

I did it! ☆

A Chariot Ride

Acts 8:26-39

One of God's angels came to Philip.

The angel told him to go to the desert road.

On his way, Philip met a man in a chariot.

The Spirit said, "Go up to that chariot."

So Philip ran up to the chariot.

There he saw a man reading a book.

It was the book Isaiah wrote.

"Do you understand that book?" asked Philip.

"No," said the man. "I need some help.

Who is this book talking about?"

　　The part the man was reading

　　　was about Jesus.

　　　Philip told him all about Jesus.

The man believed
   and asked Philip to baptize him.
So Philip did,
   and the man went on his way happy.

I did it! ☆

A Bright Light

Acts 9:1-20

Saul was against people who followed Jesus.

He tried to put them in jail.

One day, a bright light came down on him
     from heaven.

Saul fell to the ground and heard a voice say,
     "Saul, why are you hurting me?"

"Who are you?" asked Saul.

"I am Jesus," said the voice.

When Saul got up, he couldn't see.

For three days he didn't eat or drink.

He prayed. Then God sent a man
    to help Saul see again.

After that, Saul told everyone
    that Jesus is God's Son.

I did it! ☆

Peter and Dorcas

Acts 9:36-42

One day two men went to see Peter.

"Please come with us right away!" they said.

They told him about a woman named Dorcas.

Everyone in her town was upset,

    because she had died.

Dorcas had helped lots of poor people.

Peter went with the men.

They took him to the room where Dorcas was.

Some women showed him clothes she had made.

Peter prayed. Then he said, "Dorcas, get up."

Dorcas opened her eyes.

Peter helped her stand. She was alive!

Then lots of people believed in Jesus.

I did it! ☆

Animals in a Big Sheet

Acts 10:9-48

While Peter was praying one day,
    God sent a dream.
It was about animals in a sheet.
There were snakes and turtles and birds.
"Eat," said a voice.
"I can't, Lord," said Peter.
"These are animals
    you don't want your people to eat."
But the dream came three more times.
Then the Spirit told Peter to visit Cornelius.
Cornelius was not one of God's people.
He was a Roman army captain.
But he loved God and helped poor people.

Peter went to see Cornelius
and told him about Jesus.
Cornelius and his family believed.
Then Peter knew the meaning of his dream.
God loves and welcomes all people everywhere
who look up to him and do what is right.

I did it! ☆

Note to Parents: If you have the *Day by Day Kid's Bible*, read *more* about "Animals in a Big Sheet" (page 646), and read "The Same Gift" (page 648) to your child this weekend (Acts 10–11).

The Angel in the Jail

Acts 12:1-11

Peter was put in jail for teaching about Jesus.
There were guards beside him
   and more guards at the door.
But Peter's friends were praying for him.
One night, a light began to shine in the jail.
An angel tapped Peter and said, "Get up.
Hurry. Put on your clothes and shoes."

So Peter dressed and followed the angel.

He thought he was dreaming.

They walked past the guards
   and through a gate that opened by itself.

Next, they walked to the end of one street.

Then the angel left, and Peter was free!

I did it! ☆

People Try to Worship Paul

Acts 13:9; 14:1-17

Saul had another name: Paul.

Paul and Barnabas went to Lystra.

There they told people about Jesus,

and they made a lame man well.

When the people saw this,

they thought the two men were gods.

They tried to worship Paul and Barnabas.

But the men said, "We're people just like you.

Worship the living God who made the earth.

He shows you who he is by giving you rain.

He makes the crops grow in your fields.

And he gives you joy in your hearts."

I did it! ☆

365

Promised Children

Galatians 1:1-2; 4:1-9; 5:22-25

Paul wrote a letter to some friends. It said:

To Jesus' followers,

You know God.

Better than that, God knows you.

He sent his Son's Spirit into your hearts.

That's because you are God's children.

His Son's Spirit in you calls, "Daddy! Father!"

With his Spirit leading you,

> you are like a tree growing good fruit.

> Loving. Having joy. Living in peace.

> Waiting quietly. Being kind. Being good.

> Keeping promises. Treating people with care.

> Having control of yourself.

So let's follow the Spirit.

From Paul

I did it! ☆

The Earth Shakes

Acts 16:19-34

Paul and Silas were put in jail
    for following Jesus and teaching about him.
Late one night, they were praying
    and singing songs to God.
All of a sudden, the earth began to shake hard.
Everybody's chains fell off.

The jailer woke up and saw the open jail doors.

He was afraid.

He thought all the men in jail had run away.

But Paul said, "Don't worry.

We are all here."

Then Paul told the jailer about Jesus.

The jailer and his whole family believed.

I did it! ☆

To Cheer You Up

1 Thessalonians 1:1; 4:13-18

To the followers of Jesus,

We want you to know about dying.

Jesus died and came back to life.

So God will bring people back to life too.

When Jesus comes back from heaven,

an angel will shout with a loud voice.

Jesus' followers who have died

will go with him.

Then people who are still alive will go.

We will go up in the clouds

and meet Jesus in the air.

Then we will live with him forever.

Help each other remember this.

It will cheer you up.   *From Paul, Silas, and Timothy*

I did it! ☆

Note to Parents: If you have the *Day by Day Kid's Bible*, read "Paul Visits Many Towns" (page 665) and "Paul's Dream" (page 667) to your child this weekend (Acts 17:1–18:11).

Runners

1 Corinthians 1:1-2; 9:24-25; 16:13-14

To Jesus' followers,

All the people in a race run hard,

   even though only one of them will win.

They all practice a lot before they run.

They hope to win a prize.

But the prize they win will not last.

In God's kingdom, we are like runners.

We run to get a prize too.

But our prize will last forever.

All who run this race well will win.

Be careful. Be brave. Be strong.

And do everything with love.

From Paul

I did it! ☆

The Idol Makers

Acts 19:23–20:1

Idol makers got mad at Paul.
That's because people stopped buying idols
    when they began believing in Jesus.
The idol makers yelled for two hours.
"Our god is best!" they shouted.
"But Paul gets people to believe in Jesus.

So how can we make money
   by selling idols of our god?"
Paul's friends were afraid
   the idol makers might hurt Paul.
At last a city leader got the idol makers quiet.
"Go back home!" he said.
So the idol makers went home,
   and Paul left that city.

I did it! ☆

Clay Jars

2 Corinthians 1:1; 4:6-7

To Jesus' followers,
When time began, God said,
   "Let light shine."
Now God has made another light shine.
This light shines in our hearts.
We have the light because we love Jesus.
This makes us rich!

We are like clay jars
full of riches from God.
People see Jesus living in us.
He gives us power to do what's right and good.
And it is clear that this power
comes from God, not from us.

From Paul

I did it! ☆

More Than Winners

Romans 1:1, 7; 8:31-35, 37-39

To my friends in Rome,

If God is for us, who can be against us?

He gave up Jesus for all of us.

So won't he give us everything we need?

What can take God's love away from us?

Death can't. Life can't.

Angels can't. Bad spirits can't.

Nothing high. Nothing low.

Nothing today. Nothing tomorrow.

Nothing in the world

   can take God's love away from us.

We will always have God's love,

   and we'll see it in Jesus.   *From Paul*

I did it! ☆

Falling out the Window

Acts 20:7-12

One Sunday, people met to hear Paul teach.

They met together in an upstairs room.

Paul planned to leave town the next day.

So he talked until after midnight.

One young man sat in a window to listen.

As Paul talked on and on,

    the young man went to sleep.

All of a sudden, he fell out the window.

When the people picked the young man up

    on the ground below, he was dead.

But Paul hugged him and told everyone,

    "Don't worry. He is alive."

Paul went back upstairs

    and talked again until morning.

Then everyone went home, even the young man.

I did it! ☆

Note to Parents: If you have the *Day by Day Kid's Bible*, read "Crowds and Shouts" (page 719) and "Tossing Dust into the Air" (page 721) to your child this weekend (Acts 21:1-24, 26-40; 22).

The Secret Plan

Acts 23:6-35

The Jewish leaders were angry at Paul
   for teaching about Jesus in Jerusalem.
They yelled and caused trouble.
So the army captain put Paul in jail.
But 40 men got together in secret.
They made plans to kill Paul.
Paul had a sister. Her son heard
   about the plan and told Paul.
Paul said the young man should talk
   to the captain. So he did.
The captain sent 70 soldiers on horses
   to take Paul to Governor Felix.
Then Felix had Paul put in a different jail.

I did it! ☆

Felix and His Wife

Acts 24

The men who hated Paul told Governor Felix
   that Paul was a trouble maker.
So Felix ordered a guard to watch Paul.

Then one day, Governor Felix asked Paul
    to come see him.
Felix's wife was there. She was Jewish.
Paul talked to them about believing in Jesus.
He talked about how to be right with God.
After that, Felix often asked Paul
    to come and talk with him.
He hoped Paul would pay to be set free.
But Paul did not pay.
After two years, a new governor came.
And Felix left Paul in jail.

I did it! ☆

A New Governor

Acts 25

The new governor was named Festus.
The men who hated Paul told Festus
    that Paul was a trouble maker.
But Paul told Festus,
    "I did not do anything wrong."
Festus thought Paul was right.
But Paul would not go back to Jerusalem.
That's where people wanted to kill him.
Paul asked to go see the great ruler in Rome.
King Agrippa came to visit Festus.
Festus told him, "Paul wants our great ruler
    to question him about what he has done.
Maybe you can tell me what to say in a letter.
I will send it with him to the great ruler."

I did it! ☆

Your Mind Is Gone!

Acts 26:1-29

Paul told Festus and King Agrippa
   about the bright light he had seen.
He told about Jesus' voice saying,
   "Why are you hurting me?"
He told about Jesus coming back to life.

Then Festus shouted, "You've learned so much,
  your mind is gone!"

Paul said, "I am telling the truth.

King Agrippa, do you believe me?"

The king asked, "Do you think I will become
  a follower of Jesus?

How could I do that in such a short time?"

Paul said, "I hope everyone will follow Jesus.

But I hope no one goes to jail for it."

I did it! ☆

A Ship Goes Down

Acts 27

An army captain named Julius took Paul
　　on a ship. It was sailing to Rome.
But winter was coming.
Paul said, "It is not safe to sail now."
No one listened to Paul, but he was right.
The winter sea pounded the ship.
Storms ripped into it day after day.
Everyone on the ship was afraid.

One night an angel came to Paul and said,

"Do not be afraid. Everyone will live."

The angel was right. The ship was torn apart.

But everyone got to the beach safely.

I did it! ☆

Note to Parents: If you have the *Day by Day Kid's Bible*, read "What If Your Whole Body Were an Eye?" (page 685) and "Love" (page 687) to your child this weekend (1 Corinthians 12–13).

A Snake in the Fire

Acts 28:1-6

Paul and the people from the ship
    landed on an island called Malta.
It was cold and rainy there.
But the people on the island were kind.
They built a fire for the men from the ship.
Paul helped by carrying the wood.
He put the wood on the fire.
As he did, a snake crawled out and bit his hand.
Paul shook the snake off into the fire.

Everyone thought Paul would get sick
   or fall down dead all of a sudden.
They watched him, but nothing bad happened.

I did it! ☆

The Leader of the Island

Acts 28:7-10

The leader of the island of Malta
   had a big house.
He asked Paul and his friends to come in,
   and he treated them very well.
But the leader's father was sick in bed.
So Paul went to see him.
The man was hot with a fever.
But when Paul prayed for him, he got well.
Soon other sick people came to see Paul.
They got well too.
So everyone liked Paul and his friends.

I did it! ☆

389

A House in Rome

Acts 28:11-16, 30-31

Three months went by.

It was time for Paul to sail to Rome.

He and Julius and the others got another ship.

They sailed to Italy, where Rome is.

Jesus' followers in Rome knew Paul was coming.

So they traveled out of the city to meet Paul.

Paul was glad to see them and thanked God.

Paul got to live in a house in Rome.

But a guard had to be with him.

Still, people could come and visit him.

Paul was brave and wise.

For two years, he taught about Jesus,
and no one stopped him.

I did it! ☆

Thursday

Like a Plant

Colossians 1:1-2, 15-16; 2:6-7

To God's people who follow Jesus,
We cannot see God,
   but Jesus shows us what God is like.
God made everything in heaven and on earth.
He made things we see
   and things we cannot see.
He made kings, powers, and rulers.
Everything was made by him and for him.
You believed in Jesus.
So keep living in him.
Be like a plant.
Let your roots go deep into Jesus.

From Paul

I did it! ☆

392

A Slave Who Ran Away

Philemon

Paul wrote this letter after Onesimus had
    run away from Paul's friend Philemon.
(Say the names this way: oh-NEH-sih-muhs
    and fih-LEE-muhn.)

Dear Philemon,
I want to ask you something.
I am an old man in jail
    for teaching people about Jesus.

Your slave Onesimus is like a son to me.

He could help me here in jail.

But you would have to say it is all right.

Instead, I will send him back to you.

He was away from you for a while.

Maybe it was so you'll have him back forever.

Now he will not be a slave.

He will be like your brother in God's family.

I pray that Jesus' kind love will be with you.

From Paul

I did it! ☆ ◯

Note to Parents: If you have the *Day by Day Kid's Bible*, read "Super Great Power" (page 738) and "Born to Do Good Things" (page 739) to your child this weekend (Ephesians 1:1, 4-23; 2).

Putting on God's Armor

Ephesians 1:1; 6:13-18

To God's people:

Put on God's armor and stand firm.

Make truth like a belt around you.

Being right with God is like

　　having a vest that keeps you safe.

The good news of peace

　　makes your feet ready.

Hold faith like a shield in front of you.

Being saved by Jesus is like

　　putting a helmet on your head.

Your sword will be the Spirit's sword,
which is God's Word.
Pray with the Spirit's help anytime.
Pray for God's people everywhere.

From Paul

I did it! ☆

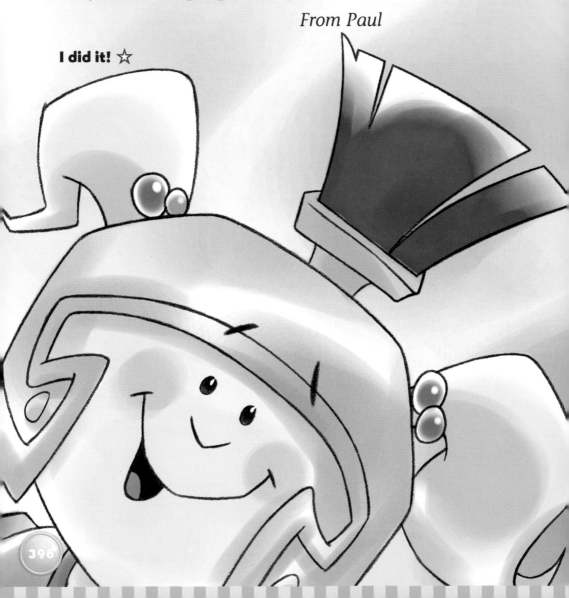

Shining like Stars

Philippians 1:1; 2:12-15

To God's people:

Keep looking up to God,

    because he is saving you.

He is helping you fit into his good plans.

Do everything without fussing and fighting.

Then you can be sinless and clean.

In a bent and needy world,

    you shine like stars in the sky.

You shine as you tell

    where true life comes from.

From Paul

I did it! ☆

Rich People

1 Timothy 6:17-18

Dear Timothy,
Tell people not to hope in their money.
Money can be here today
   and gone tomorrow.
So tell people to hope in God.

398

God is rich.

He gives us everything to enjoy.

Tell rich people to do good things
and to give a lot.

Tell them to be glad to share.

From Paul

I did it! ☆

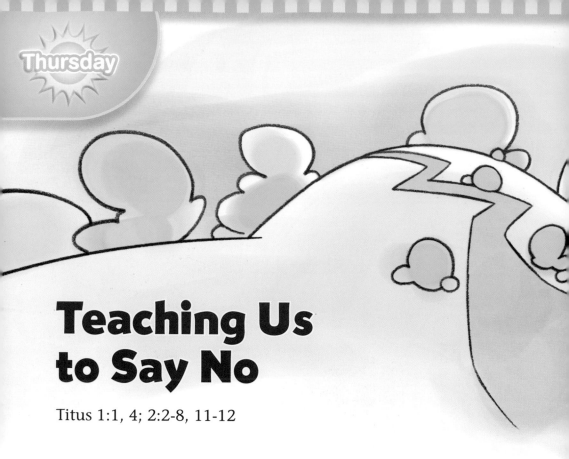

Teaching Us to Say No

Titus 1:1, 4; 2:2-8, 11-12

Dear Titus,

Teach old men to keep believing
even in hard times.

Teach older women
not to say bad things about others.

Instead, they can teach younger women
how to love their children.

Show young men how to have self-control.

Mean what you say. Say what you mean.

God's kind love teaches us to say no to bad things.

It teaches us to say yes to what's right.

From Paul

I did it! ☆

A Small Fire

James 1:1-2; 3:5, 7-10, 13

James, one of Jesus' brothers,
   wrote this letter to Jesus' followers.

To God's people everywhere:
Your mouth may be small, but it talks big!
People can train all kinds of animals.
But nobody can train a mouth.
We shout for God with our mouths.
Then we turn around and say bad things.
Good words and bad words
   come from the same mouth.
It should not be like that.
Are you wise? Do you understand?
Then show it by living God's way.

From James

I did it! ☆

Note to Parents: If you have the *Day by Day Kid's Bible*, read "Like a Fog" (page 765) and
"Rotten Riches" (page 766) to your child this weekend (James 1:1; 4–5).

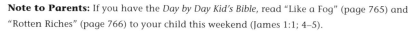

Wild Waves

Jude 1:1, 10, 12-13, 24-25

Jude, another brother of Jesus',
　　wrote this letter to Jesus' followers.

To the people God chose:
Some people say bad things
　　about anything they don't understand.
They are like clouds that don't bring rain.
They are like trees that don't grow fruit
　　and like wild waves tossing high in the sea.
Everybody sees their sin.

But you will come to God full of joy.
You'll come with a heart he has made clean
   so there is no sin.
God is our only God, and he saves us.

From Jude

I did it! ☆

A Crown

1 Peter 1:1-2; 5:4, 7, 10

To people who believe:

Jesus, the Chief Shepherd,

　　will come back someday.

He will help you shine like he does.

It will be like getting a shining crown

　　that will never fade.

So tell God about all your worries.

Then trust him to take care of you.

You can trust God

　　because he is kind and loving.

And he cares about you.

From Peter

I did it! ☆

Angels

Hebrews 1:4-8, 14; 2:7-8

(No one knows for sure who wrote this letter.
Maybe Paul did. Or Luke.)

Jesus is greater than angels.
God brought his Son into the world
   and said, "All you angels, worship him."

Here's what God says about angels:

"He makes his angels to be like wind.

He makes his servants to be like fire."

But here's what God says about his Son:

"You will be King forever and ever."

Angels are spirits God sends to serve people.

Jesus was a bit lower than angels for a while.

But now he is in charge of everything.

I did it! ☆

Like a Ship's Anchor

Hebrews 6:18-20

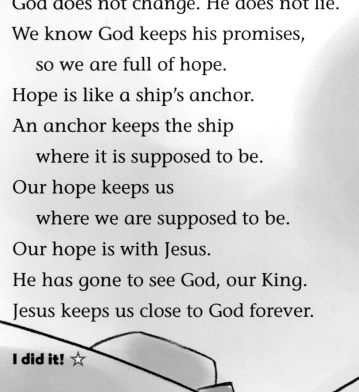

God does not change. He does not lie.
We know God keeps his promises,
   so we are full of hope.
Hope is like a ship's anchor.
An anchor keeps the ship
   where it is supposed to be.
Our hope keeps us
   where we are supposed to be.
Our hope is with Jesus.
He has gone to see God, our King.
Jesus keeps us close to God forever.

I did it! ☆

Faith

Hebrews 11:1, 6-7, 11, 29; 12:2

Faith is being sure
  that what you hope for will happen.
It is believing for sure
  in things you do not see.
People who want to know God
  have to believe that God really lives.
They have to believe that he brings good
  to people who look for him.
Noah believed and built an ark.
Abraham believed and had a son.
God's people believed
  and walked across the sea on dry ground.
So let's keep looking up to Jesus.
Our faith begins and ends with him.

I did it! ☆

Note to Parents: If you have the *Day by Day Kid's Bible*, read "Keep On Running" (page 789) and "Yesterday, Today, and Tomorrow" (page 791) to your child this weekend (Hebrews 12–13).

How God Showed His Love

1 John 4:7-11

Let's love each other.

Love comes from God.

People who love are people who know God.

Anyone who does not love does not know God.

That is because God is love.

God showed his love by sending his only Son
  into the world.

He sent his Son so that we could live.

That is love.

God sent his Son to die for our sins.

Jesus was God's gift.

God loved us that much!

So we should love each other.

I did it! ☆

A Voice like a Waterfall

Revelation 1:1, 4, 9-19

John, Jesus' friend, wrote to the churches.
He wrote about things that God showed him:

I was sent away to an island
   so I couldn't tell anyone about Jesus.
One day I heard a loud voice behind me.
It said, "Write about the things you see."

I turned around and saw a man in a robe.

A wide gold cloth went around his chest.

His hair was like wool and as white as snow.

His face was like the sun.

His voice sounded like a waterfall.

He said, "Do not be afraid.

I am the One Who Is Alive.

I will live forever and ever."

I did it! ☆

An Open Door

Revelation 4:1-3, 5-8

I, John, saw an open door in heaven.

A loud voice said, "Come up here.

I will show you what is going to happen."

Then my spirit met with God's Spirit.

I saw someone on the King's throne in heaven.

A rainbow spread out like a fan over him.

Flashes of lightning came from where he sat.

Thunder rolled and boomed.

Four living beings were near the King.

They always call, "Holy, holy, holy!

God has all power.

He lived before. He lives now.

He will live forever."

I did it! ☆

Horse and Rider

Revelation 19:1, 11-14, 16

Then I, John, heard a roaring sound.

It was like a great crowd of people in heaven.

They shouted, "Praise the Lord! He saves!"

Then I saw a man riding a white horse.

The rider is called the True One.

He is called the One Who Keeps Promises.

Many crowns are on his head.

His name is Jesus, the Word of God.

Heaven's armies follow him
  on white horses.
Their clothes are white and clean.
A name is on Jesus' clothes and on his leg.
The name is "King of kings
  and Lord of lords."

 I did it! ☆

New Heaven, New Earth

Revelation 21:1, 3-4; 22:1-5, 7, 20

I, John, saw a new heaven and a new earth.

A loud voice said,

"Now God will live with people.

He will wipe away all their tears.

People will not hurt or cry or die anymore."

A clear river flowed from where the King sat.

The tree of life grew on each side of it.

The tree's leaves make people well.

The King's people will get to see him.

There will be no more night.

People will not need lamp light or sun light.

God will give them the light they need.

"Look and listen!" said Jesus.

"I am coming soon."

Yes! Amen! Come, Lord Jesus!

I did it! ☆

My Prayer

Thank you, God, for your Word.

Thank you, God, for your love.

I see your love in Jesus, your Son,

who loved me so much

that he died on the cross.

I know that Jesus died for my sins

so that you can forgive me, God.

I am very glad that he came back to life.

I love Jesus, and I want to be his follower.

I want to live with him forever in heaven.

Thank you, God, for letting me know

what a special place heaven is.

I will see you there someday.

Yes! Amen!

Complete List of Stories in Bible-Book Order

OLD TESTAMENT

Genesis
1–2 That Is Good! 1
2–3 Adam's Helper 3
3 The Snake 4
6–8 A Big Boat 6
11 The Tower 8
15; 18; 21 A Visit 9
24 Looking for a Wife 11
25 Twins 13
27 A Trick 14
27–28 The Ladder 16
29–33 Going Home 17
37; 39 Hard Times 18
41 The King's Dream 20
41–47; 50 Joseph's Brothers 21

Exodus
1–2 The Princess and the Basket 23
3 A Bush on Fire 25
4 The Stick 26
5–6 Hay Bricks 28
7–12 Wonders 29
14–15 Across the Water 31
19–20; 24 A Thundering Cloud 33

Numbers
13–14 A New Land 34
22–24 A Talking Donkey 35

Deuteronomy
31–32 Moses' Song 37

Joshua
2–3; 6 A Wall Falls 39
10 The Sun Stands Still 41

Judges
3–4; 10; 12 Lots of Leaders 44
6–7 Fire and Horns 43
13; 16 Samson 47

Ruth
1–4 Ruth 46

1 Samuel
3 Samuel 49
3; 7 Fighting with Thunder 51
9–10 Lost Donkeys 53
10; 13–15 A King behind the Bags 54
16 Choosing a New King 55
17 David and the Giant 57

18–19 A Friend and a Spear 59
20 The Arrow 61
24 David Hides 63
31 David Becomes King 65

2 Samuel
2 David Becomes King 65

1 Kings
2–3 Solomon's Wise
Choice 113
3 A Wise King 114
4; 10 Riches for a Wise
King 120
5–6 King Hiram Helps 116
8 Solomon Prays 118
11–12 A Torn Coat 142
15 Good King Asa 143
16–17 No Rain, No Food 145
18 Fire on the Mountain 147
19 Afraid in the Desert 149
19 Elijah's Helper 151

2 Kings
2 Horses of Fire 153
4 Oil to Sell 155
4 A Room on the Roof Top 157
4 Death in the Soup 158
5 Dipping into the River 164
6 An Ax on the Water 160
6 A Great Army 162
11 The Boy King 166
20 A Shadow Moves
Backward 185
22–23 King Josiah 194
25 A City on Fire 208

1 Chronicles
12 David Becomes King 65

2 Chronicles
2–5 King Hiram Helps 116
5–6 Solomon Prays 118
9 Riches for a Wise King 120
14–15 Good King Asa 143
19–20 A Singing Army 152
21 Obadiah 161
26 Forts and Towers 173
34 King Josiah 194

Ezra
1–6 Going Home 228
7–8 Ezra's Trip 230

Nehemiah
1–2 Broken Walls 242
4 Tools and Swords 244
6 Letters and Messages 246
12–13 Singers on the Wall 247

Esther
1–2 A New Queen 238
3–4; 7–9 For Such a Time
as This 239

Job
1–2; 11–13 Job in Trouble 220
38; 40 God Talks 222
39–40 Who? 223
40 The Elephant 225
41–42 Too Wonderful for
Me 226

Psalms

1 A Tree by the Water 76
8 Children and Babies Praise 84
19 God's Way 86
20 Chariots and Horses 106
23 My Shepherd 66
24 The Great King 87
32 Not like a Horse 108
33 A New Song 89
34 Taste and See 64
37 Like the Sun at Noon 78
42 Like a Deer 110
46 Be Still 68
50 Every Animal 79
61 A High Rock 70
65 The Hills Look Glad 90
77 God Who Does Wonders 72
84 Even the Sparrow 81
92 Morning and Night 82
93 The Thunder of the Water 92
95 The Deep Earth in His
Hand 73
98 Make Music! 94
100 His Sheep 96
104 Wings of Wind 97
104 The Earth and the Deep,
Wide Sea 98
119 Sweet Words 100
121 My Eyes Look Up 74
131 Like a Well-Fed Baby 112
139 You Know Me 101
139 In the Secret Place 103
147 What Makes God
Happy 234
147 Snow and Ice 236
150 Dancing 105

Proverbs

2:1-5 Listen 121
3:21-24 Listen 121
6:6-8 Working Hard or
Being Lazy 130
10:12 Love, Hate, and
Caring 122
12:10 Love, Hate, and
Caring 122
12:25 Love, Hate, and
Caring 122
12:26 Friends 132
15:1 The Words We Say 125
15:13 Happy and Sad 134
15:17 Love, Hate, and
Caring 122
15:30 Happy and Sad 134
16:24 The Words We Say 125
17:1 Fighting and Hurting 127
17:14 The Words We Say 125
17:17 Friends 132
17:22 Happy and Sad 134
18:19 Fighting and Hurting 127
20:22 Fighting and Hurting 127
22:3 Friends 132
23:4-5 Being Rich and
Poor 129
24:30-34 Working Hard or
Being Lazy 130
25:11 The Words We Say 125
25:16 Self-Control and
Pride 124
25:21-22 Love, Hate, and
Caring 122
25:28 Self-Control and
Pride 124
26:20 The Words We Say 125

27:3 Fighting and Hurting 127
27:7 Being Rich and Poor 129
27:9-10 Friends 132
27:21 Self-Control and
Pride 124
28:6 Being Rich and Poor 129
28:20 Being Rich and Poor 129
29:6 Happy and Sad 134
29:11 Self-Control and
Pride 124
30:18-19, 24-28 A Wise Man
Wonders 135

Ecclesiastes
3 A Time for Everything 138
4 Two Are Better Than One 140

Song of Songs
2; 8 Solomon's Song 137

Isaiah
6 I Saw God 176
8 Signs from God 177
9 Prince of Peace 178
11 A Branch 180
35 Shout with Joy 182
40 Who Is like God? 187
55 Trees Will Clap 188
58 Here I Am 190
65 The Wolf and the Lamb 192

Jeremiah
1 God Chooses Jeremiah 197
35 A Family That Obeyed 199
36 The King in the Winter
House 201
38 A Muddy Well 206

39–40 A City on Fire 208

Lamentations
1; 3 Great Love 209

Ezekiel
1–2 In the Cloud 210
37 A Valley Full of Bones 212

Daniel
1 Daniel and the King's
Food 204
3 A Big, Burning Oven 214
4 A King Eats Grass 216
5 Words on a Wall 217
6 Lions! 218

Hosea
1; 4; 7; 10; 14 Hosea 171

Joel
1–2 Joel 168

Amos
1–2; 4; 7; 9 Amos 174

Obadiah
1 Obadiah 161

Jonah
1–3 A Big Fish 169

Micah
1; 5 Hope for God's People 184

Nahum
1 A Safe Place 193

Habakkuk
3 Wow! 203

Zephaniah
1; 3 Sing and Shout 196

Haggai
1 Haggai 232

Zechariah
8 City of Truth 233

Malachi
3–4 Dance like a Calf 241

NEW TESTAMENT

Matthew
1 Joseph's Dream 253
2 Wise Men 258
3 The Man Who Ate Honey 259
3 Jesus at the River 260
4 Jesus in the Desert 262
5 Jesus the Teacher 278
6 Birds and Flowers 280
8 A Sick Servant 282
8 The Storm 288
9 A Hole in a Roof 272
9 A Sick Girl 290
9 Two Men Who Could Not
See 291
12 Is It Right? 275
13 Seeds and Dirt 285
13 Seeds and Pearls 286
14 Bread for Everyone 292
14 On Top of the Water 294

17 As White as Light 299
17 Fishing for Money 300
19 Let the Children Come 315
21 A Colt 321
21 Two Sons and a Grape
Garden 323
25 Ten Lamps 326
25 Ready for You 327
26 A Jar of Perfume 320
26 Thirty Silver Coins 329
26 The Room Upstairs 331
26 Praying in the Garden 336
26 Judas and the Guards 337
27 Skull Hill 339
27 The Grave 341
28 An Angel 342
28 Into the Clouds 351

Mark
1 The Man Who Ate Honey 259
1 Jesus at the River 260
1 Jesus in the Desert 262
2 A Hole in a Roof 272
3 Is It Right? 275
3 Twelve Friends 276
4 Seeds and Dirt 285
4 Seeds and Pearls 286
4 The Storm 288
5 A Sick Girl 290
6 Bread for Everyone 292
6 On Top of the Water 294
7 Making People Well 297
9 As White as Light 299
10 Let the Children Come 315
10 By the Side of the Road 319
11 A Colt 321
12 The Most Money 324

14 A Jar of Perfume 320
14 Thirty Silver Coins 329
14 The Room Upstairs 331
14 Praying in the Garden 336
14 Judas and the Guards 337
15 Skull Hill 339
15 The Grave 341
16 Joy Again 344
16 On the Road 346
16 In a Locked Room 347
16 Into the Clouds 351

Luke

1 God's Son 251
2 A Trip to Bethlehem 254
2 In the Fields 256
3 The Man Who Ate Honey 259
3 Jesus at the River 260
4 Jesus in the Desert 262
5 Nets Full of Fish 270
5 A Hole in a Roof 272
6 Is It Right? 275
6 Twelve Friends 276
7 A Sick Servant 282
7 Perfume 283
8 Seeds and Dirt 285
8 The Storm 288
8 A Sick Girl 290
9 Bread for Everyone 292
9 As White as Light 299
10 The Neighbor 307
10 Taking Time 309
13 Seeds and Pearls 286
15 Lost and Found 310
15 Pig Food 311
17 Ten Men and One
    Thank-You 305

18 Let the Children Come 315
18 By the Side of the Road 319
19 Up in a Tree 317
19 A Colt 321
21 The Most Money 324
22 Thirty Silver Coins 329
22 The Room Upstairs 331
22 Praying in the Garden 336
22 Judas and the Guards 337
23 Skull Hill 339
23 The Grave 341
24 On the Road 346
24 In a Locked Room 347
24 Into the Clouds 351

John

1 Meeting Jesus 264
2 A Wedding Party 266
4 At the Well 267
4 A Sick Son 269
5 At the Pool 274
6 Bread for Everyone 292
6 On Top of the Water 294
6 Bread from Heaven 296
9 Seeing 304
10 The Shepherd 302
11 Out of the Grave 313
12 A Jar of Perfume 320
12 A Colt 321
13 Clean Feet 333
13–14 God's Spirit of Truth 335
18 Praying in the Garden 336
18 Judas and the Guards 337
18–19 Skull Hill 339
19 The Grave 341
20 Joy Again 344

20 In a Locked Room 347
21 Going Fishing 349

Acts
1 Into the Clouds 351
2 Wind, Fire, and Different
   Languages 353
3 A Lame Man 354
6–7 Stephen Sees Jesus 355
8 A Chariot Ride 356
9 A Bright Light 358
9 Peter and Dorcas 360
10 Animals in a Big Sheet 361
12 The Angel in the Jail 363
13–14 People Try to Worship
   Paul 365
16 The Earth Shakes 368
19–20 The Idol Makers 372
20 Falling out the Window 377
23 The Secret Plan 379
24 Felix and His Wife 380
25 A New Governor 382
26 Your Mind Is Gone! 383
27 A Ship Goes Down 385
28 A Snake in the Fire 387
28 The Leader of the Island 389
28 A House in Rome 390

Romans
1; 8 More Than Winners 376

1 Corinthians
1; 9; 16 Runners 371

2 Corinthians
1; 4 Clay Jars 374

Galatians
1; 4–5 Promised Children 366

Ephesians
1; 6 Putting on God's
   Armor 395

Philippians
1–2 Shining like Stars 397

Colossians
1–2 Like a Plant 392

1 Thessalonians
1; 4 To Cheer You Up 370

1 Timothy
6 Rich People 398

Titus
1–2 Teaching Us to Say No 400

Philemon
1 A Slave Who Ran Away 393

Hebrews
1–2 Angels 406
6 Like a Ship's Anchor 408
11–12 Faith 410

James
1; 3 A Small Fire 402

1 Peter
1; 5 A Crown 405

1 John
4 How God Showed His
Love 411

Jude
1 Wild Waves 403

Revelation
1 A Voice like a Waterfall 412
4 An Open Door 414
19 Horse and Rider 415
21–22 New Heaven,
New Earth 417

About the Author

Karyn Henley is an award-winning author and children's communicator. She is best known as the author of *The Beginner's Bible*, which has sold more than four million copies, and the *Day by Day Kid's Bible*, a chronological Bible for readers ages seven to ten. Her Child Talk Seminars and PLAYSONGS concerts take her all over the United States.

In 2001 *Children's Ministry* magazine named Karyn Henley a Pioneer of the Decade, in response to a readers' poll that identified her as one of the top ten people who have most changed the face of children's ministry. In 1997 the International Network of Children's Ministry honored Karyn with their Excellence in Children's Ministry Award.

An accomplished songwriter, Karyn's audio recording of *My First Hymnal* was nominated for a Dove Award in 1995, the same year that a video version was released. In 1990 Karyn received an Emmy Award as music composer for a children's television special.

A graduate of Abilene Christian University, Karyn also completed her Master of Fine Arts in Writing for Children at Vermont College. She lives in Nashville, Tennessee, with her husband, Ralph, where they raised their two grown sons.

About the Illustrator

Joseph Sapulich grew up in Chicago and was classically trained in fine art and design at the American Academy of Art. Joseph received several awards and honors for his conventional and digital art in advertising, which led him to the film industry. He was responsible for the conceptual designs of many characters and sets in the VeggieTales computer-animated series and served as art director for the VeggieTales feature film *Jonah*. He has also been an art director for such companies as Walt Disney Studios (Los Angeles and Asia), Tyndale House Publishers, and Focus on the Family.

Joseph travels and speaks, sharing his love of art and design. He also donates time in ministry to several organizations including the Ronald McDonald House, using art-therapy techniques. An ordained minister, Joseph says, "My art flows from my relationship with God." His passion for ministry is "to help people enter into God's presence and know Him in a personal way."

Joseph's wife, Cathy, and two children, Joshua and Sarah, are his greatest joys and God-given treasures. They live in a suburb of Chicago along with a dog, a turtle, a frog, a guinea pig, and a parakeet named Tweeter.

SURRENDER, WHITE PEOPLE!

ALSO BY D.L. HUGHLEY

How Not to Get Shot

Black Man, White House

SURRENDER, WHITE PEOPLE!

D.L. HUGHLEY

AND DOUG MOE

OUR UNCONDITIONAL TERMS FOR PEACE

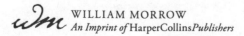

WILLIAM MORROW
An Imprint of HarperCollins*Publishers*

HarperCollins books may be purchased for educational, business, or sales promotional use. For information, please email the Special Markets Department at SPsales@harpercollins.com.

FIRST EDITION

Designed by Nancy Singer

Library of Congress Cataloging-in-Publication Data

Names: Hughley, D. L. (Darryl L.), 1963– author. | Moe, Doug, author.

Title: Surrender, white people! : our unconditional terms for peace / D. L. Hughley and Doug Moe.

Description: First edition. | New York : William Morrow, 2020.

Identifiers: LCCN 2020012324 (print) | LCCN 2020012325 (ebook) | ISBN 9780062953704 (hardcover) | ISBN 9780062953711 (trade paperback) | ISBN 9780062953728 (ebook)

Subjects: LCSH: United States—Race relations—Humor. | Whites—United States—Humor. | Race awareness—Humor. | African Americans—Humor.

Classification: LCC PN6231.R25 H84 2020 (print) | LCC PN6231.R25 (ebook) | DDC 305.89/6073—dc23

LC record available at https://lccn.loc.gov/2020012324

LC ebook record available at https://lccn.loc.gov/2020012325

ISBN 978-0-06-295370-4

20 21 22 23 24 LSC 10 9 8 7 6 5 4 3 2

To my father, Charles Hughley. I'll always try to make you proud.

CONTENTS

INTRODUCTION: **SURRENDER, WHITE PEOPLE!**   1

THE TERMS OF OUR PEACE TREATY   13

ARTICLE I: **WHITE PEOPLE SHALL CONSIDER REPARATIONS**   17

ARTICLE II: **HISTORY BOOKS SHALL BE ALIGNED**   39

ARTICLE III: **WE SHALL ENDEAVOR TO UNDERSTAND ONE ANOTHER**   71

ARTICLE IV: **WE SHALL DEAL WITH THE WHITE SUPREMACY PROBLEM**   127

ARTICLE V: **WE SHALL BE UN-OPPRESSED**   137

ARTICLE VI: **WE ARE PART OF AMERICA**   209

CONCLUSION   227

SIGNATURE PAGE   243

ACKNOWLEDGMENTS   245

SURRENDER, WHITE PEOPLE!

INTRODUCTION

SURRENDER, WHITE PEOPLE!

Surrender, white people! Time's up.

After four hundred years of oppression, discrimination, and bias, black folks are still here and we still won't shut the fuck up. And now we've got reinforcements. Just in my lifetime, the face of America has become a hell of a lot browner. In fact, we're on the cusp of being a majority-minority country. Let that sink in: whites will soon be a minority. This new reality carries consequences. White people have been in charge for a long time now, but black and brown folk are not going to take a back seat anymore. Whiteness ain't what it used to be. I'm here to say, it's time for white folks to sue for peace while the getting's still good.

Not that we won. No black or brown person can say "we won" with Trump in the White House or Tucker Carlson on the TV. Charlottesville, Botham Jean, and Atatiana Jefferson make it clear how far we still have to go. But the times *are* changing. As *The Atlantic* recently observed, "The United States is undergoing a transition perhaps no rich and stable democracy has ever experienced: Its historically dominant group is on its way to becoming a political minority— and its minority groups are asserting their co-equal rights and interests." Damn right.

So here we are. Nobody's winning, everybody's losing. We're all angry. We've been at it so long that it feels like we'll always have racial conflict and like we'll never figure out how to live together in peace and harmony. Whatever happened to ebony and ivory living side by side on my piano keyboard?

What we have here in America is a dysfunctional relationship. It's an unhappy marriage after a shotgun wedding. Oh, and after slavery, Jim Crow, and lynchings. So, ya know, we got issues.

But this country's not going to therapy, because America

doesn't want to deal with her issues. White people hate talking about race. "Why is everything about race?" they say. "Why do we always have to talk about race?" Everything's about race, because in America, it's *always* been about race here. The places we could work and live, the places we could eat, the places we could go to school.

It's the same today. How are we supposed to deal with Charlottesville if we don't know the same history? How are we supposed to trust the police if we don't acknowledge the continuing violence against us, as well as centuries of forced subjugation by white authorities? Where white people see an obsession with victimhood, black people see a willful lack of taking responsibility. When will white people let us be part of America?

Peace and reconciliation will only happen, I believe, when white people surrender their unjust privileges and their delusions of "supremacy." Look your history in the face, put aside all your visions of superiority, open up your institutions so they benefit everyone in this nation, and join the rest of us as equals. That's what I mean by surrender.

But America still has a white supremacy complex, still wants to bring black and brown people to heel. Slavery, Jim Crow, and segregation all tried to get black people to be like good little children, seen but not heard. Maybe not even seen.

And then you voted for Obama: "Fuck it, okay; I'll vote for a black guy this one time. Now this will make them shut up." But then we didn't shut up, so we got Trump as payback. Soon enough, African countries were "shitholes," brown people were in cages, and Nazis were marching in our streets.

So I'm going to solve our problems with this book. This book will do more for white people than the Obama election ever did. It'll do more than rooting for a black quarterback, more than celebrating Martin Luther King Jr. Day. You tried all these little things, hoping that we'd shut up, but it didn't quite get you there.

So fine, you don't want to hear from us anymore? This book is about how we can get black people to stop talking about oppression, discrimination, and our place in America. You give us this stuff and you get the niggers to shut the fuck up about it!

Surrender, white people! These are our terms:

WHY WE NEED A PEACE TREATY

A peace treaty, D.L.? Isn't that a bit . . . dramatic?

Don't we need one? We're clearly at war. When you can get shot in your own house like Botham Jean or Atatiana Jefferson, what else can you call it?

All deaths are tragic, but not all of them are surprising. When dudes are on the streets, running afoul of the law, the propensity for something happening is probably exacerbated. But when cops kill two people in their homes, what else can you call it but war?

You used to be able to tell yourself, "Well, he sold cigarettes," or "He wouldn't comply." But what do you say to these people who were just at home at night, and had white cops shoot them through a window or bust into their homes and kill them there? I mean, you're gonna run out of us to kill. You're killing "good ones" now.

FREEDOM, BUT NOT A FORK

There are people in America who think just not having slaves anymore was all we needed. Because you freed the slaves in 1865, we good. But it was a hundred years later before you gave us the ability to eat at the same restaurant as you. So you gave us freedom, but not a fork.

You gave us the right to not be slaves anymore, but then you changed the vagrancy laws, the housing laws, and the voting laws to make it almost impossible for us to *really* be free. All these changes were just designed to keep us slaves. You reincarnated the incarceration.

I WANT TO BE TREATED LIKE AMERICAN

I think America can do better for us. Let me tell you a story.

I travel a lot for work because I'm touring all the time. I probably spend $300,000 to $400,000 a year on airline tickets. I have maybe nine million air miles because I fly domestically every week. And because I fly American Airlines so much, I'm a ConciergeKey member. That's the top status; I don't even know how you get to be a ConciergeKey member—it's some kind of secret. There's nowhere I'm treated better. They meet me at the gate, come pick me up in a Cadillac—they're not fucking around.

I might be a god on American, but when I go other places, I'm just another black guy. Or worse, people think I work for my assistant, Derek.

Now granted, Derek looks like a model, so he's always going to get attention. I mean, I'm dope, but he looks like the Most Interesting Man in the World. So I'm used to it. But it's incredible how quickly you go from being king to just another nigger.

Recently, we were staying at the Ritz-Carlton in Orlando. Derek had my credit card and he was at the counter checking us in. I remembered that I had to give him a letter, so I walked up to give it to Derek and this white man goes, "HEY!"

Like that: *"HEY!"*

And he startled me. You know how your mouth goes like a Cheerio when you're startled? Nigga, I have never been so surprised. I just stopped short and my mouth looked like a big O. I was *startled*.

He said, "What are you doing? The line's back here." This guy's standing there with his wife and kids. And I said, "*He* works for *me*. We were in line—and I just had to get this letter." And I got mad that I was explaining myself. I said, "By the way, I would never be that rude where I would jump in front of somebody, a man with his family." He said, "Well, I apologize." I said, "Not fast enough."

Then Derek and I were waiting, having a drink while they were bringing my bags up. The dude's wife walked by on her way to the pool with her two little girls in their floats and shit. She saw me and she mouthed, "I'm so sorry." You know when a wife says something like that, she knows her husband's an asshole.

But he was showing off for his family. "I'm gonna show this nigger." And I'm like, "Man, do you see me?" White people have a psychic confusion when they see a black man in the fucking Ritz.

But at American, it's different. Like I said, I'm an American god. So recently we were leaving L.A., and Derek and I were waiting to board. There's one lane for priority boarding, one for first class. ConciergeKey members board before first class, but when they called us this old white guy walked right past us—"Excuse me, excuse me"—to get on the plane. He just shoved past us. This guy had a flag lapel pin and a navy-blue blazer, khakis and tassel loafers—like straight from the country club. He was so dismissive. So he came barreling up to be at the front and tried to go ahead of us, but the flight attendant stuck her arm out like *BAM*. She full-on blocked him and said, "No, no, *they're* boarding first." She just did him like that: *BAM*. And I just started laughing looking at him. I was like, "*Wow*." And then he said, "Well, I thought it was my turn. I thought I was first."

And that white man just could not believe it. This Asian American flight attendant made him wait while Derek and I boarded. He probably had never had that happen to him. And that's why he'll vote for Trump again: because a nigger, a beaner, and a fucking chink stopped him from taking his rightful place.

That was like a little bit of reparations right there. *I*

thought I was first. That's white America right there. American Airlines makes me feel how it feels to be a white man. That's probably the closest I get to being a white dude. So I don't blame him for being mad; I wouldn't want to give that shit up either.

I'm writing up this treaty because I want *America* to treat me like *American*.

WHY YOU HAVE TO SURRENDER

But D.L., why do I have to "surrender"? Shouldn't we be coming to some kind of a compromise?

You ever notice that whenever America makes "compromises," they're usually sacrificing black people? "Compromise" means "I'm giving up poor black people."

- **THE GREAT COMPROMISE**—gave rural states as many senators as populous states
- **THE THREE-FIFTHS COMPROMISE**—counted slaves as three-fifths of a person
- **THE MISSOURI COMPROMISE**—allowed Missouri to be a slave state
- **THE COMPROMISE OF 1850**—admitted a bunch of new slave states into the United States

Whenever there's a compromise, it's us doing the compromising. So . . . no more "compromises." We can come to an *understanding* or a *deal,* but we're not gonna compromise. *That's* why you have to surrender. Release yourselves from your racist delusions and address the real structural injustice that keeps black and brown people down. Remember, we got the numbers now.

WE'LL TRY TO IGNORE YOUR PROBLEMATIC HISTORY

If you're reluctant to sign this peace treaty, think of how we feel: we have to bargain with people who have shown themselves to be untrustworthy again and again. Let's start by acknowledging that white America's track record with upholding agreements is . . . not good. That shit has not ended well, ever since the first time a white guy offered a black guy a boat ride. *Man, I thought this was supposed to be a three-hour tour.*

No backsies, and no crossing your fingers behind your backs when you sign this thing. We'll be checking the fine print, because we know that's where you like to hide shit. And we'll be checking up to make sure you uphold your end of the bargain. Like your pal Reagan says: "Trust, but verify."

I don't want to start off too negative. I'm not trying to say that *all* white people can't be trusted. Of course, there are *good people on both sides.*

THIS ONE'S JUST LIKE THOSE OTHER TREATIES YOU SIGNED

If it's helpful, think of this treaty as something like the Indian treaties you all signed. What did the United States get from the Indians? Nothing except silence. They already took all their land. What was the goal, then? The goal was to make them not be a nuisance anymore. They were a pain in the ass. *What the fuck—you attack me with your dumb bows and arrows and now I have to kill all of you, and everybody thinks I'm an asshole.*

White people write treaties because they don't want to feel like assholes, basically. Treaties are an admission of something short of guilt. They're a way to buy peace and silence while saying, "Sorry, not sorry."

THE TERMS OF OUR PEACE TREATY

PRE-PREAMBLE

Treaties have to get written in official, fancy language: you know, "henceforth" and "having thus described" and so on. People write shit up that way to seem official, but also to be confusing. It's like the small print. That's just how treaties are. I'm not gonna try to trick you, white people, but I'm not about to get mine thrown out just because I wanted to keep it casual. So as we go along here, I'm going to put together a real *treaty* treaty, real official sounding.

And everybody knows that a treaty needs a preamble. I mean, shit: How're you gonna amble without a pre-amble?

PREAMBLE

A Peace Treaty Between White America and Black Folks

The search for peace between races must be guided by the following:

Black folks ("African Americans," "people of color," "those people") have decided, after four hundred years of oppression and discrimination, to come to the table and issue demands for a lasting peace with their oppressors. That's mighty big of them.

White people ("America"), having determined to hold a conference with the black folks, for the purpose of removing from their minds all causes of complaint, making them stop grousing, posting annoying memes to social media, and otherwise throwing shade, and establishing a firm and permanent friendship with them, recognize D.L. Hughley as sole agent for that purpose and affirm their intent to come to terms.

Recognizing that it is in the interest of all that racial harmony be established and racial animus shall no longer be the default;

Acknowledging that cooperation in this goal is of the essence and necessary, that peace may prosper, even if that means talking about things that upset the apple cart;

Acknowledging also that everyone's been a little hot under the collar for a while about all this stuff;

Convinced that the establishment of a firm foundation for the continuation and development of such cooperation on the basis of mutual understanding accords with the interests of harmony and peace;

Convinced also that a treaty ensuring this peace, by nature, must be specific and must cut the treacle;

Now, in order to accomplish the good design of this conference, the parties have agreed on the following articles, which, when ratified, shall be fully binding.

Damn, it's a pain to write like that.

WAIT, I DIDN'T AGREE TO ANYTHING!

*"But hold up, D.L.," you say. "I wasn't alive in 1846—
I wasn't even around in 1946—why the hell do I have
to pay you money for something that I didn't do?"*

I hear that. That's how a lot of white people feel. But
don't you see, it's not just about slavery. In this book I'm
going to explain how oppression keeps happening in the
most seemingly innocuous ways. I'm going to explain how
race is embedded in everything in American life today for
black people. So it's not just about slavery, and it's not all
about money.

If you want me to shut up, you have to at least hear me
out. If we're going to have peace, first you get a piece of my
mind.

WHITE PEOPLE SHALL CONSIDER REPARATIONS

R-R-R-REPARATIONS?!?

The word "reparations" is so scary to white people. They act like the idea of reparations is crazy. But support is growing, and now here we are at this treaty. Yes, so far, only 26 percent of Americans support some kind of compensation or payments to descendants of slaves. But most of them haven't read this book yet.

THE CASE FOR REPARATIONS

In 2014, Ta-Nehisi Coates made a powerful case for reparations in his essay titled, um, "The Case for Reparations." He chronicled the course of racial injustice in America and set the terms for the discussion of reparations since. Before that, everyone pretended like *Chappelle's Show* was the most serious representation of reparations: people buying liquor, cigarettes, and fried chicken. Coates argued not just for a bunch of checks being sent out, but for a reckoning with America's past:

> And so we must imagine a new country. Reparations—by which I mean the full acceptance of our collective biography and its consequences—is the price we must pay to see ourselves squarely. The recovering alcoholic may well have to live with his illness for the rest of his life. But at least he is not living a drunken lie. Reparations beckons us to reject the intoxication of hubris and see America as it is—the work of fallible humans.
>
> . . . What I'm talking about is more than recompense for past injustices—more than a handout, a payoff, hush money, or a reluctant bribe. What I'm talking

about is a national reckoning that would lead to spiritual renewal. Reparations would mean the end of scarfing hot dogs on the Fourth of July while denying the facts of our heritage. Reparations would mean the end of yelling "patriotism" while waving a Confederate flag. Reparations would mean a revolution of the American consciousness, a reconciling of our self-image as the great democratizer with the facts of our history.

If Coates's well-reasoned, eloquently presented, emotionally impactful essay didn't change your mind, what will? That shit is well said. But you all still didn't want to go for that. And the reason is, I don't think America wants to have "a national reckoning." I think what it wants is for us to shut the fuck up.

THAT'S SOME GOOD CHICKEN

I think that the closest we may have ever come to reparations was the Popeyes chicken sandwich.

Remember when reparations talk was hot and heavy? It was all over the news, the Democratic presidential candidates were all talking about it, there were hearings on Capitol Hill—and then all of a sudden, they come out with the Popeyes chicken sandwich.

It hooked our communities like the crack epidemic. Man, we were not prepared for it. Black people standing in line for an hour and a half for a chicken sandwich? How can anyone focus on reparations when all you can think about is whether you're gonna get your fix?

And this was no ordinary sandwich. It was diabolical. They must have studied our habits for years to get a sandwich that tapped into nigga-ness so succinctly. The *thought* that went into it! Sure, chicken; that's a basic element. That's a given. *Well, we got to give them soft bread. Black people love soft bread. And sauce with that.* But then to add the pickles? That's evil-genius-level shit. I mean, this sandwich is fucking irresistible. I don't know nobody who doesn't like this sandwich. It hit all black people like a plague: people with refined tastes and without. Rich and poor. People who love fast food and people who should know better. My daughter went to culinary school and she had to have it. And I know professors who cut class just for a taste. I heard they closed Foot Locker early. We were not prepared for it.

And we haven't heard anything about reparations since.

But you couldn't just let us have the sandwich, right? That'd be giving too much away. Then *you ran out of chicken*? How do you run out of chicken? Right now I have a dozen eggs in my refrigerator. That's twelve would-be chickens right there.

So it was purposeful. It was a conspiracy. You ran out of chicken just to keep us unsteady and on edge. The niggas wanted reparations, then they got their chicken sandwiches. And then the chicken ran out—so now it's all "When will the chicken come back?" instead of "Where's our money?"

And they won't even tell us when it's coming back. It's like your father. You know what I'm saying? They *say* it's because it was "experimental." That's two experiments I'll always hold against white society: the Tuskegee Syphilis Experiment and the Popeyes Chicken Experiment.

Well, I'm onto you. So that's the first article of this treaty: since the Constitution only counted us as three-fifths of a person—we should only have to pay three-fifths of the price of that sandwich.

Reparations Article 1a. Chicken Discount

It is thus decided that due to the Popeyes chicken sandwich being much beloved in the black community, but in suspiciously short supply, all such sandwiches shall be offered to black folks at a three-fifths discount.

THE MITCH McCONNELL PROBLEM

But before we got distracted, reparations was in the news. Four hundred years after the first slaves were brought to America, the Democrats in Congress held the first hearings on reparations in decades, taking up Representative John Conyers's H.R. 40 bill. First introduced thirty years before, this bill sought to establish a commission to study the institution of slavery and make recommendations for amends.

And in the 2020 presidential campaign, Democrats were at least discussing it. You could get fucked up in the primaries if you didn't have a reasonable answer to the issue. Candidates at least had to say, "Well, we have to put an exploratory committee together, do some research, etc." Nobody could just say, "Fuck it, it's unnecessary."

Predictably, there was pushback because a lot of white people thought they *already* gave reparations. Mitch McConnell, the Republican Senate majority leader, probably put it best:

I don't think reparations for something that happened 150 years ago, for whom none of us currently living are responsible, is a good idea. We've tried to deal with our original sin of slavery by fighting a civil war, by passing landmark civil rights legislation. We elected an African American president. . . . I don't think we should be trying to figure out how to compensate for it. First of all, it would be hard to figure out whom to compensate.

First of all: "*We* elected an African American president"? No, I guarantee *you* didn't. I guarantee you had nothing to do with it. *We* didn't do anything. For Mitch McConnell to put himself in a sentence like that is telling. McConnell spearheaded *opposition* to Obama. He's the one who said, "The single most important thing we want to achieve is for President Obama to be a one-term president." He blocked Obama's Supreme Court nominee Merrick Garland. So forget about McConnell taking responsibility for stuff that happened 150 years ago; how about taking responsibility for stuff that happened nine years ago?

White people want to claim credit for electing Obama, even if they voted against him. They want to take credit for civil rights legislation, after they opposed it. And they want to take credit for ending the Civil War, when all they did was lose it. We've moved forward *despite* their actions, not because of them. Everything black people got from

America, we got over the protests and anger and vitriol of white supremacy. Everything we can do, everything—playing baseball, going to dinner, using a bathroom—everything we've ever wanted to do, we had to do over the protests of old white men like McConnell.

And is it really that hard to figure out whom to compensate, Mitch? McConnell's lucky because NBC News did his homework for him. They found that both his paternal and maternal great-great-grandfathers, James McConnell and Richard Daley, owned slaves. According to county "Slave Schedules," they owned at least fourteen slaves in Alabama, all but two of them female. Four are classified as "mulatto." The only way you get a mulatto is for a black person and a white person to have sex, right? So that would mean that if his relatives owned those slaves, it's likely that they raped them. So right now, there's somebody sharing Mitch McConnell's name that is a relative of his. So "it would be hard to figure out whom to compensate"? Well, you could start at your next family reunion, actually. "Pass the potato salad and the reparations."

The sad part is that McConnell can say whether we have the conversation or not. He's the majority leader of the Senate. And I think it's weird that a dude whose great-great-grandparents owned slaves gets to decide whether we're gonna have a conversation about what they did. Shouldn't he recuse himself?

But whether you're in charge of the Senate or not, a lot of white folks feel like this. They weren't around, they didn't have anything to do with it. It isn't *their fault*. Well, it was *someone's* fault.

Sometimes history is important to white people and sometimes it isn't. They want to have their Confederate statues, right? But they weren't here for that. They want the patina of the war; they want to pay to remember it, just not pay to rectify it. They preserve battlefields, they re-create Civil War battles because they like the glory of it, just not how gory it was. They have selective amnesia. How did white people get to be who they are today? On whose backs? They want to remember when it suits their purposes and not remember when it doesn't.

WHAT KIND OF REPARATIONS?

But like I say: We're not gonna shut up about it. This unpleasant state of affairs will continue if you just want to put your fingers in your ears. If you want everything to stay the same, with all the conflict and bad feelings, what can I say? But if you want change, try to engage in at least the thought experiment of what reparations might look like.

It's incredible what white people can accomplish when they want something. *I believe in you!*

So are we talking about cash payments? Is everybody affected by slavery getting a check? Maybe. But there are other ways to pay reparations too. You don't have to give money, but you could give low-interest loans. You could cut the tax rate. You could make sure everybody receives an equal education. You could make sure everybody gets fairly financed for a house. It's at least worth talking about, right?

And it's not like nobody's ever tried to figure out reparations. Republicans act like it's just too complicated. But look around: somehow you worked out how to pay other people before.

REPARATIONS ALREADY HAPPENED, SORT OF

Mitch McConnell is right about one thing: in fact, historically, payments for slavery have already been paid. Unfortunately, those reparations were paid the other way: they were paid to former *owners* of slaves.

For example, in 1825 France forced the government of Haiti to pay reparations to former slave owners after Haiti's slaves revolted against their colonial rulers and founded an independent government. Under threat of being invaded,

Haiti had to pay 150 million francs for the loss of French "property." Haiti had to take loans and pay this ransom with interest for 124 years, from 1825 to 1947. It's pretty easy to become a "shithole" country when a rich country has a gun to your head.

And you know, when your property gets took, you file an insurance claim. It was routine practice to have insurance on "cargo," in this case, slaves. So if you throw your slaves overboard, who's to know that your insurance claim isn't right? How many millions of black people were killed in the Middle Passage between Africa and the New World is unknown, but one documented incident was the Zong Massacre in 1781. After an outbreak of illness, the ship's captain decided to murder 132 enslaved people by throwing them overboard. Fifty-four people were chained together and then drowned, and over the next few days, another seventy-eight were thrown overboard. We know about it because the owners filed an insurance claim for the "loss."

And when slavery was banned in England in 1833, the British government paid three thousand families that had owned slaves for the loss of their property. So reparations for slavery isn't such a crazy idea, it's just that white folks tend to get the check.

WHERE'S MY FORTY ACRES AND A MULE?

So fine, weren't we all promised "forty acres and a mule"? Spike Lee didn't just make that shit up, right? Everyone's heard of that, but what the hell was it?

At the tail end of the Civil War, General William Tecumseh Sherman issued Special Field Order No. 15, which called for giving four hundred thousand acres of coastline to freed slaves in forty-acre increments. A little later, he added the mule part.

Sherman wasn't just being a nice guy; he was trying to stick it to the white rice farmers of the South and solve a problem at the same time. The problem was what to do with all the freed peoples of the South who had no resources of their own. Sherman consulted with a group of black preachers from Savannah, Georgia, to come up with solutions. The leader of the group, Garrison Frazier, a Baptist minister and himself a former slave, argued for land: "The way we can best take care of ourselves is to have land, and turn it and till it by our own labor." Giving everyone forty acres was a way to keep ex-slaves self-sufficient and allow Sherman to keep marching northward. People were actually given land from this order. By June 1865, approximately forty thousand freedmen had settled four hundred thousand acres.

But you know there's no way they're gonna give niggas beachfront property. I think Lincoln got killed by Century 21. Somebody check and see if John Wilkes Booth was wearing a gold blazer. After Lincoln's assassination, President Andrew Johnson came in and he was like, "No. Fuck that," and he made everyone give everything back.

It must have been awkward. Stepping up to some old white guy's plantation, ringing the bell: Ding-dong. *Hey, man, thanks for letting me borrow your mule.*

And that was the end of that first bit of reparations. So let's start there. I mean, I don't know if it makes sense for all the black folks to get forty acres and a mule anymore, but *it's something.*

Let's see: If all the black folk in America each get 40 acres, that's 40 × 42 million people. That's 1.68 billion acres, and America only has like 2.43 billion. That would be most of the lower forty-eight states. And black people are not gonna live in Alaska, so we already got a problem. If you give us all the land you owe us, where the fuck are you all gonna live? The last thing we need is to deal with a bunch of angry white folks renting property from us, not paying rent on time, making a mess and being shitty tenants. Without that pride of homeownership, you just can't trust white folks to not trash the place and leave us holding the bill.

Plus, with global warming, half this land's gonna be underwater in a few years. And you know black folks don't like to swim. No, I think it's too late to hand out all that land.

And without the land, what's the point of handing out forty-two million mules? First of all, mules are actually a cross between a donkey and a horse. Without getting into a whole biology lesson—do you know how a mule is made? *Sometimes when a horse and a donkey love each other very much* . . . So how the hell are you going to find enough horses and donkeys to make that many mules? I'd think it'd take a special horse to love a donkey that much. And forty-two million of them—I don't see it.

So fine; you don't have the land and you don't have the mules. So you reneged on that and it's time to renegotiate. We need a new deal. A New New Deal.

RADISH MONEY

After President Johnson canceled the order providing land for ex-slaves, many of them were relegated to poverty and forced into sharecropping for their former masters and landowners. Thousands of people were removed from land they had been given under Sherman's Special Field Order No. 15.

But it wasn't like reparations talks were *over*. It was still discussed. On one side were the former slave owners who wanted to be compensated for their lost "property," never mind that they just lost a war over it. And on the other side were the formerly enslaved, whose labor had enriched America over the previous several hundred years.

Groups of former slaves pushed for reparations in the form of pensions in the 1890s and early 1900s. The main group spearheading this was the National Ex-Slave Mutual Relief, Bounty and Pension Association, the MRB&PA, led by Callie House. Callie House was a widow, a former slave, a mother of five, and a badass. Her plan called for pensions based on an ex-slave's age: people seventy and older would get $500 and $15 per month for life; those in their sixties would get $300 and $12 per month; those in their fifties would get $100 and $8 a month, and anyone under fifty would get $4 per month. Not much, but you know in 1899 you could buy yourself a delicious plate of radishes for fifteen cents or some green apple fritters in rum sauce for sixty cents, whatever those were.

The plan was similar to Civil War pensions for disabled soldiers, so it should have seemed reasonable. Y'all could have gotten off cheap back then. But instead, the government infiltrated and undermined the MRB&PA, accusing its officers of fraud. Hmm, the government investigating a black organization and seeking to undermine it? Where have I heard this before? The Bureau of Pensions, the Post Office Department, and the Justice Department all actively worked against the movement, especially after Callie House brought a class-action lawsuit against the U.S. Treasury in 1915 asking for $68 million, the amount of tax revenue earned from slave labor on cotton from 1862 to 1868.

The lawsuit failed, and eventually the Post Office Department charged House with mail fraud. I like my post office delivering mail, not indictments. After an all-white-male jury convicted her, she spent a year in jail. Even though it was a frame-up, the slave pension movement fell apart after.

LOOK AT THE GERMANS

So America has fucked up on reparations a few times, but we can look around and see how other countries have used reparations to apologize and atone for their behavior. For instance, West Germany paid money to Israel after World War II. At the time, the first Israeli prime minister, David Ben-Gurion, argued for reparations "so that the murderers do not become the heirs as well."

But many Israelis didn't want to take money from Germans, because they felt like they'd be taking blood money. And many Germans felt like they hadn't done anything. According to *The Jewish Press,* "only 34 percent of the German public believed that Germany owed Jews anything at all, and 21 percent still believed that *the Jews themselves were responsible for what had happened to them during the Holocaust*" (emphasis in original).

But the agreement ended up passing, and today more than $70 billion has been paid in reparations. These weren't warm and fuzzy negotiations, there wasn't total agreement, but still they got paid. And in 2000, German companies that had used slave labor in the war created a foundation to compensate people. It's not like this has made up for the Holocaust or made many Jews want to spend their vacations in Baden-Baden, but it's *something.*

If former Nazis and Jews can sit down and hammer out a settlement, why can't white America and black people?

SOME PEOPLE GOT PAID
JAPANESE GOT PAID

It's not like the American government hasn't ever paid anyone money or apologized to *anyone.* In 1988, President Reagan signed the Civil Liberties Act, compensating people of Japanese descent who were imprisoned in camps during World War II. During the war, 120,000 people were put in internment camps because of racist fears after the Pearl Harbor attack. After years of pressure from people whose property and livelihood had been taken away, the government issued a formal apology and $20,000 to compensate each surviving victim.

AND ITALIANS...

Oh, and did I mention that Italians were given reparations? I'll tell you about that one later, but damn—Italians? Japanese, Italians, Jews—I mean, we gotta be in line before the Irish, right?

AND OTHERS

Some white people get hung up, or like to pretend to get hung up, on the mystery of who might have been enslaved by whom. How can we know who benefited from slavery? How can we know who was enslaved? How can we possibly figure it out? It's too hard, so why try?

Except this didn't all happen thousands of years ago! We're not trying to figure out if King Tut liked sausages for breakfast or if Julius Caesar had a horse named Betsy. This isn't ancient history. Slavery ended just 150 years ago.

And just because the government is sitting on its hands, that doesn't mean that nothing can be done. Some people have tried to do the right thing, after they did the wrong thing. At Georgetown University, students voted to increase their tuition to pay reparations to descendants of 272 slaves who had been owned by the school. In 1838, the Jesuits who ran Georgetown sold their slaves to raise money. This sale stands out because of the large number of slaves sold and the fact that it was *Catholic priests* doing the selling. That's fucked up, but maybe not even in the top ten most fucked-up things Catholic priests have done.

After student protests and a financial push from alumni, these 272 people were researched and their history traced, and genealogists were able to find almost four thousand descendants of the slaves sold in 1838. It's not some abstract, unknowable history. It's not always easy, because paper trails are scarce, but with some effort it can be done.

So now, along with the students' vote to increase tuition, Georgetown has issued an apology, renamed several buildings, and provided admissions preference to descendants. Is that enough? Who knows? But it's a start, and an acknowledgment of wrongdoing.

While we're renaming buildings, I want to make sure that we're not picking all the obvious people. Sure, we could name another building for Sojourner Truth, and she deserves every building she gets. But I think we should name some buildings or scholarships after people who never really got to reach their full potential because of slavery and the oppression of racism. Not the people who triumphed and overcame racism. It's easy to name buildings after people who were triumphant.

Nipsey Hussle should have a building, for example. It should be all cats like him. The ones who, if not for systemic oppression, might have been something. They would never have gotten accepted into genteel society, but I'm sure their shit gets played at homecoming games.

Reparations Article 1b. Nipsey Hall

In recognition of the fact that buildings are named after old white guys, some of whom were involved in the very systemic racism and oppression that have brought us to this fraught moment of racial tension, we hereby establish a new naming criterion for buildings in universities, cities, and other public institutions. Consideration shall be given to badass, dope niggas whose time passed too soon and who might not previously have been accepted as people to bear in tribute.

With students and activists pushing them, a bunch of different colleges, including Harvard, Brown, Columbia, and the University of Virginia have put together commissions and issued apologies for their ties to the slave trade. And some religious institutions, like churches and convents, have done work to figure out their slave-owning past and make amends.

The Virginia Theological Seminary just set up a $1.7 million reparations fund. And the Catholic sisters of the Society of the Sacred Heart created a fund to finance scholarships for descendants of the 150 slaves the society once owned in Louisiana and Missouri. This is moral leadership from institutions that preach morality. But it wouldn't have happened if the people in charge just threw up their hands or shrugged off the responsibility of the past.

These institutions are facing up to history. Why won't you?

I think a big problem is that white people and black people have totally different perceptions of America. Everyone feels emotional about the whole thing, and yet in so many ways our interests align. Try not to think of this as a lose-lose. What if I could get you to see it our way? Would that take away the sting of surrender?

HISTORY BOOKS SHALL BE ALIGNED

OUR HISTORY BOOKS AND YOURS

Suffice it to say, black people's history books and white people's textbooks wouldn't match up. But let's try to get on the same page. A lot of people don't really know the history of how we got here, or they got bad facts. It shouldn't be surprising that some of the same people who enslaved us or justified oppressing us also wrote the history books.

So let's look at the history of slavery and oppression in America. How can we judge what we owe each other if we aren't operating from the same facts? Let's see if you can put yourself in our shoes, see if you think you'd still be pissed if this were your history.

IN THE BEGINNING . . .

The deal for black people in America changed almost overnight.

In 1619, the first enslaved Africans were brought to Virginia, where they were sold to colonists of Jamestown. These were people seized from a Portuguese slave ship by an English ship, then sold to colonists in exchange for food.

Initially, slavery was a bit *informal;* everyone, black or white, was considered an indentured servant. It was something of a handshake deal, or maybe a *handcuff* deal. Maybe it wasn't a lot different from slavery. If you were a black indentured servant in 1619 Virginia, I bet you *felt* like a slave. Probably nobody said, "Hey, man, don't feel so bad—you're only an indentured servant!" *Feels pretty slave-y.* That said, some of the first slaves brought to America were able to buy their freedom or have kids who weren't slaves.

But after a little while, the deal got switched up on black folks. It must have been pretty fucked up to be a black man in colonial Virginia when these new laws were getting passed, taking away freedom after freedom. Look at this list from Historic Jamestowne's website:

- **1630s:** "Customary practice to hold some Negroes in a form of life service." *Some. Okay, all right. At least it's not like every Negro is a slave . . .*
- **1639:** "All persons except Negroes are to be with Arms and Ammunition." *It does make me nervous that us black folk can't have guns, but they said, "Look, we got you—you don't need to hold on to a piece."*
- **1640:** "John Punch, a runaway indentured Servant, first documented slave for life." *John Punch got slapped, I guess.*
- **1662:** "Slavery was recognized in the statutory law of the colony." *Oh, okay, now it's a little less informal.*
- **1667:** "Baptism does not bring freedom." Baptized Africans are no longer exempt from slavery. *White people think they're bigger than God. What would Jesus do?*
- **1680:** "Blacks could not congregate in large numbers." *Huh, why are there only four other brothers at this party?*
- **1692:** "Negroes must give up ownership of horses, cattle or hogs." *How am I gonna ride the fuck out of here without my horse . . . Oh, I see . . .*

So the picture we have of black people being brought over as slaves is one that didn't have to be. It was a devolution of rights, taken away in pieces. By 1705, the Virginia Slave Codes were passed, and slavery was codified in America. In only a few decades, slavery became a thing America relied on, and the subjugation of black people began.

LIFE, LIBERTY, AND THE PURSUIT OF HAPPINESS

So from the very beginning of America, we were being cut out of the deal. It's interesting that when Thomas Jefferson was writing the Declaration of Independence in 1776, he had slaves. He wrote the words:

> We hold these Truths to be self-evident, that all men are created equal, that they are endowed by their Creator with certain unalienable Rights, that among these are Life, Liberty and the pursuit of Happiness.

"All men" seems straightforward enough, but what's this asterisk here? I don't even know where they put the fine print on a scroll, but if you find it, it says, *All men are created equal . . . except you niggers. Get me some tea!* Right?

Apparently, Jefferson's first draft did have some shit about slaves in it. One of the things he accused King George of was:

> He has waged cruel war against human nature itself, violating it's [*sic*] most sacred rights of life & liberty in the persons of a distant people who never offended

him, captivating & carrying them into slavery in another hemisphere, or to incur miserable death in their
transportation thither.

So he blamed King George for slavery, called it a "cruel
war against human nature itself," all while owning slaves.
Jefferson was . . . a complicated guy. But we knew that from
his "relationship" with his slave Sally Hemings. So the other
part about slaves that didn't make it into the final draft was
about the king inciting slaves to rise up against the colonies:

He is now exciting those very people to rise in arms
among us, and to purchase that liberty of which he
has deprived them, & murdering the people upon
whom he also obtruded them: thus paying off former
crimes committed against the liberties of one people,
with crimes which he urges them to commit against
the lives of another.

Yeah, that's complicated: slave owner hates on slavery,
but doesn't want slaves to be freed because they might murder their owners. White people worried about black people
rising up for freedom? Sounds familiar.
But none of that made it into the final draft anyway;

Jefferson had to keep the Southern delegates happy to get the thing signed, so everyone agreed to scrap that part. They had to come to a *compromise*. Once again, some old white guys from the South cut us out of the deal.

THREE-FIFTHS OF A MAN

And when the Founding Fathers got together to write up the Constitution, things didn't get any better for black people. See, what happens when you get a bunch of white guys in a room is you get things like the Three-Fifths Compromise. When the Founders were trying to come up with the legislative branch, they had to figure out how to account for everyone. Some people argued for not counting slaves at all; others wanted them counted. So everyone met in the middle to count each slave as three-fifths of a person. I bet a lot of us have felt like three-fifths of a person after a late night out, but that shit usually lifts around noon.

This worked well enough for everyone—well, the *white* everyones—along with a couple of extra promises that importing slaves was okay for another twenty years and that fugitive slaves would be returned to their owners. Ultimately, it would take the Civil War to undo the slave trade in America, but we're still stuck with the compromised form of representation that gives every state two senators, regardless of how many people live there. So Wyoming gets two senators and California gets two senators. This continues to skew power to the South centuries later. More Americans live in Los Angeles than live in Mississippi, but Mississippians get to elect a redneck like Senator Cindy Hyde-Smith, who made jokes about public hangings and went to a segregation academy. Meanwhile, I don't get to vote for an extra Senator Magic Johnson.

SLAVERY WAS BAD

I shouldn't need to say this, but let's all get on the same page about something: slavery was bad.

I do need to say it, however, because even though I never see any white people *signing up to be slaves,* I still hear people trying to make it seem like slavery wasn't, you know, *bad.* Some of these people aren't saying it was *good* so much as they're saying it wasn't *that bad. Look on the bright side, black people!*

Take the criticism of the movie *12 Years a Slave,* which conservatives seemed to think was going to be about twelve great years. James Bowman, film critic for *American Spectator,* complained about director Steve McQueen's choices: "If ever in slavery's 250-year history in North America there were a kind master or a contented slave, as in the nature of things there must have been, here and there, we may be sure that Mr. McQueen does not want us to hear about it." *Why wasn't there a nice slave owner in the movie about abducting someone and forcing him into slavery?*

And sure, it's shameful that slaves helped to build the White House, but it wasn't all that bad according to Bill O'Reilly: "Slaves that worked there were well fed and had decent lodgings provided by the government." *It wasn't so bad: they got a lunch break and a shack to live in!*

The cool thing is that we don't have to rely on conservatives to tell us what it was like to be a slave. We can read for ourselves. In the 1930s, writers working for the Works Progress Administration interviewed many of the still-living former slaves and recorded their stories.

I know when I'm reading about slaves, I use Morgan Freeman's voice. I don't know what you all use, but feel free to fill in Samuel L. Jackson, Viola Davis, or Whoopi Goldberg as necessary.

Does this sound "bad" or "not so bad":

One day I remembers my brother, January, was caught over seein a gal on de next plantation. He had a pass, but de time on it done gib out. Well sir, when Massa found out dat he was a hour late, he got as mad as a hive of bees. So when January he come home, de massa took down his long mule skinner and tied him a rope to a pine tree. He strip his shirt off and said: "Now, nigger, I'm goin to teach you some sense."

Wid dat he started layin on de lashes. January was a big, fine lookin nigger, finest I ever seed. He was just four years older dan me, an when de mass begin a beatin him, January never said a word. De massa got madder and madder cause he couldn't make January holla.

"What's de matter wid you, nigger?" he say. "Don't it hurt?"

January, he never said nothin, and de massa keep a beatin till little streams of blood started flowin down January's chest, but he never holler. His lips was a quiverin' and his body was a shakin, but his mouth it never open; and all de while I sat on my mammy's and pappy's steps a-cryin.

—*William Colbert, 93, Alabama*

Bad or not so bad:

Aunt Cheyney was jus' out of bed with a sucklin' baby one time, and she run away. Some say that was nother baby of massa's breedin'. She don't come to the house to nurse her baby, so they misses her and old Solomon gits the nigger hounds and takes her trail. They gits near her and she grabs a limb and tries to hoist herself in a tree, but them dogs grab her and pull her down. The men hollers them onto her, and the dogs tore her naked and ate the breasts plumb off her body. She got well and lived to be a old woman, but nother woman has to suck her baby and she ain't got no sign of breasts no more.

—*Mary Reynolds, 105, Texas*

Bad or not so bad:

My grandmother, and my mother were both freed like this, but what they called "nigger traders" captured them and two or three others, and they took them just like they would animals, and sold them, that was how "Ples" Holbert got my mother. My grandmother was sent to Texas. My mother said she wrote and had one letter from my grandmother after that, but she never saw her again.

—*Clayton Holbert, 86, Kansas*

Bad, right? So let's just put this to rest: slavery was bad.

WAS SLAVERY THE CAUSE OF THE CIVIL WAR?

D.L., was slavery the cause of the Civil War?

Yep. But don't take my word for it. Take the word of Alexander Stephens, the Confederacy's vice president:

> Our new government is founded upon exactly the opposite idea; its foundations are laid, its cornerstone rests, upon the great truth that the negro is not equal to the white man; that slavery subordination to the superior race is his natural and normal condition. This, our new government, is the first, in the history of the world, based upon this great physical, philosophical, and moral truth.

Wasn't it about states' rights or something?

Yeah, the states' rights to have slaves! Here's what the states said when they declared their secession from the Union:

> **MISSISSIPPI:** "Our position is thoroughly identified with the institution of slavery—the greatest material interest of the world."

SOUTH CAROLINA: "A geographical line has been drawn across the Union, and all the States north of that line have united in the election of a man to the high office of President of the United States, whose opinions and purposes are hostile to slavery. He is to be entrusted with the administration of the common Government, because he has declared that that 'Government cannot endure permanently half slave, half free,' and that the public mind must rest in the belief that slavery is in the course of ultimate extinction."

TEXAS: "In all the non-slave-holding States, in violation of that good faith and comity which should exist between entirely distinct nations, the people have formed themselves into a great sectional party, now strong enough in numbers to control the affairs of each of those States, based upon an unnatural feeling of hostility to these Southern States and their beneficent and patriarchal system of African slavery, proclaiming the debasing doctrine of equality of all men, irrespective of race or color—a doctrine at war with nature, in opposition to the experience of mankind, and in violation of the plainest revelations of Divine Law."

To pretend that the Civil War was about states' rights beyond the "right to have slaves" is nonsense. A lot of this bullshit was originally a way to make Southern people feel better about themselves after they got their asses kicked defending chaining people up, forcing them to work, raping them, and tearing apart their families. Yeah, that can *feel bad*.

That's why so many people still cling to the "Lost Cause" ideology that tried to reframe the secession of the South as a struggle to maintain a Southern way of life, to maintain states' rights, and *definitely, definitely* not just about slavery. Even though the leaders of the Southern states said it was about slavery, Lost Cause proponents pretended it was about a noble conflict, instead of a white supremacist economic model.

White people don't want the blame for slavery. And you don't get credit for ending it either. On the Fox News show *Outnumbered,* conservative commentator Katie Pavlich said, "They keep blaming America for the sin of slavery. But the truth is, throughout human history, slavery has existed, and America came along as the first country to end it within 150 years. And we get no credit for that, to move forward and try and make good on that."

Only 150 years? That's slower than Interstate 405 on a Friday.

And Newt Gingrich wants to get credit for the "several hundred thousand white Americans who died in the Civil War in order to free the slaves." See, I thought Newt represented Georgia. Isn't Georgia in the South?

Or take Ben Shapiro: "There was a national apology for slavery. It was called the Civil War where 700,000 Americans died." Um, Ben—that's a *total*. It didn't seem like half of those people were apologizing. Next time send flowers.

RECONSTRUCTION: A NEW HOPE

I'm not going to relitigate the whole Civil War. But you know the end of the story: we got our "freedom."

With the end of the Civil War, America had to figure out how to put all its pieces back together. Reconstruction, the period right after the war, from about 1865 to 1877, was a time when our basic rights got established, as did a lot of the lies still told about us. Embittered Southerners tried to reassert white supremacy after their loss. A racist, horrible president tried to let them do it. And finally, white people just got tired of the whole thing and let black folks down. It's the same kind of shit we're trying to prevent with this treaty!

After Lincoln's assassination, it was up to President Andrew Johnson to oversee Reconstruction. He wanted to let the Southern states dictate their own terms, even though they lost the war. Maybe it had something to do with the fact that he was, um, an unlikely champion for ex-slaves. "This is a country for white men, and by God, as long as I am President, it shall be a government for white men," he wrote in 1866. *Okay.*

So-called Radical Republicans opposed Johnson and pushed for stricter terms for readmitting former Southern states back into the Union and for ensuring ex-slaves had rights in the postwar era. You have to remember that back then Republicans were basically Democrats and Democrats were basically Republicans. That's why Republicans nowadays are always trying to claim that they are "the party of Lincoln" when they pretend to care about black people. If you gotta go back to the motherfucker on the penny, you've gotta update your résumé.

Right after the war ended, the Southern states had passed "black codes" that gave black people some rights, but didn't allow them to vote, work freely, serve on juries, or testify against white people in court. Using "vagrancy" laws, local governments could round up black people they felt weren't employed enough and force them into involuntary labor. *You're not a slave; you're an ex-slave doing involuntary labor.*

But the Radical Republicans pushed back, passing the Civil Rights Act of 1866, overriding Johnson's veto. The Thirteenth Amendment, banning slavery, had passed a year earlier. They then passed the Reconstruction Acts, again over Johnson's veto, setting harder terms for the states to reenter the Union. These included creating new state constitutions, which had to be approved by Congress. They passed the Fourteenth and Fifteenth Amendments, ensuring legal equality and giving the vote to black men.

Over the next few years, a newly empowered black political class emerged. Blacks voted in large numbers and elected interracial governments that had never been seen before. The number of black people in government went from zero to about two thousand—everyone from sheriffs to senators. It wasn't exactly Wakanda, but it was still pretty incredible.

This new political power led to big achievements like in South Carolina, where a biracial legislature came together to write a new state constitution and pass reforms like creating the first public school system of the South. It's crazy to think about now: several years before, blacks were enslaved, and now they were sitting at the table as equals in government.

It didn't last long. Violence and terrorism by the Ku Klux Klan and other groups spread and suppressed blacks.

In 1868, about a thousand black people were killed in racial violence. And in the 1868 U.S. presidential election, Republicans lost Georgia to Democrats because voter intimidation prevented black turnout. In Colfax, Louisiana, in 1873, 150 black people were killed by white supremacists to overturn an election.

By the time of the 1876 presidential election, the handwriting was on the wall. After years of war, then several cycles of white supremacist violence, the Northern Republican advocates for Reconstruction were fed up. Then there was a contested election where nobody got a majority of electoral votes. It was crazy—a constitutional crisis ensued, and a deal was struck. You know, a *compromise*. The Compromise of 1876. This put the Republican Rutherford B. Hayes in the White House but forced the withdrawal of all federal troops from the South, ceding effective control back to the white supremacists.

It's these white supremacists, the same motherfuckers who lost the Civil War and created the Klan and the Jim Crow laws of the South, who wrote the history books. They portrayed Reconstruction as a failure of black self-rule, instead of the violent oppression of a black minority. They rewrote history with their "Lost Cause" as the winner.

THE TOTALLY DUMB, WACKY LAWS OF JIM CROW

The era of "Jim Crow" laws had begun. Roughly speaking, these were laws and rules asserting racial segregation and white supremacy. They imposed restrictions on voting, transportation, marriage, and every other facet of life in America for black people, all the way through until the civil rights movement. You already know that people had to ride on different parts of the bus, use different water fountains, and so forth. But white supremacy is so virulent that laws were made about shit you'd think wouldn't even be worth fucking with:

MENTAL HOSPITALS (GEORGIA): "The Board of Control shall see that proper and distinct apartments are arranged for said patients, so that in no case shall Negroes and white persons be together." *If you had a crazy black dude who thought he was Napoleon, which ward did you put him in?*

BARBERS (GEORGIA): "No colored barber shall serve as a barber [to] white women or girls." *Barbershops remain segregated to this day, but you know, it's okay by me.*

CIRCUS TICKETS (LOUISIANA): "All circuses, shows, and tent exhibitions, to which the attendance of . . . more than one race is invited or expected to attend shall provide for the convenience of its patrons not less than two ticket offices with individual ticket sellers, and not less than two entrances to the said performance, with individual ticket takers and receivers." *They keep the lions and the elephants in the same tent, but the blacks and the whites in different ones?*

THE BLIND (LOUISIANA): "The board of trustees shall . . . maintain a separate building . . . on separate ground for the admission, care, instruction, and support of all blind persons of the colored or black race." *If there's anywhere that color shouldn't matter, it's in a house for blind people, right?*

GAMES (ALABAMA): "It shall be unlawful for a negro and white person to play together or in company with each other in any game of cards or dice, dominoes or checkers." *Damn, it's fucked up that you couldn't play a game of Boggle together.*

WELL-KNOWN UNKNOWNS

But nobody was in much of a Boggle mood anyway.

The history of racial violence in America is so crazy that white people don't believe it when they see it. The first episode of HBO's *The Watchmen* started with the Tulsa Race Massacre, but a lot of people thought that it was made up. They didn't know that it was depicting a real event where hundreds of black people were killed and thirty-five city blocks of Tulsa, including "Black Wall Street," were destroyed by white vigilantes. Why isn't this in the history books? Why don't more people know about it? It only happened in 1921—but it was buried and whitewashed. Not a single person was punished. So they won't give us justice, but they'll give us a TV show.

Donald Rumsfeld once said, "There are known knowns; there are things we know we know. We also know there are known unknowns; that is to say we know there are some things we do not know. But there are also unknown unknowns—the ones we don't know we don't know."

I'll add a category: there are well-known unknowns. There's shit that's unknown to all you white folks but is well-known to us. And because of that, you need a little education before you can judge whether your understanding of race in America is well informed. A lot of times you don't know it because it's so horrible, no one would admit that it happened. It's so horrible, you go, "That's bad—it can't be right." It is right. All of this shit happened in *America:*

1811: NEW ORLEANS SLAVE REVOLT

A group of slaves rallied an army of almost five hundred slaves to take over plantations north of New Orleans and then march to conquer the city. They battled the U.S. military and a white planter militia but were overwhelmed. In the brutal aftermath, militia members chopped off the leader's hands and burned him. They then executed and beheaded more than one hundred slaves, put their heads on spikes, and lined them along the river so when people came by, they would see the heads. "Their Heads, which decorate our Levee, all the way up the coast . . . look like crows sitting on long poles," wrote one traveler.

It was such a well-organized rebellion that it was basically erased from the history books.

1831: NAT TURNER'S REBELLION

Nat Turner led a slave revolt in Virginia, gathering almost one hundred slaves in an uprising that killed fifty-one white people. He was able to stay at large for almost two months before getting captured and killed. Throughout his rebellion, the rebels killed white people, but spared a few homes because Turner believed the poor white inhabitants "thought no better of themselves than they did of negroes." Southerners lived in terror that another Nat Turner might rise up and kill them in a similar organized attack.

1887: THIBODAUX MASSACRE OF SUGARCANE WORKERS

A group of striking black sugarcane workers was attacked in Thibodaux, Louisiana, after white vigilantes were brought in to break the strike. Gunmen ordered black men out of their houses and shot them. The posses killed sixty black Americans and yet no one was prosecuted or brought to justice.

1893: THE PUBLIC TORTURE OF HENRY SMITH

Lynchings weren't necessarily spontaneous outbreaks of violence. In 1893, a seventeen-year-old black man was captured by a mob after having been accused of raping and murdering a white child. He was brought by train back to Paris, Texas, where the townspeople had assembled a platform in the middle of town. He was then tortured and burned alive in front of ten thousand people. The *Fort Worth Gazette* reported the horrifying details:

A tinner's furnace was brought on with IRONS HEATED WHITE.

Taking one, Vance thrust it under first one and then the other side of his victim's feet, who, helpless, writhed as the flesh SCARRED AND PEELED from the bones.

Slowly, inch by inch, up his legs the iron was drawn and redrawn, only the nervous jerky twist of the muscles showing the agony being induced. When his body was reached and the iron was pressed to the most tender part of his body he broke silence for the first time and a prolonged SCREAM OF AGONY rent the air.

Slowly, across and around the body, slowly upward traced the irons. The withered scarred flesh marked the progress of the awful punishment. By turns Smith screamed, prayed, begged and cursed his tormentors. When his face was reached HIS TONGUE WAS SILENCED by fire and thenceforth he only moaned or gave a cry that echoed over the prairie like the wail of a wild animal.

Then his EYES WERE PUT OUT, not a finger-breadth of his body being unscathed. His executioners gave way. They were Vance, his brother-in-law, and

Vance's son, a boy of 15 years of age. When they gave over punishing Smith they left the platform.

This was all done with the approval of law enforcement, the media, and the public.

1917: THE EAST ST. LOUIS "RACE RIOT"

After a car of white occupants drove through the black neighborhood of East St. Louis, Illinois, randomly shooting at people, two white policemen were mistakenly killed by residents who thought they were the shooters. In retaliation for this and amid labor tensions, a group of white rioters killed one hundred black people and destroyed over $400,000 in property. A reporter from the *St. Louis Post-Dispatch* described the indiscriminate killings:

I saw man after man, with hands raised, pleading for his life, surrounded by groups of men—men who had never seen him before and knew nothing about him except that he was black—and saw them administer the historic sentence of intolerance, death by stoning. I saw one of these men, almost dead from a savage shower of stones, hanged with a clothesline.

1919: THE RED SUMMER

During a year of widespread white mob attacks in more than three dozen cities, hundreds of black people were killed. Black soldiers returning from duty in World War I were especially targeted and fought back. A partial list of the violence:

- **JENKINS COUNTY, GEORGIA:** A mob burned a church down, lynched several people, and destroyed three black Masonic lodges.
- **CHARLESTON, SOUTH CAROLINA:** White U.S. Navy sailors led a riot that killed six black men and injured many more.
- **LONGVIEW, TEXAS:** Whites attacked the black area of town, killing people and burning property before the National Guard took control.
- **WASHINGTON, D.C.:** White soldiers rioted and beat black people on the street; the National Guard was called in after four days and fifteen deaths.
- **CHICAGO, ILLINOIS:** A black teenager was stoned for being on the wrong side of a segregated beach, sparking violence. There were at least 38 fatalities, 537 injuries, and 1,000 black families left homeless.

- **OMAHA, NEBRASKA:** A crowd of ten thousand white rioters surrounded and burned down a courthouse to lynch a black prisoner. They hanged him and burned his body, then attacked black businesses and homes before troops restored order.
- **ELAINE, ARKANSAS:** White planters organized a militia against black sharecroppers who sought to unionize. Over several days, they killed between 100 and 237 black people.

1921: TULSA RACE MASSACRE

A white mob attempted to lynch a black teen being held on bogus charges. They gathered around the courthouse and tried to force their way in. A group of armed black men arrived to defend him but was outnumbered by a huge crowd of whites. After a battle, black residents retreated to the Greenwood District, the black neighborhood of Tulsa containing "Black Wall Street." Thousands of white residents then attacked Greenwood, shooting unarmed black residents and burning homes and businesses. All of this was done in plain view of law enforcement and with the participation of whites who had been "deputized." When the National Guard arrived, they imprisoned the black Tulsans and kept them at a local fairground. Between one hundred and three hundred people were killed and more than eight thousand people were made homeless.

1943: DETROIT RACE RIOT

In 1942, white resistance to allowing black families to move into the Sojourner Truth Housing Project sparked racial tension. A year later, fighting, riots, and attacks escalated after false rumors of an assault on a black woman and another false rumor of a rape of a white woman. Twenty-five black people were killed, many by police and National Guard. Seven hundred people were injured and $2 million worth of property was destroyed.

1985: THE PHILADELPHIA FIREBOMBING OF MOVE

After a daylong confrontation with a radical black-liberation group called MOVE, the Philadelphia police dropped a bomb on the West Philadelphia row house that the MOVE members lived in, killing eleven people, including five children. The fire caused by the police bombing destroyed sixty-five houses in the neighborhood. Two hundred people were made homeless. Nobody involved ever faced any repercussions—not the mayor, not the police.

These are people who were *bombed* in 1985. *In America.*

AN APOLOGY FOR LYNCHING

So fine, maybe we'll never get reparations for being slaves. But what about the violence and lynching directed at us? After slavery ended, it's not as if the former white supremacists who ran the place welcomed black folks to the lunch counter.

According to researchers from Tuskegee University, more than 4,700 people were lynched between 1882 and 1968. That's 4,700 people killed in the reimposition of white terror, especially in the South. And almost none of the perpetrators of that violence were brought to justice, nor were their victims' families compensated in any way.

In 2020, mob lynching still isn't a federal crime. It was only at the end of 2018 that Senators Kamala Harris, Cory Booker, and Tim Scott got their Justice for Victims of Lynching Act of 2018 passed. The Senate had previously failed to pass federal antilynching legislation two hundred times. At the time of the act's passage, Republican senator Cindy Hyde-Smith of Mississippi was the presiding officer; this was the same lady who said she'd be in the front row of a "public hanging" if invited. And even though the House has approved a version of this bill, President Trump has yet to sign it into law.

So the Senate has been slow to recognize the damage done by lynching. Maybe we shouldn't hold our breath for an apology or a payout. But then again, Italians got both.

That's right: the U.S. government paid $25,000 in reparations for Italian Americans who were lynched. Now granted, this was in 1892, but still, $25,000 could buy you a lot of wagons in 1892. And, hey: that's $25,000 more than the United States has paid to us.

You see, in 1891, a mob broke into a New Orleans prison and murdered eleven Italian Americans whom they blamed for the death of the police chief. You have to remember that at the time, Italians were considered basically almost niggas. People in New Orleans did *not* like Italians. People felt like they were taking "American jobs," and Italian immigrants were discriminated against for their darker complexions. Sound familiar?

When the New Orleans police chief, David Hennessy, was killed in an ambush, rumors spread that he had blamed Italians in his dying breath. Hundreds of Italians were arrested, and nineteen people were indicted. None of these people were convicted of the crime, but eleven were lynched by the mob that broke into the prison. The payment of reparations was made to Italy, to distribute to the families affected. As the *New York Times* quoted the secretary of state in 1892: "While the injury was not indicted directly by the United States, the President nevertheless feels that it is the solemn duty as well as the great pleasure of the National Government to pay a satisfactory indemnity. Moreover, the President's instructions carry with them the hope that the transaction of today may efface all memory of the unhappy tragedy."

How is it that President Benjamin Harrison was more enlightened in 1892 than President Trump is in 2020?

And you know how white people hold a grudge. How when they get irritated, they yell "HEY" and startle you. When white people feel irritated, they go looking for an apology and usually get it. So when Michael Santo of the Order Sons and Daughters of Italy in America asked the City of New Orleans for an apology this past year, Mayor LaToya Cantrell decided it was the right thing to do. "At this late date, we cannot give justice, but we can be intentional and deliberate about what we do going forward," said Mayor Cantrell. She asked the crowd "to be the kind of people that our children are not apologizing for 128 years from now."

There's something fucked up about a LaToya apologizing

for a lynching, right? Why is it always up to black people to do the right thing?

So our history books and yours don't match up. What you've done is you've co-opted truth. These false notions get stuck over time and are never challenged. According to my history classes, we didn't do anything but invent the peanut. I mean, the only black person I ever learned about in school was George Washington Carver. You know how hard it was during Black History Month, learning all the aspects of one motherfucker for twenty-eight days? *Wow, normally I like Skippy, but all this history has made me think about checking out Jif.*

So of course you believe we were always slaves and that we didn't do anything else. This country has heard only one side of the story. And then people don't ever want to go back and fix it. We just stop talking about that part of the story because it makes white people uncomfortable. They think we just go right from slavery to playing basketball.

WE SHALL ENDEAVOR TO UNDERSTAND ONE ANOTHER

HISTORY TODAY

So you can understand why we don't understand each other. There's a long history of "misunderstandings." But because we've had these separate histories, here we are today trying to understand each other without a common language.

History is history, but it's also today.

WHY DIDN'T YOU TELL US YOU WERE UNHAPPY?

A lot of old white people agree with what one weird old reality TV star said about the "good old days." No, not *Trump*—the *Duck Dynasty* dude, Phil Robertson. He reminisced about the old days in an interview with *GQ:*

> I never, with my eyes, saw the mistreatment of any black person. Not once. Where we lived was all farmers. The blacks worked for the farmers. I hoed cotton with them. I'm with the blacks, because we're white trash. We're going across the field. . . . They're singing and happy. I never heard one of them, one black person, say, "I tell you what: These doggone white people"—not a word! . . . Pre-entitlement, pre-welfare, you say: Were they happy? They were godly; they were happy; no one was singing the blues.

Why didn't you tell us you were unhappy? You seemed so happy! Never mind that the difference between Phil Robertson, white trash cotton-picker, and any black person in the South was that nobody was trying to lynch Phil Robertson or beat him or prevent him from voting.

Phil Robertson was born in 1946, but even then there was a big difference between white sharecroppers and black sharecroppers. The difference between white trash and niggas is niggas didn't have employees. You know what I'm saying? You can't be that poor when poorer people are working for *you*.

Why does he think they called their music "the blues"? It's called the blues for a reason. White people didn't have the blues before we came along. And singing don't mean you're happy. One of Billie Holiday's signature songs was "Strange Fruit":

> *Southern trees bear a strange fruit,*
> *Blood on the leaves and blood at the root,*
> *Black body swinging in the Southern breeze,*
> *Strange fruit hanging from the poplar trees.*

Maybe white people like Phil Robertson wouldn't hear that this was a song about lynchings. It's a protest song. Black people working out in the fields as slaves used songs as a way to keep themselves connected as a community and to communicate with one another. Songs like "Follow the Drinking Gourd" and "Go Down Moses" contained coded messages. "Follow the Drinking Gourd" refers to the north star and a route to escape. Songs were very subversive; they weren't always happy. They could teach and provide information that white masters wouldn't detect or understand. Black people sang work songs and spirituals to bond. They sang songs when they revolted too. These songs weren't all songs of joy and happiness. They were "When Israel was in Egypt's land, let my people go." They weren't "Sunday, Monday, happy days."

THE GOOD OLD DAYS

So it's really only white people waxing poetic about "the good old days." Because black people don't really have them. When we talk about "the good old days" it's generally the time before we knew we were black. Or it might be "Oh, the good old days were when my dad and mom were together," but there's not a cultural "good old days" for us.

The only reason there used to be a Black Wall Street before it was burned down was because no one would do business with us and we couldn't live anywhere else. So we don't have "good old days," but we do have "kind of good days."

If a black man could use a time machine, he would go

back to 2008. "The good old days" are that recent. Our time machine wouldn't waste no gas. It wouldn't waste no fuel at all.

Beep-beep—"Oh, we're here already? It seems like just yesterday"—it was. Because the further we go back, *the further we go back.*

Take the 1950s. White people are so nostalgic for the 1950s. Isn't that the Great America that we're all supposed to be Making Again? But it's a Great White America.

IHOP recently had a promotion celebrating the "Panniversary" of its founding in 1958. You could get fifty-eight-cent short stacks of pancakes while enjoying a retro menu. As the restaurant's Facebook page promised: "We don't just have 1950s prices, we've got 1950s lingo too. So cruise on through, daddy-o. It's gonna be the bees' knees. The cats' pajamas. Totally aces."

Cute, right? But don't they realize that in the 1950s, I couldn't eat at their restaurant? Let's get real about the 1950s! If you're going to serve up fifty-eight-cent pancakes, they should also come with a waitress who says, "No coloreds served here." I would rather pay eight dollars for my Rooty Tooty Fresh 'N Fruity and keep the progress. Because a nigga would have to eat in the alley. So, no thanks—I don't want to go back to the '50s. The prices were lower, but so was the tolerance.

LIMITATIONS OF STATUES

So forgive us if we don't want to walk down memory lane with you. History means different things to you and me. Just look at how much time we've spent arguing about statues, especially ones of Confederate war "heroes." White people like to pretend that it's important to keep these statues up, to not "lose history." But a lot of these statues were put up in black neighborhoods during the Jim Crow era. Isn't it strange that they decided just at that moment to start "preserving history"?

The only reason we're able to live freely is because those motherfuckers on the horses lost. So, to you, it's part of your heritage. To me, that's the motherfucker who was so inept, I'm free.

How many statues of Robert E. Lee do you want? Is it worth killing people over? A young woman was murdered in Charlottesville just because people were so worked up about a statue of a Confederate general put up in 1924.

Let's put it this way: if you have to Google who a statue is, you weren't that attached to it. You really still want that statue of the guy who led a charge in 18-whatever where everybody was killed but him in the Battle of Who Cares? Don't pretend it's your favorite statue and that you can't live without it. If I cover your eyes and you can't remember whether it was General Nathaniel Bartholomew Hayes or Corporal Hayworth Bartholomew Nathan, that statue can go.

At least in Philly, they got a statue of Rocky. Everybody knows Rocky. That's a fun statue. That's an Instagrammable statue. I guarantee you more people know Rocky than Nathan Bedford Forrest.

It's pretty safe to say that when you see a bronze statue, you know it's of someone who didn't like black people. I've never seen a bronze statue yet of someone who liked black people. Maybe we shouldn't make statues out of bronze; maybe it's not the people who are racist, it's that alloy.

Let's stop making bronze statues: it's expensive and maybe racist. Why do we gotta keep all these statues forever anyway? Let's make statues out of something easy to get rid of. Statues should be temporary, like your emotions. If you're feeling so excited about someone that you want to put a statue up, you should put it up in something easy to knock down in case you change your mind. You know? It's like a tattoo: you don't get a tattoo for every girl you go out with. You might love somebody one day, but then things change . . .

That's why we propose a time limit on statues. A statue of limitations. I mean a Statute of Statue Limitations. We gotta limit statues, is what I mean.

Let's call it seven years. Seven years per statue, then you have to re-up. That way no one statue gets too comfortable clogging up a park where people don't want it anymore. After seven years, give another statue a chance!

Reparations Article 3a. Statute of Statue Limitations

White people having gotten overly attached to bronze statues of racists, and having erected statues anywhere they could in an effort to remind black people of who was in charge, now agree to end the practice of erecting new bronze statues. Bronze, a possibly racist alloy, will be replaced as a building material by plaster of Paris, Play-Doh, or some other temporary building material. New statues will be limited to a seven-year erection, which is more than you need anyway, in most instances.

And if you want to add more statues, we have to limit new ones and get rid of old ones. We know white people hate quotas, but don't you think that there are too many bronze statues of Confederates? Be reasonable. I'm not advocating for a statue affirmative action policy, but I am advocating for more diversity of statues. We gotta make some room.

Think of all the fun statues we can put up, knowing that we won't have to look at them forever. It's 2020 while I'm writing this, so let's put up a statue of Lil Nas X—what the hell, if that shit doesn't seem right in a few years, we'll just take it down.

BUT WHAT THE HECK, GO AHEAD AND KEEP BLACKFACE

It's weird how much white people like to wear blackface. You all like blackface about as much as you like statues. It feels like every politician who lived through the '70s and '80s dressed up in blackface for their yearbook photo. There are a lot of contenders for "Most Likely to Resign in Disgrace."

The latest example was Ralph Northam, the governor of Virginia, who was about to resign because a picture of him in blackface turned up. At first, he apologized for the picture from his 1984 med school yearbook, but then he said he couldn't be sure that it was really him. Then he changed his mind again. "It was definitely not me," he said at a news conference. "I can tell by looking at it." He was also pretty sure that he wasn't the guy dressed up in the KKK outfit standing next to the dude in blackface.

He could explain: "That same year, I did participate in a dance contest in San Antonio in which I darkened my face as part of a Michael Jackson costume." So he knew that it wasn't him in blackface because he had used shoe polish a different time to look like Michael Jackson. It's weird because in the '80s Michael Jackson was whiter than him. Michael was so white he used to confuse black people: *How does this white woman know how to moonwalk?*

And Northam isn't the only one to have a blackface problem. In the last few years, many different candidates for office around the country have had old blackface pictures turn up. Mississippi governor Tate Reeves and his frat brothers were dressed in blackface and Confederate flags in his 1995 yearbook. Michael Ertel, Florida's secretary of state, resigned because of pictures of him wearing blackface and a "Katrina Victim" T-shirt. And that was from 2005.

Some white people think that photos like this are just youthful mistakes and shouldn't be disqualifying. I mean, haven't we all worn a racist costume now and again in the 1980s? Or in the '90s? Or in 2015?

We won't make you feel bad for all the poor choices you made in the '80s and '90s. That was a long time ago and we all wore some weird shit back then. We'll stop bringing up blackface if you don't bring up our parachute pants and high-top fades.

I think that if you want to dress in blackface, that's fine. If being black appeals to you, go ahead and wear the blackface. But I think the minute you do, your credit score should go down and your blood pressure should go up.

And if white people want to dress in blackface on Halloween, we should have Halloween be on Election Day, so they don't count your vote either.

Reparations Article 3b. Blackface for White Folks

White people, having embraced blackface as a fun dress-up tool, having enjoyed Halloween parties in the 1980s, having engaged in racist skits during fraternity parties of the 1990s, and having celebrated such problematic frivolity by documenting blackface in uncountable yearbook pages, shall henceforth be

held blameless. Their love of Michael Jackson is hereby
affirmed, and their right to wear blackface is retained.
This privilege is restricted, however, to Election Day,
bank loan interviews, and any other occasion where
historical discrimination against people of color has been
exhibited.

BBQ BECKYS

You don't have to wear blackface or a hood to be part of
white supremacy's legacy. That's a thing white people don't
always understand—they think, just like Trump, that they
"don't have a racist bone in their bodies." So why are they
always calling the cops on black people for selling water, or
having a barbecue?

These days we're living with each other with greater fre-
quency. White people are living near black people where
there didn't used to be any white people. Because of gentrification, all of a sudden you have this clash of cultures.

I'll admit: Black people have always done things a little
outside the lines. Like opening up a fire hydrant, or climb-
ing up on a pole to steal cable. You know, little things. And
for a white person, new to the neighborhood, they're not

used to seeing these things, and it's an affront to their sense of justice.

Take BBQ Becky herself: She called the cops on people barbecuing in Oakland at Lake Merritt. People are always barbecuing there, and her outsized beef with a group of black people trying to enjoy their day has everything to do with both gentrification and white people's feeling that they can police black people.

First, she came up and harassed them about being in "her park," then she told them they couldn't have a *charcoal* grill there. Apparently, the grill was in one of several barbecue areas, but this one was for *non-charcoal* grills. Even so, I mean, what the hell? It's in a barbecue area, people are always grilling there. Yeah, it might technically be illegal, but I'm not feeling ready to go up here and arrest all these niggas because they're barbecuing—you'd have to round people up every weekend.

White people are always policing black people. That's why I liked that movie *Bird Box*. In *Bird Box,* there's this force, and if you actually see it, it shows you your greatest fears and sorrows and makes you kill yourself. It's the first thing that I've ever seen that can make white people mind their business. Finally, something to stop you from looking out the window at us. *What is this nigger doing?* I'd welcome that *Bird Box* force into our neighborhoods. And it wouldn't affect black people because we never see anything anyway. *What happened? I didn't see nothing.*

There's so many white ladies calling the cops on black folks, we're running out of names: we got BBQ Becky, Permit Patty, Cornerstore Caroline, Pool Patrol Paula, and a whole lot of others—all trying to regulate black people and using the police to do so. Even if some of the people calling the police aren't racist-bone-having racists, they're not thinking through how police encounters can go bad. Eric Garner got choked out for selling loose cigarettes, not for robbing a bank.

Misunderstandings can happen, of course. Everyone gets things wrong. My housekeeper's been with us for twenty-five years. She came right from Guatemala. We love her, so my wife made her a big meal for Cinco de Mayo and she's like, "I'm Guatemalan." So?

Cinco de Mayo is just for Mexicans, turns out. I guess now we have to cook another big dinner for Día de la Asunción, which is fucked up because cooking is my housekeeper's job.

So how do we get to understanding each other better? I think we probably need better writers. Because when

I look at the LGBTQ community, shows like *Ellen* and *Will & Grace* really changed people's opinions about gay people. Suddenly gay people felt familiar, not threatening. Straight people got to know gay characters whom they liked and could laugh at. Maybe we can talk to the people who write for *Queer Eye*. Because none of them got hanged or assassinated, not even that one guy, Antoni, who doesn't even know how to cook. *Queer Eye for the Black Guy? Black Eye for the White Guy?* Not sure that works, but I'd like to see the way a bunch of black guys fixed up some dude's apartment.

Reparations Article 3c. Black Eyes for the White Guy

It is thus decided, Hollywood's top writers and producers must be brought together in pursuit of a relatable black comedy or makeover show for the masses. We need some of that creativity put in service of making people like us more. We want some shit on Netflix, on NBC, heck, even something that can run on CBS to catch some old white people after *NCIS*.

JUST DON'T CALL ME THE N-WORD WHILE I'M EATING

Still, some white people *do* need to scale back the overt racist shit.

Like, I never understood how Papa John could be racist, because it's black people who keep him in business. He gets on a conference call and says "nigger." And then tries to defend himself? All these fast-food places depend on black people. If you serve shitty food at low prices, niggas buy it. How are you racist to *me*? White people do not eat Papa John's.

And Buffalo Wild Wings had an incident recently where a bunch of black people were told to move because this racist dude didn't want to sit next to niggers, which is ridiculous. Because anytime you have wings, it's like the fucking Field of Dreams: *If you build it, they will come.* You thought you could be at a restaurant with wings and black people wouldn't show up? It's a self-fulfilling prophecy. How the fuck are you gonna get hoity-toity at Wild Wings, motherfucker?

So just don't call me a nigger while I'm eating, all right?

I'm not calling for a boycott; I'm not saying we're going to stop eating your shit. I'm saying we are going to keep eating it, a lot. Just . . . be respectful. Just don't be racist to me while I'm eating. Because, trust me, if I keep like this, I won't be at your restaurant long anyhow. If I'm gonna lose my arm and my eye to diabetes so that you can get rich, at least be nice to my face.

> ## Reparations Article 3d. Don't Call Me the N-Word While I'm Eating
>
> Racism has no place in America, and certainly not in a Buffalo Wild Wings or a Papa John's. Herewith, black people shall eat in peace, without having to deal with slurs and antagonism. Polite dinner conversation only, please.

Plus, you don't want to get rid of us. Because white people never believe in racism unless it's them getting denied a position or a school admission. They don't believe in racism until they're in the unusual position of being on the flip side of the coin. But you need us: you need us to have somebody to blame shit on.

If you live in these really homogenous enclaves with no black people, who can you blame for your problems? If you have a high drug problem, but it's all broke white people, who you gonna blame? If your average-ass kids can't get into an elite school, don't look at me. You need us!

FROM MY COLD, DEAD HANDS

Black people love Buffalo Wild Wings. White people love shootin' things.

Owning a gun is really a "white thing." There's a reason you only see white guys standing around at rallies with assault rifles. Guns are linked to white identity now, not black identity. The Second Amendment doesn't really apply to us.

I live in California, which has the strictest gun laws in the country. It didn't used to be so strict, but in 1967, thirty Black Panthers occupied the California statehouse with shotguns, .357 Magnums, and pistols.

See, "gun rights" are just another thing that white people copied off of black people. It was the Black Panthers who first advocated for gun rights; not so they could go around shooting people, but to protect themselves from a racist government and police force. Bobby Seale, one of the leaders of the Panthers, read a statement that day at the state capitol:

The Black Panther party for self-defense calls upon the American people in general and the black people in particular to take careful note of the racist California Legislature which is considering legislation aimed at keeping the black people disarmed and powerless at the very same time that racist police agencies throughout the country are intensifying the terror, brutality, murder and repression of black people.

After that, Ronald Reagan and the NRA did something they had never done before. They went, "You know what? Did we say Second Amendment? Well, how about a second thought—niggers with guns in the statehouse? I don't think that's what the Founders had in mind." So they passed the Mulford Act, repealing open carry in California.

That's why now a white guy walking into a Walmart with an assault rifle is a "patriot," but a black guy walking into Walmart with an assault rifle is a "target."

Maybe you can't fix everyone's heart, but you can probably make it harder for him to get an AR-15. Unfortunately, white people won't let that happen. They need *protection*. But you know who the most likely person to get killed by a mass shooter is? Another white guy. So for every Dylann Roof who plans out a specifically racially motivated attack, there's another white guy popping off indiscriminately. All those people who got shot in Vegas: Who were they? A bunch of country music fans. The only black people at a country music festival were cleaning up the grounds.

But still, white folks want to hold on to their assault rifles. They won't change the gun laws even though their "independence" and "freedom" are getting them killed. And every time there's a shooting, it's treated like an aberration. Everything is blamed but guns. I saw somebody blame mass shootings on *Call of Duty*. Blaming mass shootings on *Call of Duty* is like blaming our obesity problem on *Pac-Man*.

If you're collecting ammunition and guns, you're not a good guy. You're a bad guy waiting to happen. You're waiting for the end of the world, for a race war, or for the black helicopters to come take your land. Most people don't stockpile weapons in anticipation that Jesus is coming back. You don't need guns for the Rapture. If you're being raptured, guns aren't going to help you where you're going.

And for the privilege of owning these guns, white people are dying. Not from mass shootings and not from gang violence. President Trump and the Right like to make a big deal about how dangerous the inner cities are. Like how in July 2019 Trump tweeted about Representative Elijah Cummings's district in Baltimore, calling it a "very dangerous & filthy place."

But the majority of gun deaths in America are white men committing suicide. Approximately twenty-five thousand Americans kill themselves with guns each year. So it's this "protection" that's killing white people. When it comes to guns, you all should be a bit more like us black folk.

LET'S BE APPROPRIATE

It's weird when I see a black woman with a blond wig and blue contacts complain about cultural appropriation. That's a little strange. It's a complicated topic. But we can't talk about cultural appropriation and then invite somebody over for spaghetti.

I think anytime you have cultural intermingling, there are gonna be natural kinds of exchanges. Like some of the stuff we eat, we got from you. I know a lot of black folks think we invented everything, but it's not *totally* true. We all sing each other's songs, shit like that.

So I think that we're gonna have to let you off the hook for "cultural appropriation." Because I don't think all of us wanna go back to looking like we did in the '70s. We've all been stealing from each other long enough that I think it'll be too hard to sort it all out. If we're gonna fuck with white musicians who sound like niggas, then we're also gonna have to tell Mom to stop making her "great macaroni and cheese."

So if you all just accept Lil Nas X, I won't have to give up Hall and Oates, you know? We'll call this a draw. In return, we'll stop complaining when a Kardashian puts braids in her hair. Deal?

> ### *Reparations Article 3e. We Keep Mac and Cheese and Hall and Oates*
>
> Lest the foodstuffs and music much adored by all peoples become the subject of continuous wrangling and conflict, we heresoforwith declare cultural appropriation to be approved for use by all peoples. Just don't be a big jerk about it.

WHITE PEOPLE CAN'T JUST SAY SHIT

That doesn't mean that white people can just say shit.

Maybe, if we're lucky, Trump will have been imprisoned by the time this book comes out. But in the lead-up to an impeachment inquiry, Trump tweeted out:

So some day, if a Democrat becomes President and the Republicans win the House, even by a tiny margin, they can impeach the President, without due process or fairness or any legal rights. All Republicans must remember what they are witnessing here—a lynching. But we will WIN!

A *lynching.* No one should expect Trump to be careful with his words, but he's symptomatic of how white people act like they're the victims. You gotta stop comparing yourself to black people when it's convenient for you. Trump: You ain't black. You orange.

Impeachment is a political remedy that the Founding Fathers put there for a reason. It's like an emergency exit that's available if we need it. They wanted to make sure that if there were high crimes and misdemeanors, we weren't permanently stuck with a president. They were concerned about people using the levers of government to enrich themselves or to oppress somebody and get away with all kinds of malfeasance. An impeachment is carried out by men and women in suits and it's very official. A lynching is where mobs come and string you up.

Four thousand seven hundred people were lynched between 1882 and 1968. Only three presidents have been impeached. And none of them has actually ever been convicted by the Senate and removed from office. So there's a difference in kind and scale. It's actually nothing like lynching.

So you gotta stop comparing yourself to black people when it's convenient for you. You can't quote Martin Luther King Jr. when you've just said the most racist shit ever.

So you're banned. You lose the ability to play the black card when you think it works for you.

HELP YOURSELF

I don't want you to do any of this stuff just because it's right or because you feel bad. Don't do it to help us. When black people get anything, it invariably benefits white people more. Help yourself!

Take affirmative action. Tucker Carlson equated it to Jim Crow:

> The other factor that colleges don't like to talk about is affirmative action. The Supreme Court banned the use of racial quotas in admissions some years ago, but in real life, that decision meant nothing. Skin color remains a central consideration at every level of the process. The average admissions office is every bit as

race conscious as any institution in the Jim Crow South, and far less transparent about it.

—Tucker Carlson Tonight, *April 18, 2018*

Perfect example. Affirmative action helped white women more than it helped us. More women became part of the workplace due to affirmative action than black people. It increased their access to contracts and jobs that were closed to them before. And that's still true. Affirmative action primarily benefits white women, so don't get rid of it! Help yourself!

Or welfare. When Trump met with members of the Congressional Black Caucus, after he made sure everyone had met Ben Carson, he was taken to task by a congresswoman about proposed welfare cuts. She told him that the cuts would harm her constituents, "not all of whom are black." Trump replied: "Really? Then what are they?"

That's typical of Republicans who hate welfare, food stamp programs, and benefits for poor people. With nearly every budget proposal, they attack these programs. But when they do things thinking that they're embarrassing us or taking us down a notch, it hurts white people. In 2018, the Trump administration sought a 20 percent reduction to spending on SNAP. When they do that shit, it hurts

Walmart more than black people. In 2017, $33 billion of SNAP benefits were spent at big-box stores like Walmart and Target.

So don't be so quick to cut shit. You better keep welfare, not because you like us, but because you want to help yourself!

Any "handout" invariably helps you more. Whatever you give us, you get to steal anyway. Who knows, maybe you all will get some reparations too . . .

WHITE PEOPLE DON'T LIKE TO FEEL BAD

The fact of the matter is that white people are always uncomfortable talking about race. They don't want to talk about race—they like *not* talking about it. Because in the end, white people don't want to feel bad.

An extreme example of this is the review left by a couple who felt upset during their tour of Whitney Plantation, which explicitly bills itself as "the only plantation museum in Louisiana with an exclusive focus on the lives of enslaved people." Leaving a two-star review, the couple complained that the tour guide made them feel bad:

> My husband and I were extremely disappointed in this tour. We didn't come to hear a lecture on how

the white people treated slaves, we came to get this history of a southern plantation and get a tour of the house and grounds. The tour guide was so radical about slave treatment we felt we were being lectured and bashed about the slavery. My ancestors were from Sicily, never owned slaves, and my husbands were German, and none of his ever owned slaves. I am by far not racist or against all Americans having equal rights but this was my vacation and now we are crossing all plantation tours off our list, it was just not what we expected. I'll go back to Louisiana and see some real plantations that are so much more enjoyable to tour.

You don't even want to feel bad about slavery on a tour of enslaved people's quarters? You felt "lectured and bashed about the slavery" on your vacation? Maybe you need to reflect a bit on your expectations. History is allowed to make you uncomfortable. I just have one suggestion for this couple: Cancel your honeymoon trip to Auschwitz. Florida can be nice.

Also, as we've seen before: Are you *sure* that none of your ancestors owned slaves? Believe it or not, some of the people who owned slaves were from Italy, some from Germany.

People always act like it could never have been possible. *My ancestors never owned slaves.* Well, somebody's ancestors did! Who were these owners if they weren't Germans and Italians and Irish? Who were they? "Oh, I'm from Scandinavia." You can't all be from Scandinavia.

White people don't know our history, and they willfully ignore it. Steve King, a Republican congressman from Iowa, said that black people never contributed anything to society or civilization: "I would ask you to go back through history and figure out where are these contributions that have been made by these other categories of people you are talking about [nonwhite people]. Where did any other subgroup of people contribute more to civilization?" You know, not math or plumbing or astronomy or science or agriculture. None of that. I guess that all started from Iowa, just outside of Jerusalem.

But it's easy to feel that way about people when you're so ill-informed about who they are and where they came from. Because, in truth, America's point of reference for black people is slavery. To white people, our story started with enslavement, with us being here in chains. So that's the thing: The African American story starts in the middle. Never at the beginning.

Here's our offer: We'll pretend like we don't know the

things we know. We agree to participate in this selective amnesia with you. And because history and Google are incompatible, we hereby move to Bing for all web searches.

Reparations Article 3f. Bing Only

In consideration of Google's accurate search results, which serve only to dredge up true, horrible, unpleasant facts that make white people feel bad, all black people are hereby sentenced to use Bing only for searches, so that the information is less true, less accurate, and less painful.

YOU PRETEND TO LIKE BLACK PEOPLE

You pretend to like black people, but you don't treat us with respect or kindness. It just feels like when white people talk about black people, it's never about love. It's always about *tough love*. Never *love* love. Why is that?

It always comes from a place of discipline and bringing the hammer down. It's never about understanding or empathy. It's always about correcting defects, always about bringing black people to heel.

WE GET TO BE AVERAGE

We're always judged by the exception, not the rule. Everybody always goes, "Why can't you be like Michael Jordan?" But there are fourteen other people on that team. And guess what? None of them are Michael Jordan either.

Or: "Why can't you be like Barack Obama? He did it. He was raised by a single mother and he went to school, got educated, and became president. Why can't you do it?"

Do you know how much good karma and kismet you need to get through the maze? With the obstacles of discrimination and history, you have to celebrate the success stories but not pretend they're the norm or act like nobody else has to be exceptional to succeed. We're always held up to the exception, as opposed to the rule.

The rule is that you should be able to make a living just being mediocre. It should be okay to be average. Look at all the average white men who made it. Take Donald Trump: Donald Trump is very average.

Even with every advantage, think of how many average white folks there are like Donald Trump. They had better schools, more resources, more money, and the ultimate luxury: being allowed to be average and have it work out. That's all we want: to be able to be average, to make a decent living and live a safe, average life. As it is, we have to be exceptional and you get to be average. But if we fail, if we have a hard time because the obstacles were too great, you blame *us* and say, "Well, we tried."

Reparations Article 3g. We Get to Be Average

Until such a time as the number of average black folks equals the number of average white folks in positions of power, acclaim, and wealth, black people shall herewith be allowed to be "normal," "average," and "unremarkable" without being deemed deficient. Until such a time as the amount of "remarkable" white people in charge of things, held up for praise, or otherwise regarded as successful increases, black people shall enjoy the same respect for being average as their white peers, suffering no penalty.

And anyway, society doesn't like strong black people. They didn't like Martin Luther King Jr. till he was dead, right? They didn't like Muhammad Ali till he was holding the Olympic torch. Remember? He was shaking so bad, people went and blew their pilot lights out. Like, "This motherfucker ain't blowing my house up."

WE GET TO PICK THE BLACK PEOPLE

That's not to say you don't like *any* black folk. You do. You just don't like the ones we like. So for the purposes of this treaty and just to be clear: we get to pick the black people. Y'all have forfeited the right to pick. Because we know how you like to play it: you like to pick weak and unremarkable black people. If we let white people pick black people, we know what we'll get.

Whenever Republicans need a black person, they always pick someone unremarkable. Name me one black man they'll ever pick who will have a street or a library named after him. We can go down the list. Need a black guy for the Supreme Court? Don't worry, you've got Clarence Thomas—totally unremarkable. You already fill thirteen of your sixteen cabinet slots with white guys, so you need a black guy to run Housing and Urban Development? After all, it says "urban" right in the title. Why not take former brain surgeon Ben Carson? Trump even tried to put Herman Cain, a pizza chain mogul, into the Federal Reserve.

Ben Carson, Clarence Thomas, and Herman Cain are

remarkable only in how much they are unremarkable. And you never see them at the same time. That's weird, right?

Sometimes I think I'm being unfair to Ben Carson. I mean, supposedly he's a bright guy. Sure, it's weird to have a neurosurgeon without any housing policy experience run a huge housing agency like HUD. That's crazy. But maybe if you're bright it doesn't matter; a bright guy could look at the problems of HUD and say, "This is fair, this is not fair." Maybe chopping into brains is just like chopping into budgets, I don't know.

Isn't that the Republican argument all the time? Those analytic skills should translate to something new. That's why Trump's supposed to be good at being president— because he's a genius businessman. Or Rex Tillerson should be a good secretary of state because he ran Exxon. Success at one thing should be able to be applied to something else. Indeed, it's *more* valuable than expertise in a given field.

But tell me, if Ben Carson's so bright, how come he went before Maxine Waters's Financial Services Committee and didn't know what "REO" stood for? Now, granted, I didn't know that it stood for "real-estate owned," but I'm not HUD secretary. This is his job!

Representative Katie Porter asked him, "Do you know what an REO is?"

"An Oreo?" Carson replied. An *Oreo*? He thought he was being insulted. He thought she was calling him an Oreo. I bet he's heard that before. And then instead of admitting he didn't know what he was talking about, he got mad and acted arrogant. If a black man talked back to the cops the way he talked to the committee, Republicans would not cheer. They would advocate for him being shot or tased.

So what is that about? That's about desire. He doesn't care about HUD; he doesn't care about learning his job. Either he's not as bright as they say he is or he's a lazy brilliant person. If you are intelligent, it should travel. Some of that intelligence should have followed you. Maybe he's a brain surgeon like Donald Trump is a business tycoon.

And why doesn't Clarence Thomas ever say anything? Clarence Thomas decided to shut up to show people: he didn't want to sound stupid, so he stopped talking. "It's better to be silent and thought a fool, than to speak and remove all doubt."

Donald Trump and the Republicans of this ilk like black people the same way they like their dogs: obedient. *Slap me five and don't shit on the carpet.*

All this is to say: we get to pick the black people.

But since you guys love him so much, you can have Kanye. We're tired of him.

> ### *Reparations Article 3h. Take Kanye*
>
> Kanye is yours. He's an honorary white guy now. Since he likes to hang out with Trump so much and spout a bunch of crazy nonsense all the time, we trade him to you.

Since we're picking our own black folks, let's make some trades to keep it simple. We'll give you some black people and you can give us some white people.

Unfortunately, there's probably only three white people we like. One is Gary Owen. Come on over, Gary. Two is that dude who plays Tommy on *Power*. Three is . . . Michael something. He's a white scholar, and niggas quote him all the time. You know the guy . . . Look, I'll send out a final list later. Oh, and Teena Marie too. Like how the Mormons can baptize dead people, we'll convert her to black posthumously. She's dope.

And in return, you can have Kanye, you can have Candace Owens. You can have Ben Carson and Herman Cain too. You can have Diamond and Silk, you can have Stacey Dash, you can have any of them shoe-bootie creatures.

And this isn't just about trading famous white people for famous black people. We want to help poor white people too. Mortality rates for virtually every group have been dropping over time for the last hundred years. But for poor, uneducated whites, the mortality rate is going up. You can't attribute this to war or famine; the increase is because whiteness ain't enough.

Poor white people are under the illusion that they're like the rich white people they see on TV, but they're not. With no jobs, no support system, they can't deal with the fact that they aren't getting what they were promised from the American Dream. They're supposed to be in charge, respected and revered. Instead, they're ignored and forgotten. That strain, that disconnect, is making them do drugs, commit suicide, and drink themselves to death. The Blue Book value on "white" just ain't what it was.

But we can't have that. After all, this state of affairs gave us Trump. So we will take your poor white people and teach them how to adjust. We'll make them niggas for free. Since we have so much in common, we'll grandfather all you poor white people in and make you honorary black people. So come on—no more killing yourself! We'll teach you how to manage disappointment, poverty, and living with the stress of having rich white people look down on you. I promise that we can turn things around for you. You too can be black!

Reparations Article 31. White Black People

On the condition that you live like a black person but are in all other respects white, if you're forgotten, ignored, disrespected, economically disadvantaged, picked on, and stressed, you are henceforth, for all intents and purposes, a black person.

We get to decide who's black, but also some of these people have tried to jump ship before their time. You know? While we're trading, we can't have some people pretending they're white *already*. I get it, it's inconvenient to be black. But damn—if everyone tries to become white, what the fuck am I negotiating this treaty for? Know what I mean? If everyone is white, including black people, who's gonna sign this thing? I guess that if you could be transracial just like being transgender, then all black people should become white people and then we won't have this problem anymore. Until then, we gotta keep shit sorted.

So there's a few people who *think* they're white or *pretend* they're white, but who are, and shall remain, black:

Like Mike Tirico, the sportscaster. He's such a nigga, it's ridiculous. "Why do I have to check any box?" he said in an interview with the *New York Times*. "If we live in a world where we're not supposed to judge, why should anyone care about identifying?" Okay, you don't have to check the box, I'm checking it for you. Nigga, you be so sub-Saharan. You gotta stay with us.

Reparations Article 3j. If You're Black, You're Black, Unless You're Not

Excluding those already denoted by name (Kanye et al.), if you are black, you are black. No trading in your blackness until we've sorted this whole thing out.

And don't make us revoke your black status. Houston Rockets general manager Daryl Morey tweeted out, "Fight for freedom. Stand with Hong Kong," and the NBA was like, "Hey, man, it's the largest emerging market in the world. We wanna sell our product. Shut up about that freedom shit."

You can't expect the NBA to do the right thing because they're all about making money. But then you heard black people say the same thing. James Harden of the Rockets said, "We apologize. You know, we love China. We love playing there." And then LeBron tweeted: "My team and this league just went through a difficult week. I think people need to understand what a tweet or statement can do to others. And I believe nobody stopped and considered what would happen. Could have waited a week to send it." Right on, LeBron—making money is more important than freedom for the people of Hong Kong?

I mean, I can't imagine black people ever not saying yes to freedom. That's the weirdest shit ever. They can't say yes to freedom because they wanna sell shoes? We wanted freedom and got it. LeBron has been able to build incredible wealth. Then we don't want to talk about freedom for other people because that fucks up the bottom line? That almost makes us white guys.

I mean, freedom to niggas is like catnip. It's our thing! When "freedom" comes up, we gotta chime in. We gotta lead the conversation.

VERY BAD PEOPLE ON BOTH SIDES

We know how you all want us to "cancel" black people when they do something bad, but you keep making excuses for people you revere. People say, "Can we just draw the line at rapists and murderers?" For us, history is rife with horrible men, and then we've learned that we have to sing praises to those horrible men, and we see them on our money and their names on our schools, on our bridges.

So "horrible man" is not a disqualifier. Our lives are imbued with them. When they ask us about Michael Jackson ("How can you sing those songs?") and R. Kelly—it's complicated. I will get rid of Michael Jackson when you get rid of Andrew Jackson. At least you can dance to "Beat It."

But our stories are so full of irredeemably horrible people that it's something that we can compartmentalize. Literally, if Bill Cosby was a priest, he wouldn't be in prison.

TAKE COLUMBUS DAY OFF

But before we get rid of history, let's stop celebrating holidays we know are bullshit. How can you defend Columbus Day? It's like those stupid statues: nobody ever wants to admit that a holiday has outstayed its welcome. It's like we moved, but we already bought the stationery. But come on.

Who really believes nowadays that Christopher Columbus discovered America? No one celebrates it really. One time I had to get to my radio show on a Monday and traffic was so light, it was like the apocalypse. I was like, "Why?" But then it turned out that it was Columbus Day. So thanks to this murdering rapist, I got to work on time.

Think I'm exaggerating or that Columbus wasn't all that bad? I mean, after all, "In 1492 / Columbus sailed the ocean blue" is a pretty cute little rhyme. And what about the *Nina,* the *Pinta,* and the *Santa Maria*? Why the hell was I taught all those ship names if Columbus was really a genocidal maniac?

Historians have firsthand accounts of some of Columbus's worst acts. He forced natives into slavery, to find gold for him. Those who didn't had their hands cut off. He enslaved more than 1,500 people and rewarded his men by allowing them to rape the native women and girls. Columbus himself wrote to a friend, "There are plenty of dealers who go about looking for girls; those from nine to ten are now in demand, and for all ages a good price must be paid." It's estimated that in 1493 there were eight million indigenous people in the Caribbean islands. By the time Columbus left in 1504, there were only about one hundred thousand. Not a good dude.

So we've got Martin Luther King Jr. Day and Columbus Day, and everybody else has to share, huh? So how the hell did it get to be a holiday? Well, weirdly, it has to do with those Italians again! You know, the other black folk who graduated into white folk. As I told you before, Italians were an unpopular bunch of people, especially as their numbers grew in America between 1880 and 1914. Remember how those Italian immigrants got lynched in New Orleans in 1891? Well, a year later, in 1892, President Benjamin Harrison made a proclamation honoring the four hundredth anniversary of Columbus's voyage, in a bid to link Columbus to the great progress America had made since then. This was all part of the plan to smooth things over with the Italian government and signal that Italians *mattered,* and that lynching was wrong (at least for Italians). Italians at the time were thought of as almost black, described in the press as "swarthy" and "kinky-haired" and sometimes as "white niggers." But Italians, seeking to be viewed as Americans in good standing—you know, white people—glommed on to Columbus as a famous Italian to be celebrated. And finally, the Knights of Columbus, a Catholic fraternal organization, pushed President Franklin Delano Roosevelt into declaring Columbus Day a holiday in 1934.

So Columbus started the slave trade and helped a bunch

of Italians stop being niggas. *In 1492 / Columbus sailed the ocean blue / But now in 2019 / Columbus Day is real obscene.* Getting to work on time and buying a mattress—that's all Columbus is good for now. I feel like Columbus's ship has sailed.

And it's weird that all the woke black people who pooh-pooh Columbus Day turn around and then six weeks later celebrate Thanksgiving. That's a little weird. I guess Indians with turkey and cranberries are different.

Now come on, D.L.! Don't fuck with Thanksgiving. We gotta keep this one—I like the football and sometimes even eating with my family.

All right, all right. But the only reason Squanto (his real name was Tisquantum) was around to help the Pilgrims is because he had been kidnapped, shipped off to Europe, and sold into slavery before they had arrived. He knew English because he had lived in London. When he finally got back to his village, everyone had been wiped out by an epidemic that white people had brought over. So enjoy your candied yams, but don't forget that poor Squanto helped a lot of lost white people survive the winter, even though he'd been a slave. We gotta make sure white people get where they're going!

Reparations Article 3k. Personal Days

All holidays must herewith be evaluated as a whole; i.e., all holidays will be put on a probationary period to ascertain their relevance and value to all Americans. Acknowledging that days off are nice and that mattress sales must occur, a number of holidays shall be continued, but no current holiday will by reason of tradition be kept without scrutiny. MLK Day excluded, because you already tried to take that shit away.

THE GREATEST AMERICANS

The people you admire, the most popular, the most note-worthy people of the last two hundred years: we know these motherfuckers have said and done some horrible stuff. I'm telling you: if we take a look at the greatest Americans of all time, you'd see that they did some great shit and some racist shit. That's why we've had to make allowances; we can't throw out everyone in America, be-cause even the "great" Americans have said horrible things about us.

We Googled it up (I can't use Bing for this, come on), and sure enough there was a four-part TV special in 2005 called *The Greatest American,* where millions of people voted for who they thought deserved the title of "Greatest American." Hosted by Matt Lauer, apparently when he wasn't busy harassing women.

So here's the top twenty-five, back in 2005:

25. Neil Armstrong

24. Henry Ford

23. The Wright Brothers

22. Rosa Parks

21. Muhammad Ali

20. Lance Armstrong

19. Eleanor Roosevelt

18. Bill Gates

17. Bob Hope

16. JFK

15. Thomas Edison

14. Albert Einstein

13. Walt Disney

12. Thomas Jefferson

11. Billy Graham

10. FDR

9. Oprah

8. Elvis Presley

7. Bill Clinton
6. George W. Bush
5. Benjamin Franklin
4. George Washington
3. MLK
2. Abraham Lincoln
1. Ronald Reagan

Let's set aside the black folks from the list and also Albert Einstein, because he was born in Germany. Oh, yeah, let's also pull Lance Armstrong, because come on now—the list was made in 2005. But even the fact that he was included is instructive, right? People—probably a lot of white people—voted for *Lance Armstrong* to be in the top twenty-five Greatest Americans over people like Maya Angelou or Frederick Douglass.

So I guarantee you that most of these people said some racist shit. I won't do all of them because by the time we finish the list, Matt Lauer will be accused of raping somebody else, but here are a few examples.

HENRY FORD

He once said: "Don't find fault, find a remedy; anybody can complain."

He also said: "The Jew is a race that has no civilization to point to, no aspiring religion, no great achievement in any form."

FDR

He once said: "The only thing we have to fear is fear itself."

He also interned Japanese Americans and put Hugo Black, a former KKK member, on the Supreme Court.

JFK

He once said: "Ask not what your country can do for you, but what you can do for your country."

He also dropped Sammy Davis Jr. from his inauguration guest list after Davis married a Swedish actress in 1960 because he wanted to keep Southern racists supporting his agenda.

WALT DISNEY

He created Mickey Mouse and Goofy.

He also created *Song of the South* and a racist crow in *Dumbo* literally named "Jim Crow."

THOMAS JEFFERSON

He wrote: "We hold these truths to be self-evident, that all men are created equal, that they are endowed by their Creator with certain unalienable Rights, that among these are Life, Liberty and the pursuit of Happiness."

He also owned more than six hundred slaves, was a rapist, and wrote, "Blacks are in reason much inferior . . . and in imagination they are dull, tasteless, and anomalous . . . never yet could I find that a black had uttered a thought above the level of plain narration."

BILLY GRAHAM

He said: "God has given us two hands, one to receive with and the other to give with."

He also said: "The only hope for enduring peace is Jesus Christ," and "Only when Christ comes again will the little white children of Alabama walk hand in hand with little black children."

ABRAHAM LINCOLN

He said: "Four score and seven years ago our fathers brought forth on this continent a new nation, conceived in liberty, and dedicated to the proposition that all men are created equal." And he freed the slaves.

But he also said: "I will say then that I am not, nor ever have been, in favor of bringing about in any way the social and political equality of the white and black races. . . . And inasmuch as they cannot so live, while they do remain together there must be the position of superior and inferior, and I as much as any other man am in favor of having the superior position assigned to the white race."

RONALD REAGAN

He said: "Mr. Gorbachev, tear down this wall!"

And he also said to Nixon, in talking about UN delegates: "To see those, those monkeys from those African countries—damn them, they're still uncomfortable wearing shoes!"

So even your heroes—the heroes you hold in high esteem—have been instrumental in keeping us where we are. Isn't it funny that the people who the country loves hate us?

BIG LOVE / BIG HATE

And who hates us more than Trump? The president you all chose set out to undo everything Barack Obama did.

Obama cared more about America than he cared about himself. He's the one who put "America First." He epitomized what a president should be. He read the manual and went, "Imma be that." And he did it to the *n*th degree. You didn't catch him cussing or involved in sex scandals. He was pristine. I mean, obviously he had the kind of small problems that everybody else has; it's a big job. He made a ton of mistakes. But what you can't ever question is that he was very earnest. And he took the weight and the pomp and circumstance seriously—those traditions meant something to him, and the idea of being president meant something to him. He ain't trying to have his personal merchandise in the gift shop and shit. He don't have his own cigarette line. You know what I mean?

That's shit he wasn't gonna do. And that extends up to talking about the current sitting president. He hasn't gone on the talk shows, talking trash about Trump. It'd be so easy for him to do that, especially because Trump has tried to unwind all of Obama's policies. It's long-standing precedent to not bad-mouth your successor and so that's what Obama is going to do, because precedent and high standards are more important to him than scoring political points. He's what a president is supposed to be and now he's what an ex-president is supposed to be.

Obama was the kind of president you always said you wanted. He was the kind of black man you always said you respected, yet you do everything to disrespect him. So how can we take you seriously when you tell us how to be? I find it totally disingenuous: Everything he was was what you told us we had to be. And yet you opposed him at every opportunity and then elected his opposite.

Obama believed in America more than America ever believed in itself, because it had never been challenged. Before Obama, all the presidents looked a certain way. I mean, they might've checked a different box politically, but they all pretty much had the same background: Skull and Bones secret society, blue blood, you know? They were all the same. But he was so different, and he expanded what this country could be.

The first time I can remember black people calling

ourselves "American" was when Barack Obama was in office. Because otherwise, hearing us talk, it sounded like we were describing a place we were visiting. We've always been American, but Obama made us feel like Americans for the first time. He proved that we belong here.

MOST RACIST PRESIDENT

So how can you elect Trump after that? How can you say he's anything but a rejection of everything that Obama represented? Obama made us feel like we belong; Trump makes sure we don't.

According to Pulitzer Prize–winning presidential historian Jon Meacham, Trump ties Andrew Johnson as "the most racist president in American history." And look: that's hard to do. As Meacham describes, Johnson believed "that African-Americans were incapable of self-government and relapsed into barbarism if they weren't closely supervised." So that's pretty stiff competition. The conversation around reparations was stopped under Johnson, but maybe Trump is our opportunity to get it right. When those ministers spoke to God and consulted and came up with "forty acres and a mule," it took a racist president to stop that conversation. Maybe it's like a cycle, now that we have the second-most-racist president.

Now, not everyone agrees that Trump is racist. One of Trump's supporters is New Hampshire state representative Werner Horn. He refused to call slavery racist, claiming that "human beings have been owning other human beings since the dawn of time. It's never been about race." In an interview with *HuffPost,* he clarified that "it's never okay to own another person. But to label the institution as racist is a false narrative." Horn said slave masters weren't considering race but were making "an economic decision" based on who was available. Auction inventory lists simply didn't have "white names," or "Native American" or "Hispanic" names.

Interesting. It's like going to the store and seeing they only have Crest toothpaste. You would have enslaved Aim, but they were out of it. I wonder how so many black people became "available"? And why is it that they only have black people for sale?

If you don't want to call *slavery* racist, then you really don't want to call *anything* racist. I really think that some people only believe you're racist if you say "nigger." But the most racist N-word I've ever heard is "no." No, you can't vote. No, you can't own a home here. No, you can't go to this school.

It shouldn't be too hard to believe that Trump is racist, because he grew up in a racist household. His dad, Fred

Trump, had a long history of racial discrimination in housing. As one of New York City's biggest developers, he was sued for refusing to rent to blacks. In 1967, a state investigation found that of 3,700 apartments in Trump Village, one of Fred Trump's developments, only seven were occupied by blacks. One superintendent testified that he was told to attach a piece of paper with a big letter *C* on it (for "colored") to applications from blacks.

Recently, an article in the *New York Times* from June 1927 was uncovered describing Fred Trump's arrest at a Klan rally in Queens, New York. One thousand Klan members marched in a parade through Jamaica, Queens. After a riot with police, Fred and six other people were arrested. That's not necessarily proof that he was in the Klan; he might have just been an innocent bystander or Klan parade enthusiast.

Of course, President Trump denied that this ever happened: "He was never arrested. He has nothing to do with this. This never happened. This is nonsense and it never happened." Clearly the *New York Times* was already part of the Fake News Conspiracy against Trump as early as 1927.

And half the shit that Trump does, most niggas I know are in jail for. Witness tampering. Intimidation. Lying. Obstructing justice. When Michael Cohen testified, Trump said, "But he should give information maybe on his father-in-law, because that's the one that people want to look at," trying to intimidate him by bringing his family into the matter. And the dudes I know who are in jail weren't even as overt as he is.

Maybe if we're lucky, he'll be in jail by the time this book comes out in paperback.

WE SHALL DEAL WITH THE WHITE SUPREMACY PROBLEM

"WHITE SUPREMACY IS NOT A PROBLEM"

Even if you think Trump isn't racist, he at least exacerbates the white supremacy problem. Everybody knows that the first step to healing is *admitting* you have a problem. But rather than try to address the problem, some on the Right want to deny that there even *is* a problem. According to Fox News's Tucker Carlson, white supremacy is a *hoax:*

But the whole thing is a lie. If you were to assemble a list, a hierarchy of concerns of problems this country faces, where would white supremacy be on the list? Right up there with Russia, probably.

Okay, so I actually *do* think that Russia is a problem, but go on . . .

It's actually not a real problem in America. The combined membership of every white supremacist organization in this country would be able to fit inside a college football stadium. . . . You know, I've lived here fifty years, I've never met anybody—not one person—who ascribes to white supremacy. I don't know a single person who thinks that's a good idea.

Really? Like you never have? You work at Fox, right?

And this was right after a gunman killed twenty-two people in a mass shooting in El Paso, Texas. The shooter posted a racist, xenophobic manifesto online *explicitly* detailing his white supremacist views. Even Ted Cruz tweeted, "What we saw yesterday was a heinous act of terrorism and white supremacy." When a gunman says that he's shooting up a place because of a "Hispanic invasion of Texas," *yeah,* I'd call that a white supremacist.

You'd think after the various mass murders of the last few years, it would be impossible to deny that white supremacy is a problem, but here's a partial list of recent mass shootings by white supremacists:

- The Walmart shooting in El Paso, Texas
- The shooting at a food festival in Gilroy, California
- The shooting at a synagogue in Pittsburgh
- The shooting at a synagogue near San Diego
- The shooting at a supermarket in Kentucky
- And so on (sadly this list will already be out of date by the time you read this) . . .

Now maybe what Tucker meant is that the white supremacy problem isn't a *problem.* And that might seem true; it might not be a problem for white guys like him.

THE REAL WHITE SUPREMACY PROBLEM

My main problem with white supremacy is there's not enough actual *supremacy* in it. What I mean is, where are the *exceptional* people at? You can't be a white supremacist living in a trailer on government assistance. The white supremacists marching in Charlottesville were chanting "You will not replace us." But if you have time to check into a hotel, march for three days, go to a rally, and you didn't take a vacation, you've pretty much been replaced already, right?

I mean, come on, man! You're fucking up the *brand*.

My white supremacy problem is it ain't truth in advertising. Stephen Miller? Steve Bannon? Mitch McConnell? Have you seen these motherfuckers? You wanna continue the white race? Well, you've gotta be able to get laid. Damn, the white supremacists these days look like shit. Nobody looks at Bannon and thinks, *That's a supreme specimen of humanity.*

Didn't there used to be a certain standard? Like an entrance exam or something? If you're gonna claim to be better than the entire rest of humanity, put some effort into it. Keep up appearances at least.

And I get it, you thought it was just gonna be enough to be white, and it ain't anymore. It's a rude awakening. I've always loved America for what it was: the good parts and the ugly, the kindness and the brutality—all of it. White people are just now getting to know the reality, and they don't like it. They don't want to hear about the ugliness; they don't care as long as they can stay feeling good about being white.

But whiteness ain't enough now. You should buy low, sell high, but at a certain point you have to cut your losses. I had this house in Rosemont in L.A. that I bought for $100,000 and it went down to $90,000 and stayed there. I lost some money, but I sold when I could. That's whiteness right now.

The market ain't what it was. Nothing is what it was. Radio is not what it was. TV is not what it was. America is changing, whether you like it or not. We're getting fatter and dumber; the rest of the world is catching up, fast.

JOBS FOR RACISTS

White supremacists are lashing out at the wrong people, convinced that their dwindling economic opportunities are black and brown people's fault. I'm not saying that racists shouldn't have jobs. I'm saying that they shouldn't have jobs where they control other people's fates, like judges or jailers or police officers. I'm not saying they can't be hired for anything. They abuse their positions of power and their views are loathsome, but they're still people.

Maybe some of these racists have skills that can translate

to new jobs. There are a lot of "soft skills" that racists have that employers are looking for:

- **BEING A TEAM PLAYER:** Racists are actually pretty good at being a team, whether it's the Klan or the Republican Party, so maybe they can work together to help a business instead of working together to assemble a torch-carrying mob.
- **FLEXIBILITY:** Racists aren't normally shown respect for their flexibility, but their *moral* flexibility is astonishing, if you think about it. The "moral majority" will wrap themselves up in righteousness, then cheer on a twice-divorced, adulterous liar who cages children like he's the chosen one.
- **EFFECTIVE COMMUNICATION:** Racists have stayed "on message" for the better part of two centuries. And they've proven they can adapt to today's fast-moving media landscape, setting up *Breitbart* and 4chan while retweeting racist memes and repeating Trump's talking points as quickly as they come.
- **DEDICATION:** Racists aren't real good at problem-solving, having been working on the "race" problem for the last few hundred years without success. But they are *persistent*. Effort counts for so much in life, doesn't it?

- **DISCRIMINATING TASTE:** Racists are rightfully regarded for their "discriminating" eye. What if we directed their talents toward more productive ends? Since racists are great at discriminating based on color, maybe they can be put to work in photographic color correction, identifying printing errors, or stoplight testing.

Plus, we want to keep people employed and busy. China and India are breathing down our neck. I'm looking for solutions here. We can't have a bunch of unemployed racists sitting around West Virginia. We've all got to pull our weight.

Reparations Article 4a. Full Employment for Racists

Acknowledging that "idle hands are the devil's playthings," and in consideration of the long history of idle racists stirring up trouble, ascribing their woes to the gainfully employed of other races, all efforts shall be made to keep racists employed, with job training to put their "skills" to good use.

But if you *are* a white supremacist, let me save you some time: you're gonna lose. You always have. Take the Civil War—all those people died, and you lost. The civil rights movement? You lost. And fifty years later, you had a black president. So all the hanging and shooting and violence just delayed the next loss for you. Let's save you some time and declare your loss now. White supremacy is a losing proposition because progress doesn't yield. Literally, you went from blowing up a black church to having a black friend in your lifetime. So, you lost.

JESUS, WHITE PEOPLE'S FAVORITE POC

And it's funny how white nationalists love quoting the Bible, because there are no white people in the Bible. None, not any white person. Jesus never saw a white person.

Y'all know Jesus wasn't white, right? We don't have any Polaroids of him, but he was a Palestinian Jewish man living in the first century, so he didn't have blue eyes and blond hair. Forensic anthropologists have reconstructed what he probably looked like based on skulls of people who lived in the same area at the same time, and they found that he most likely had dark olive skin and short, curly black or brown hair.

So Jesus looked a lot more like *me* than like Brad Pitt in

Legends of the Fall. But the white Jesus is the only one you ever see. That's not Jesus, that's Tristan. Sure, it'd be great if Jesus could kill sinners off with his bowie knife, but I don't know if he needs that.

I mean, we can't know for sure. The only thing that made me think Jesus could be white was that he did turn over all those tables in the temple and didn't go to jail. But I know he was black because he got convicted and killed for a crime he never committed. And he went around with twelve dudes with him all the time.

"Christian values" have caused a lot of pain in the world. You see, I have a problem with the church because the very same people who came up with "nigger" also want to tell us about Jesus. At the same time that they didn't actually believe we had a soul, they taught us about their Lord and Savior. I haven't seen God in a lot of places that niggas are. And Jesus: I find it ironic that the Bible says that we were all created in God's image, but white people had to create him in theirs.

The Jesus that white people worship is amazing. He may not come when you want him to, but he's always on call. Our Jesus takes a lot of weekends off. Maybe, like the cops, Jesus responds quicker to white folks.

I think that's wrong. White people co-opted Jesus in

their image, so when black people pray for salvation, they're asking for help from a white dude. That doesn't usually go so great. I think we gotta make Jesus look like he used to, like 50 Cent in "In Da Club."

Reparations Article 4b. Jesus in Da Club

To restore historical accuracy to the Jesus beloved by white nationalists and black folk alike, and to hopefully make Jesus a bit more accountable to everyone, regardless of the color of their skin, blond-haired, blue-eyed Jesuses shall henceforth be replaced with black Jesuses, modeled after 50 Cent. Jesus will still have abs, just black abs. Also, when there's a manger scene: let's get some black sheep up in that shit too.

WE SHALL BE UN-OPPRESSED

In America, we are still oppressed. In housing and wealth we are left behind. In health, we suffer. The South is still a big fucking problem. In justice and policing, we are discriminated against and abused. This oppression must be countered and lifted!

WE DON'T GET THE SAME EDUCATION AS YOU

Take education: There's never been an honest effort to educate black folks. Never. When the South Carolina Legislature funded the first public school system, they did it because they knew that education is a way out of poverty.

But we don't go to school in the same America as white folks.

FUND OUR SCHOOLS

Local control of schools means that there are huge discrepancies in school funding in different places. Small, rich towns can fund their small, rich—mostly white—schools. Big, poor cities have to make do with less.

On average, nonwhite school districts receive only $11,682 per student each year, compared to $13,908 in predominantly white school districts. Nationwide, that's $23 billion less than white districts for the same number of students. Due to segregation, historic inequities are built into school district borders and the way those school districts are funded.

You can tell a bad school from the name. If you're going to a school named after the KKK founder Nathan Bedford Forrest, I don't have to tell you that it's a shitty school. The way it's funded makes it seem like the KKK is running it. Can you imagine being somebody who hated black people and now the school named after you is full of them? I'm trying to stop your ancestors from rolling over in their graves.

YOU'RE CHEATERS

So let's say that despite the lack of funding, we rise above our shitty schools. Then what? White people always tell us to work hard, get good grades, and then we can go to a good college and get a good job, just like them. And that's true. But it's not the only way.

Let's say that you're a shitty student, but your dad has a lot of money. And let's say your name is Jared Kushner. Then, if your dad donates $2.5 million to Harvard University, it might not be a coincidence when you get in. Big donors get special privileges. People like Les Wexner, the billionaire in charge of Victoria's Secret, donated millions of dollars to Harvard and got three kids in.

But even if you don't have millions of dollars to throw at Harvard, you can still get lucky as long as you're white and your great-grandpappy went to school there in 1789 or whatever.

Take Brett Kavanaugh. According to him, he got into Yale fair and square: "Senator, I was at the top of my class academically, busted my butt in school. Captain of the varsity basketball team. Got in Yale College. When I got into Yale College, got into Yale Law School. Worked my tail off." All that hard work, and still no mention that his grandfather, Everett Edward Kavanaugh, also went to Yale. That's privilege for you: it's all hard work, nothing to do with family connections, it's all a meritocracy—except it isn't.

So a white dude who gets drunk and is accused of sexual assault by multiple women can still become a Supreme Court judge. A black guy who gets a parking ticket and works his way through junior college, goes to law school, what he gets is a TV show about judges. He's Judge Kevin Ross. Judge Kevin Ross is actually a friend of mine. He's like one of the brightest dudes ever. He went to Morehouse, became a judge in Inglewood, and then went on to the California Superior Court. Now he's had a TV show about being a judge for ten years. That's the best we're gonna get.

That's fine, but there's still a difference: Supreme Court or *America's Court*. Judge Kevin Ross might make money, but nobody gives a shit about his opinions. It's all "Pay this bitch her five hundred dollars and let's go home. We ain't got time for this." The difference in the kind of cases you hear is stark: *Citizens United* or *Kayla didn't pay the electric bill*. Come on, man.

And legacy college admissions naturally accrue benefits to white folks whose families were able to attend schools that we weren't allowed in. It's another way that black people get shut out for having the wrong ancestors. Being a legacy can increase your chances of admission by about 20 percent. That's a huge advantage.

I always wanted one of my children to go to the University of Southern California. So I was so happy when my daughter called and she said, "I got accepted to USC." I was on the radio and I started crying. I was able to save the money, my daughter worked hard, played by the rules, and here she is going to the school I always dreamed of. I wish I knew that all I had to do was bribe a motherfucker to say she was on the rowing team. Who knew it was that easy? In March of 2019, the feds busted a bunch of rich parents who shelled out a lot of money to get their kids into schools like USC. For $1.2 million, a girl got into Yale for soccer even though she didn't play soccer. With a lot of cash and a little Photoshop, a girl got admitted to USC as a water polo player. Just put her face on someone else's body and make sure the cash is on the way.

Lori Loughlin and Felicity Huffman paid money to get their kids into schools where slots could have gone to other, more deserving kids. Olivia Jade Giannulli, daughter of Loughlin and fashion designer Mossimo Giannulli, was literally floating around on a yacht when her parents got busted. That yacht, which happened to be owned by Rick Caruso, the elected chair of USC's board of trustees, was probably as close to being on the rowing team as she got.

Now, when you get busted on a yacht for pretending to be on the rowing team—that's some privilege. And Felicity Huffman only served fourteen days in prison for paying to have her daughter's SAT scores fixed. Her lawyers argued that it was her first offense, though the judge neglected to consider her part in *Christmas with the Kranks,* which was an offense to cinema. That shit is the *real* war on Christmas.

Fifteen thousand dollars for good SAT scores and she got fourteen days in jail. You know that has everything to do with her being a rich white lady, because we just gotta look at Tanya McDowell to see that shit is different when you're poor and black. Tanya got charged with "stealing education" because she lied about her address while homeless so her kid could go to a good elementary school. And she was sentenced to prison for five years. Not five days. Five *years*.

At the time there were at least two dozen other families who were found to be violating the residency rules in the district where Tanya enrolled her kid. But because she also had pending drug charges, the authorities threw the book at her. It's fucked up.

So okay, you might not be able to stop rich people from bribing their way into good schools. But even if you don't *bribe* the water polo coach to get your kid into USC, a lot of these sports are just rich-white-kid affirmative action. They're another bit of reverse reparations where black basketball players and football players subsidize sports teams that are full of rich white kids.

Sailing. Water polo. Rowing. What do these sports have in common? They're all white-people sports for kids named Chet, Mitt, or Travis. I mean, with our history, you really want to put a bunch of niggas in a boat and yell at them to row?

And even though nobody's going to the women's water polo matches, somebody's gotta fill that team. So coaches are able to stack these slots on these sports teams with people who wouldn't otherwise get into these schools.

Bribes or no, unpaid black athletes on the money-making football and basketball teams are supporting the admission of white water polo players. We got a problem when Trevon's paying for Tucker. You know what I mean? Kids who grew up shooting hoops are supporting kids who grew up sailing sloops.

And if white people want to pretend that water polo and sailing are real sports, they have to commit to it. I think

that every white season-ticket holder for an NCAA basketball or football team should also have to be a season-ticket
holder for the water polo team. You can't get in to see the
Crimson Tide if you haven't been in to see the sailors go
out on high tide.

Reparations Article 5a. Sailing Season-Ticket Holders

All supporters of sports of dubious import, the sole
purpose of which is admitting their children into college,
shall be subject to season-pass requirements. Archery,
rowing, fencing, jousting, dressage, or any other stupid
sport shall be canceled if there are not enough white
parents in attendance at the matches. In addition, every
white season-ticket holder for an NCAA basketball or
football team shall also be a season-ticket holder for the
water polo team.

NO ONE LIKES BAD SPORTS

And while white athletes are playing tennis, black athletes are playing the sports that actually fund the colleges.

So even before this treaty, some people have been thinking about how fair a bargain black athletes are involved in. Are athletes being treated with respect and compensation commensurate with what they bring to universities?

Chris Broussard and Jemele Hill are among the sportswriters thinking about this, calling on minority athletes to "fight power with power" and start going to historically black colleges. Black athletes bring both money and recognition to their schools, so why not keep it in the fam?

Jemele Hill's argument was this: Why do we know about the University of Texas? Why do we know Alabama? Because of their football. All these black kids, these exceptional five-star athletes, go to schools like Texas or Alabama. For years and years, before *Brown v. Board of Education,* black athletes had to go to black schools because they couldn't go anywhere else. But now, the best athletes go to mainstream, majority-white schools.

So when these athletes go to predominantly white schools, they bring resources with them. The athletic programs at Michigan, Ohio State, and Notre Dame pay a ton of bills. Twenty-seven schools make at least $100 million a year from their athletic departments. Michigan State makes $54 million in licensing, $59 million from football, and $18 million from basketball. Look at all the money generated from athletes: from parking to concessions to merchandising. So if you're Magic Johnson, you go to Michigan State and all those boosters come to see you play in those games and you pay for a lot of shit just running that ball. Imagine if those same monies were in black schools. The buildings would be better. The professors would be better. The facilities would be better.

And these schools really are white schools, run on black athletes' money. Black men are only a tiny percent of the student population, but they're the majority of the athletes. Without that money, these schools' teams would be nothing. Jemele Hill argued in an *Atlantic* article that a concerted movement back to historically black colleges and universities (HBCUs) would benefit the places that have the greatest impact on the black professional class in America: "Despite constituting only 3 percent of four-year colleges in the country, HBCUs have produced 80 percent of the black judges, 50 percent of the black lawyers, 50 percent of the black doctors, 40 percent of the black engineers, 40 percent of the black members of Congress, and 13 percent of the black CEOs in America today."

These games are giant advertisements for the schools. A lot of white people know about USC only because it's got great basketball and football traditions. I don't care how many Pulitzer Prize or Nobel Prize winners come out of your school; you don't get no commercials on Saturdays. Black athletes are bringing in that money.

And you know what else? Everybody loves niggas on a Sunday, because that's when the football games are on. And most people's sports heroes are black. If that's where we gotta start—if that's what gets some white people to respect or admire a black person—I don't want to take that one day away from them. You know what I mean? Let's build from there. Pretty soon we got people liking us Sunday through Wednesday, at least.

So here's the deal: We want a fair share of the revenue coming in for our efforts. And we want funding for our HBCUs, which, after all, benefit everyone. With all the problems in education, you want to be sure there are places educating black people effectively. The endowments of these schools are far below those of Ivy League schools, but their impact on diversity in the professional class is huge.

And in return, we'll play ball. If you have a college sports program, you need black people in it if you want people to watch it. When people sit out in the snow with paint on their faces, they don't want to see some bullshit. If black people didn't play football, it would be rugby. You don't want that. The only time you watch rugby is when you lose your fucking remote.

Reparations Article 5b. Pay Up, or Rugby

The sport of rugby, being abhorrent in nature, undesirable to both black and white, who do both enjoy the Sundays spent watching "the Big Game," shall henceforth be set aside in favor of keeping black athletes playing ball. Black athletes will play ball if white supporters will likewise play ball, financing historically black colleges and universities, paying athletes their worth, and generally respecting the fact that nobody would give a fuck about Alabama without Tua Tagovailoa.

WE CAN'T LIVE WHERE WE WANT TO

The oppression continues in education, housing, and banking to this day. We still can't live where we want to, and we still don't share in America's wealth.

WHERE THE BLACK PEOPLE AREN'T

A few years ago, Jon Stewart tried to call Bill O'Reilly on his white privilege. O'Reilly, of course, wants to deny that such a thing exists and wants to pretend that he's some kind of Johnny Lunchpail, a self-made man from a tough working-class background who pulled himself up by his bootstraps. Bill O'Reilly talks in his book *The O'Reilly Factor* about growing up in Levittown, Long Island, the iconic post–World War II suburban development. Levittown was built as one of the first suburban communities for returning GIs, who could pick up a house for $7,990 with TV included. Using a GI loan, you paid 0 percent interest. Well, you know what my father couldn't get? A GI loan.

That's because the GI Bill was deliberately structured to shut black veterans out. The chair of the House's committee on veterans, Mississippi congressman John Rankin, made sure that it was administered by states, not the federal government, thus making sure that racist state governments would have control of it. Rankin was a capital-*R* racist, on the record for saying civil rights would destroy "the white man's civilization throughout the world." Jim Crow was alive and well at the time, and Rankin thought that warm feelings for returning GIs would generate gains for blacks that he couldn't tolerate.

The local administration of the bill denied opportunities to black veterans. Racist policies of the states ensured that loans were given out to whites, not blacks. Many white-run banks refused mortgages and loans to black people, even though the VA would cosign the loan. So even after fighting a war, black veterans were shut out of the honor they deserved. According to the Equal Justice Initiative, "A survey of 13 Mississippi cities found that African Americans received only 2 of the 3229 home, business, and farm loans administered by the VA in 1947." This didn't just happen in the South; in New York and New Jersey, fewer than 100 of the 67,000 mortgages insured by the GI Bill were for black people's homes. Yet black people's taxes financed that shit for you too. We paid taxes but didn't get shit.

But even if my dad had the money, he wouldn't have been allowed to buy the same house as Bill O'Reilly's dad's. At Levittown, no niggers were allowed. It was written right into the original charter that no "non-Caucasians" could own or rent in Levittown. Eventually, that got struck down in court, but discrimination continued and even today the suburb is 94 percent white. Charters like this were widespread. The executive producer for my show dug up the old charter for his neighborhood and it says you can't sell to black people. That's two miles from where I work right now.

So the GI Bill was designed for white people and Levittown was designed for white people.

And this isn't ancient history—the same thing is still happening today. *Newsday* just did a three-year investigation of the real estate industry on Long Island and found that black people are still being discriminated against, steered away from white neighborhoods and into black neighborhoods.

One real estate agent told a white buyer to stay away from a mostly minority neighborhood because of gang violence but didn't discourage a black buyer who had the same budget. Agents sent white buyers to Merrick, a white area. And when talking to a black buyer about Brentwood, a black and Hispanic area where there's MS-13 gang violence, an agent said that residents there were the "nicest people."

The undercover investigation showed that real estate agents treated black people unequally 49 percent of the time, compared to white people. A lot of this treatment was subtle—discrepancies in what houses people were shown or requiring preapproved mortgages before showing listings.

The black buyers would really have no idea that they were being treated differently. But they were given fewer listings and were steered into different areas than white people.

When I was a brand-new young dude, twenty-four or twenty-five, looking to buy a new house, the same thing happened to me in L.A. I specifically said I wanted to move out of the neighborhood and yet they only showed me houses in Compton or in deep L.A. I must have looked at ten houses that day and none of them was four miles away from where I was currently living. It was like: you take a left, then another left, then another left, and we're back where we started. I almost rebought my own house, except my price was too high.

So the discrimination is different, but it's real. It's biased real estate agents. And it's unfair practices.

It's not like people put ads in the paper anymore that say, "Whites Only," but then again, people don't put any ads in papers. It's all online now. In March 2019, the Department of Housing and Urban Development sued Facebook for allowing housing discrimination by way of targeted advertising. It allowed users to target ads excluding people by race, just like in the old days. When *ProPublica* did an investigation of similar practices in 2016, it found that Facebook discriminated based on "ethnic affinity." A spokesman pointed out that ethnic affinity is not the same as race—but I'm gonna guess that when you discriminate against "African American affinity," you're not just targeting Eminem and Vanilla Ice. Turns out that the people with the greatest African American affinity are black people. If that ain't racist, it's at least affinity-ist.

So fine, if you want to keep saying that you come from a hardscrabble town and modest means and built yourself up from nothing, go ahead. Tell everyone you came from Levittown or Steelburg or Old Scranton. We understand how important these old places are to your sense of belonging and to your story.

But if you're going to do that, we want you to make a slight modification, a clarification to your origin story. Please only refer to these towns with the preface "All-White." So if you want to say you came from Levittown or Steelburg, you must now call it "All-White Levittown" or "All-White Steelburg," as in, "Yes, I came from humble beginnings: my dad used to dig for potatoes in the fields of All-White Potatotown," or "It weren't easy for me ma and pa, all day me ma would cook meals and run the PTA and me pa would commute to an accounting firm in the city. At night, we'd all huddle around the dining room table and enjoy a big dinner in the traditional All-White Levittown way."

Reparations Article 5c. Truth in Advertising

White people, being beneficiaries of racist housing policies, having written the rules to ensure all-white suburbs, and having extended opportunity to whites only, shall henceforth retain their cherished lies about the lack of privilege and opportunity that they had. Not having lacked for privilege and opportunity, they shall nonetheless henceforth have the privilege and opportunity of lack: that is, they shall retain the opportunity to say they did not have much, grew up in humble circumstances, are self-made in every way. However, if a place is named in such recollections, if an anecdote of their upbringing is in the offing, they must amend the place-name with the preface "All-White" to bring a bit of truth to the lie.

WE FELL INTO THE GAP

And policies like this have created a wealth gap, even in the modern era. The original homes in Levittown only cost you $7,990, but the median price today is $400,000. That's what building wealth in real estate gets you. And it's what we missed out on.

According to McKinsey & Company,

the median white family had more than ten times the wealth of the median black family in 2016. In fact, the racial wealth gap between black and white families grew from about $100,000 in 1992 to $154,000 in 2016, in part because white families gained significantly more wealth (with the median increasing by $54,000), while median wealth for black families did not grow at all in real terms over that period.

Home ownership is one of the biggest generators of family wealth over time, because you can buy a starter home, it (hopefully) accrues value, and you sell it to buy a bigger home. That's been a part of the American Dream for decades. But it doesn't work for us.

Just being in a black neighborhood costs you money.

The Brookings Institution found that in neighborhoods that are at least 50 percent black, the homes are valued at half the price of homes in nonblack neighborhoods. And it's not because the houses or neighborhoods are worse. According to Brookings, "Homes of similar quality in neighborhoods with similar amenities are worth 23 percent less in majority black neighborhoods, compared to those with very few or no black residents." And even when you adjust for crime rates, commute times, etc., it only explains about half of the undervaluation. On average, having a "black" house costs you $48,000. Across all majority black neighborhoods, that's a $156 billion loss. Let that sink in. That's $156 billion that racial bias pulls from our pockets.

When I was selling my house in West Hills, Los Angeles—a brand-new house—this shit happened to me. We had lived there for three years and my wife wanted to move. So we remodeled the house, and we were getting an appraisal and my real estate broker told us to put our family pictures away during the appraisal. I said, "I'm not taking my fucking pictures down." And I didn't do it.

And the appraisal came in so low that the bank called us and they're like, "Is the property in disrepair?" I mean, this was a new house, only a few years old, and I had put in a pool and hardwood floors and new counters. There were still houses being built on my street. The bank couldn't understand why the appraisal was so low; the comps in the area were much higher. So they talked to the appraiser and asked why it was so low and he said, "Because I just thought it was accurate. Because it is what I say it is."

So he tried to take $160,000 of real value from my home. They fired that appraiser and got another one, and my house ended up selling for the comps. And I was able to take the profit from that and buy another house. I was lucky, luckier than most black people. But damn if it wasn't a wake-up moment.

So you all freed us, but then wouldn't let us live where we wanted. You restricted where we could move, then wouldn't give us loans for the places you let us go. And now, you steer us back to those same places, those same neighborhoods.

When we do have a house, it gets devalued because we live in it. And we get offered worse mortgages. Wells Fargo had to pay $175 million in 2012 because of their predatory lending practices. Researchers found that black borrowers in Baltimore were given loans that cost an average of $15,000 to $16,000 more over the thirty-year term than white borrowers' loans.

All of this has led to where we are now: the lowest black home ownership rates since the 1960s. The Urban Institute showed a huge gap between black and white home ownership: from 2001 to 2016, the black home ownership rate dropped five points to 41 percent, as opposed to a one-point decline for whites to 71 percent.

Then when you need to run a highway somewhere, or build an airport, you take our houses.

EMINENT DOMAIN AND HIGHWAYS

In L.A., there's this freeway, the 105. It goes right through our neighborhoods. The 105 is like a lot of highway projects: The government comes in and takes your house by eminent domain. If you bought a house for thirty grand, they say, "I'll give you thirty-two, now get out."

My wife's grandmother owned a house along the freeway's proposed path, and they took it from her forty or fifty years ago to build the 105. She had bought this home for $15,000, and today a shitty house in that area is $350,000. Just the property is worth that much.

All the time these highways go through poor neighborhoods inhabited by people of color. So even when you have a big chip in the game, the powers that be are able to take it away. Imagine how much wealth you'd have if you had just been able to keep that house and accrue the benefits over time. There are houses now in Inglewood that are worth more than $750,000 that were originally $20,000. They could have changed people's lives.

All of this is made possible even though the Fifth Amendment of the Constitution specifies that the government can't take private property. The exception to this rule is taking property for "public use." But a lot of the time, this "public use" is for "urban renewal," itself a disguised bit of racist code for "take black people's shit."

Because all the highways go through black neighborhoods, I think that black people shouldn't have to pay any tolls. By this agreement, we'll create a new E-ZPass for black folks—let's call it a Take It Easy Pass.

Reparations Article 5d. Take It Easy Pass

Until such a time as highways are put through white neighborhoods, and in consideration of the inequal use of eminent domain, the building of highway projects in black neighborhoods, and the drawbacks that accrue therefrom, black people shall be issued Easy Passes that provide discounted (free) tolls for all highways.

And furthermore, the toll roads need to be adjusted to prioritize black drivers. High-Occupancy Vehicle lanes gotta change. Not HOV, but BOV lanes: Black-Occupancy Vehicles. Of course, we do run a risk putting all the black drivers in one lane, 'cause the cops will know exactly who to pull over. I don't feel like helping the cops that much, so tell you what: In some places, you can pay to use the HOV lane even if you're just driving alone, right? So maybe we can incentivize some white people to use the lane, making a little money on the deal and mitigating the risk of everyone in the lane getting pulled over. Finally, some white people will get pulled over for DWB.

Levittown was built for white people, but there's never been a housing development built for black people. None. Except jail. Even the projects weren't originally built for black people. They were built for people coming back from the armed services. And it's funny that all the places that are the roughest are named after cool shit. It's always "gardens" and "terraces" and "villages." If you heard the names of the places we live; all the projects sound beautiful. Hacienda Village, Cabrini-Green, and Nigger-Free Gardens . . . but the prettier the name, the shittier the neighborhood.

There's never been anywhere that was designed with the

idea of attracting a lot of black people. So even the homes that we have, people didn't want us to have. Compton is called the Hub City because it's in the center of all of L.A. But before World War II, Compton was 95 percent white. By 1970, due to white flight, 65 percent of the population was black. Compton has an airport. They didn't build the airport because they knew niggas was gonna be there. They didn't know Dr. Dre was gonna be there. I mean, Kevin Costner lived in the neighborhood. So everywhere we go, one nigga moved in and white people moved out. There was nowhere we were invited to live.

THE COLOR PURPLE

And black neighborhoods don't have stores that fit our needs. We only get stuff when we leave, and then we aren't there to enjoy it. When we move out, white people move in and bring everything with them. Gentrification is funny because those are the same structures, just new people. Gentrification is black people having enough money to move out and white people having enough money to move in, but they bring Starbucks and grocery stores and opportunity with them. But we don't have that shit. You can go to the Magic Johnson Theatre, but how many times can you watch *Juice* or *Boyz n the Hood*? If you're a black person, you'll never see an independent film in your neighborhood.

I mean, we can live without seeing *The Royal Tenenbaums,* but we can't live without grocery stores. It's seventeen miles on average before black people can access fresh produce or fresh meat. Grocery stores just don't open in our neighborhoods the way that dollar stores and liquor stores do. The Greenwood section of Tulsa, former home of Black Wall Street, went from having dozens of grocery stores to having none. But it does have eight dollar stores. Dollar stores are replacing grocery stores in poor communities of color throughout the country. These sorts of stores have a very limited amount of fresh food, if any.

So we can't get fresh fruit, but we can get Fabuloso. Black people love Fabuloso for some reason. We used to have grocery stores where you could get Pine-Sol or Ajax. But when dollar stores came, they brought the cheapest bullshit, so all you can get is Fabuloso. It's a Spanish name, but we're probably their biggest customer. So now niggas is buying shit they can't pronounce. Fabuloso virtually killed Pine-Sol for niggas. You ain't gonna smell a fresh pine scent in a black neighborhood. Black neighborhoods smell purple.

It wasn't like that ten years ago. I didn't used to know

what Fabuloso was. My housekeeper brought it into my house, and I was like, "What the fuck is Fabuloso?" But then all of a sudden, every black person's house that I'd go over to would have Fabuloso. All because of dollar stores. Dollar stores have become our corner store, our hardware store, our grocery store.

And who knows what the hell is in Fabuloso? Nature don't make shit that purple, so you know it ain't plant based. According to its website, it's got sodium dodecylbenzenesulfonate in it. Sodium dodecylbenzenesulfonate? That looks like a Word Jumble, not an ingredient. You're not gonna find that shit at Whole Foods or Trader Joe's. They don't make organic sodium dodecylbenzenesulfonate. So one of the things that happens to us is we use things that are not environmentally safe. And we only have access to food that's bad for us. And then, who becomes the burden on society? Meanwhile, all these people getting rich off of folks who they made sick are like, "You're on your own." It's a weird nexus.

Black and brown neighborhoods are more likely to have hazardous compounds in the air. The highways that cut through and surround poor neighborhoods cause nitrogen oxides from exhaust fumes. Air pollution from industrial sites, truck routes, and ports contributes to higher asthma rates and other poor health outcomes. According to a Yale University study, black people had a higher exposure than white people for thirteen out of fourteen pollutants.

So black people get more:

- Air pollution
- Lead
- Asthma
- Dollar stores
- Fast food
- Fabuloso

And we get less:

- Nature
- Grocery stores
- Art-house cinemas
- Fresh food
- Pine-Sol

So what do we want? We want fair access to the shit you all got. We want facilities: grocery stores, movie theaters, and better food.

Reparations Article 5e. Near Our Houses: Actual Food

We need actual food in our neighborhoods: quality grocery stores with fresh fruit, vegetables, and meats. For the purposes of this agreement, neither a pile of bananas by the cash register nor any meat in a can shall constitute "fresh," regardless of the packaging's claims. We want real restaurants and coffee shops; the McCafé section of a McDonald's shall not count. We want environmental justice, so that we don't have to use Fabuloso to scrub out the pollutants in our homes. We want that fresh pine smell and that fresh clean air you all got.

And now it's moving in reverse. African Americans are moving to the outlying areas. They're not living in the cities no more, because cities are becoming untenable for us. And we're not moving to the good suburbs; we're moving to places far away and shitty. Like San Bernardino is suburban, but it's all niggas and it's horrible. So they just moved the projects to San Bernardino and moved all the bullshit with them. All you did was change the background on *Cops.*

But we live where we can. The only reason we're in the

hoods is because we have to be there. My parents *had* to live where they lived; they were not allowed to live anywhere else. Most black people lived where we were forced to live. Between being told that you can't have a house here and facing charters against selling to black people or banks refusing to lend, the places that we live in are the places we had to live in.

In the '70s, people thought there was a CIA plot to cordon black people into concentration camps: the King Alfred Plan. The King Alfred Plan came from a novel, *The Man Who Cried I Am* by John A. Williams, and was invented as part of his publicity campaign for the book. He left copies of these "secret" plans on subway cars and they spread to activist communities, who were unsure whether the plans were real or not. So it's fictional, but we actually *do* live in areas cordoned off by the government. King Alfred is nothing like Fat Albert, and maybe both are fictional, but they represent something real. Some people call it redlining, some people call it camps. But the bottom line is you can't get loans there. And you're only shown certain houses. And you can only get approved to live in certain places. So how is that demonstrably different from a "fictitious CIA-led plot"? Who needs the CIA? You have Coldwell Banker or Bank of America.

WE'RE NOT AS HEALTHY AS YOU

And when you have to live in a bad neighborhood, when you don't have money or access to good food and resources, you're not as healthy.

GET THE LEAD OUT

The only person who still uses lead pipes is Mrs. Peacock, in the conservatory. It was either her or Colonel Mustard in the billiard room with the rope. But I digress.

Well, also black people and other people of color in Flint. Oh, and in Newark. And Pittsburgh, Baltimore, and who knows where else.

Everybody knows that lead is dangerous. Lead exposure has been linked to increases in crime, lower IQs, and behavioral disorders. If you look at most people in prison, they have a couple of things in common: they're illiterate and they have high concentrations of lead in their blood.

The fall in violent crime beginning in the 1990s wasn't due to "broken windows" policing or "zero tolerance" policies. It wasn't stop-and-frisk. It was a drop in people's lead levels. Higher childhood blood lead levels are associated with higher adult arrest rates for violent crimes. The drop in crime corresponds with the banning of leaded gasoline emissions that caused the majority of lead exposure in children.

The impact on black urban populations can't be over-stated. Your environment has an impact on you physiologically and physically, but it's easier to blame illiteracy and crime on "cultural" problems than on environmental factors. The black culture is violent, prisons have to be built, and so on.

But let's not get off track. So you say there's a cultural problem, we say there's a lead problem. Tell you what: let's at least take care of one of the problems that we all agree on—nobody thinks lead is a good idea anymore. It's out of gas, but there's still a lot of old lead paint and a lot of old lead pipes.

In Flint, in Newark, and elsewhere they keep fucking things up by trying to add chemicals to the water and then send everyone a bunch of filters and water bottles when it doesn't work. Well, enough. We want new pipes. No more lead pipes, no more bottled water deliveries. I don't care if it's Fiji or Poland Spring, it's got to go.

And we need a big paint job, a Sherwin-Williams' March to remove lead paint from our homes. Y'all love home renovation shows: Think of this like one big HGTV project. The flips have flopped—now we need Chip and Joanna Gaines to come out and fix shit up. You won't find a bigger fixer-upper than the neighborhoods that still have lead paint.

Reparations Article 5f. Black Neighborhood Rehab

It's makeover time for black neighborhoods, due to the lead pipes and paint. We hereby demand that the HGTV network send some of their experts in to get the lead out and spruce the place up, preferably that Chip and Joanna couple, as long as Chip keeps the corny jokes to a minimum. If they are busy, we'll take the Property Brothers.

This treaty might be a bitter pill, so I want to throw you a few easy wins: things that you can agree to that will take the sting out. Some of this shit will even *save* you money, instead of costing you money. Kevin Drum of *Mother Jones* estimates that cleaning up lead could cost about $20 billion a year but would still save us all money in higher IQs, higher incomes, and drops in crime to the tune of about $200 billion a year. Doing something that everyone agrees is a good idea *and* saving money? Yep.

You don't want another white governor getting blamed for another lead pipe problem. You don't want another "the next Flint." Trust me: there's not a big enough Brita filter to take care of this shit.

KEEP MEDICAL RACISM

I've spent a lot of this book criticizing racism, but I don't want to seem totally negative about it; I mean, maybe some good has come of it after all.

For example, because of racism, we didn't get hooked on opiates like white folks did. Doctors, traditionally, don't believe black people feel as much pain, so they prescribe them less medication. Multiple studies have shown this to be the case. When black patients complain of pain similar to that of white patients, they are less likely to be given pain meds, and if they are, it's at a lower dosage than whites.

Some part of this is probably overprescription of medication to white people, of course. But part of it has been shown to be due to bias and misguided beliefs about biological differences between the races, including beliefs that black people are stronger and feel less pain than whites. The only time I feel no pain is when I've had a little too much Rémy Martin. I mean, when a doctor says, "You know, I hate niggers," it's not good. But because he hated niggas, I didn't OD in a bathroom. So, you know—in this one way it kinda worked out for us. Because of institutional biases and racism, we missed that whole scene.

Doctors have never believed black people can feel pain. In a way, it's put black people at the forefront of many medical breakthroughs, although maybe not in the way you'd usually like. For instance, take the experiments of the "father of modern gynecology," J. Marion Sims, who relied on the contributions of black women to perfect surgical techniques. His achievement was marked, until recently, with a statue of Sims in Central Park across from the New York Academy of Medicine. I probably don't have to tell you that someone called the "father of modern gynecology" has turned out to have a problematic past. Did you see that coming? Well, unfortunately, these surgical techniques were perfected on enslaved black women without anesthesia. His statue was pulled recently because, as the New York City Public Design Commission said, "Free consent to participate in the experiments was not obtainable from women who were not free." *Another fucking statue we had to deal with!*

So yeah, we were at the forefront of medical discovery, but as test *subjects*.

And it's not just experiments like this and the Tuskegee syphilis experiments that make black people distrust doctors. There's something about white guys in white robes that makes us nervous, you know?

Black people don't have a high trust of doctors for good reason. Take Serena Williams: she nearly died after childbirth because doctors didn't believe she had a blood clot. The day after her C-section, she felt short of breath. Because she's a badass, she was able to advocate for herself and alert the medical staff. She walked out of her hospital room and told the nurses that she needed "a CT scan with contrast and IV heparin right away." How many people would know to order that shit? When they did the scan, it showed small blood clots in her lungs that could have killed her.

Medical bias is a real thing. The Centers for Disease Control and Prevention reported that black women were three times more likely than white women to suffer a pregnancy-related death. Serena's experience isn't uncommon for black women; a lot of these deaths happen the day after delivery, or even several weeks later.

When medical care is less available and doctors exhibit bias, the outcomes are worse. Black women are more likely to go into pregnancy with underlying health problems because they don't have as much health care access. And it's not just because of less insurance coverage; studies have shown that mothers avoid prenatal care when they feel like they face bias and bad treatment from medical staff.

Black women and white women get breast cancer at about the same rate, but black women die from it at a higher rate than white women, as an example. Why? They've only recently tried to figure it out. The institutional bias in the medical industry is to study white people and not black people. Only recently, after other studies included mostly white women, did a Black Women's Health Study get launched out of Boston University to specifically study the health of fifty-nine thousand black women. This study figured out that black women are more likely to develop the most aggressive form of breast cancer. And it turns out that being born in a Southern state that used to have Jim Crow laws raised black women's risk of being diagnosed with breast tumors. Racism kills.

But again, I don't want to sound like the lack of medical care and institutional biases of the Southern states are all bad.

Let me thank the Republican Party, especially Republican governors who fought so hard against expanding Obamacare. Because if you don't have health insurance, you're not getting opiates. Lack of health coverage has been a huge help here. And you'll never guess who's lagging behind in health coverage. Just prior to the launch of Obamacare, black people had a much higher uninsured rate than white people, and since its passage that gap has narrowed a bit. But in states where Republicans blocked the Medicaid expansion, that uninsured rate is still nearly twice as high as in states that passed the Medicaid expansion. That's basically the South and parts of the Midwest, ya know, where most black people live.

Have you ever noticed that only rich niggas OD on opiates? That's why. Nobody can afford the coverage it takes to get hooked on opiates. I mean, $2,500 a month with a $500 copay? You need money to get hooked like that. Prince? Come on, now. Prince died because he started taking pain meds for hip pain. If only people had been more racist toward Prince, he might have lived. You know, if you can die the same way as Tom Petty, you're dying like a white guy.

Reparations Article 5g. Stay Racist, Medically

White people, unable to eliminate racism and bias in all forms, are hereby allowed to remain racist in matters of prescribing medicine, especially opioids and pain medications. With expanded access to health care, we understand that risks to us increase, but we'll worry about that when y'all approve Obamacare's Medicaid expansion anywhere in the South at all. In the meantime, if a wealthy black person requires pain meds, please remember that he "Got the Look" of a black dude, so he ain't "Free Fallin'" into a coma.

THE SOUTH MUST SURRENDER PROPERLY

You know, it seems like I've spent a lot of the book criticizing the South. Well, the South has a lot of problems for black people. And if the white people in the South had surrendered properly the first time around, we might not even need this treaty.

YOU LIVE FOR LESS IN THE SOUTH

The largest percentage of black people in America live in the South. You can live for less in the South. But the *chance* to live is lower.

It doesn't cost you money, it costs you years. In California, your life expectancy is 81 years. But if you live in Mississippi, it's 74.5 years. That's less than the life expectancy in

Bulgaria or Malaysia. The average life expectancy in America is 78.6 years. But all across the South, you'll live less than that on average: North Carolina, Georgia, South Carolina, Tennessee, Louisiana, Kentucky, Alabama, West Virginia, and Mississippi.

Black people who live in more diverse areas live longer, make more money, and are better educated. When the Associated Press looked at county-level data of life expectancy, they found that a lot of the same issues that plague the black population generally are also correlated with life expectancy. Life expectancy increased with an increase in median income and decreased with increases in unemployment or lower education levels. It decreased by eight months with a 10 percent increase in the black population. Of the areas with the lowest life expectancy, about half are majority-black populations, 51 percent have low education, and 61 percent have low incomes. Most of the places where people die the earliest are black places.

MEET THE FLINTSTONES

It's like America's made up of the Flintstones and the Jetsons, and the Flintstones are running the country. They want to stop cars with their feet instead of jetting around. You think the Green New Deal is a stupid idea, but coal mining's smart? Come again? You like working for Mr. Slate when you could be working for Cosmo Spacely? They're so backward, they want to deport Rosie the Robot.

Who benefited more from the Civil War: black people or white people in the South? Even the losers of that war benefited more than the people who the war was fought over. And these states are still run by white legislatures and governors.

The South is still a mess for black people. Fifty-four percent of African Americans live in the Southern region of the United States, but somehow, it's still run by white people. Eighteen percent of black folks live in the Northeast, 19 percent live in the Midwest, and 10 percent live in the West. Republicans are in charge all across the South, even though more black people are concentrated in the South than in all the other regions combined. And for some reason, this region is primarily the poorest, the most in need of government assistance. If white people are so smart, why can't they get their shit together in the South? Maybe if the white governments of these states worked a little harder on making things good for their constituents instead of trying to knock black people down, they'd get more done.

The South has been set up to take away freedoms from black people. India's constitution is 177,000 words and they've got billions of people. The U.S. Constitution is 4,543 words with 27 amendments. The Alabama State Constitution has more than 300,000 words and 892 amendments. The United States learned a long time ago that taking freedoms away is problematic. They tried to do Prohibition and it was repealed. Most of the amendments have given people more rights, not less. Alabama's constitution is all about restrictions. When it was written, it was specifically designed to retain white supremacy in the state, including sections against interracial marriage and maintaining the segregation of public schools. I really don't understand how you have 300,000 words and you're fiftieth in education. All them words and you still can't read? You cut out the words "no" and "hate" and you're down to 150,000 words, easy.

The South is still about oppressing black people. Have you ever noticed that all of these states where they frown more on doctors who perform abortions than they do people who commit rape and incest are the same states where it was okay to rape slaves? A woman's body wasn't ever really her own. I wonder how many white people in the South would be for abortion when they find out they're going to have a black grandbaby.

And Mississippi only officially outlawed slavery in 2013.

Mississippi was one of the only states to not ratify the Thirteenth Amendment banning slavery. When three-fourths of the states ratified the amendment in 1865, it became law. Every other state ratified the amendment, but Mississippi didn't. It was only after a Mississippi resident saw the movie *Lincoln* and did a little research that he realized that even though Mississippi had voted to ratify the amendment in 1995, it had failed to make it official by notifying the U.S. archivist. They were like, "Hey, fellas, we'll be right back. There's something we forgot to do." And so they finally ratified it 148 years late.

That's how backwards shit is. Just last year, they found the last slave ship to reach the United States in Mobile, Alabama. Researchers found the remains of the *Clotilda*, the boat that carried 110 slaves to Alabama in 1860, in the mud of the Mobile River. And the crazy thing is that it was still working. They had to tell the skipper to get off. "Why? I got deliveries to make."

In parts of the South, people are still trying to defend the "traditional" Southern way of life. "Tradition" is a great way to keep stuff the same as it always was—i.e., racist. Segregation has been outlawed in the United States, but in some places in the South, racially segregated proms have been a "tradition" that's only recently been challenged. Mississippi fully integrated its schools in 1970, but some places still had "black proms" and "white proms." In 1997, Morgan Freeman offered to pay for a racially mixed prom in his hometown of Charleston, Mississippi, but it took until 2008 for it to happen. The same is true in places like Rochelle, Georgia, which had its first mixed prom in 2014.

The reason for these separate proms? "Tradition." So when do you decide to get rid of "traditions" like this? When do we get the full rights of American citizens?

Virtually every city that black people are doing well in is either in a blue state or the blue city of a red state. I think it's gonna stay that way. Even when it seems like a black politician is going to take charge, the old racist voter suppression machine kicks into high gear. If not for voter suppression, we'd have at least two black governors in the South: Stacey Abrams in Georgia and Andrew Gillum in Florida. In Georgia, Abrams's opponent was the secretary of state overseeing the election, a clear conflict of interest. He purged 670,000 voter registrations in the year before the election and another 53,000 right before. And in Florida, Gillum lost by fewer than 30,000 votes after a recount and a campaign where his opponent, Ron DeSantis, urged people not to "monkey up" the election by electing Gillum.

It's always hilarious to me how all these MAGA-hat-wearing red-state Republicans are always complaining about taxes, about "makers and takers," and about "draining the swamp," when they're the ones *getting* the tax money, *they're* the takers, and the swamp benefits them more than anybody.

Mississippi, Kentucky, West Virginia, Alabama, and South Carolina are all in the top ten states that depend the most on federal funds to support their government and residents. As far as "makers" go, Alabama, West Virginia, Arkansas, and Mississippi all have the lowest gross domestic product of the states, and yet Mississippi and West Virginia still get the highest amount of money in federal grants—pretty swampy!

I think America would be better off if we moved most of the black folks out of the South and let white people have it. Sell this shit back to white people and get a credit on our statement. We'll give you a discount and move some of you white folks from California and other nice spots to the South, your treasured homeland. We're handing it back to you, gently used. This land is your land, this land is made for you and you.

Reparations Article 5h. Reverse Louisiana Purchase

White people, having worked very hard to retain the South during the Civil War and having used voter suppression and other tactics to retain power, shall be given the South—just not all the good parts—to do with as they wish. No federal funds (handouts) nor voting powers beyond local control shall be retained, to make sure that the South can credibly claim the right to say they are self-sufficient. Let them build pride in their work, allow them the dignity of work.

In the South we'll establish a territory for white people. It might be a little swampy, a little humid, and I can't guarantee that you won't have problems with global warming. Let's hope your conservative leaders are right about it being a hoax.

Now, you might have some reservations about this plan, but hear me out. Excuse my choice of words. Come to think of it, that's a good name for this territory: a reservation. This'll give you the opportunity to help you prove your theories about states' rights and the value of local control. We won't be sending you federal dollars, because we know you hate handouts. This time we'll let you out of the Union with our blessing, without our free labor. Let's see if you can be self-sufficient. Will the South rise again? I'll wait and see.

FREEDOM, BUT NOT FREE

It's a shame that the most underused, the most undervalued part of the word "freedom" is "free."

Now that we've got the Southern states squared away, let's talk about the state of justice in America. Slavery is over, but we've basically gone from slavery to prisons. There's still no justice for us.

FREE LABOR

See, black people get a little sensitive about "free labor." When your ancestors were enslaved and then forced into labor under vagrancy laws, you tend to be *touchy* about being forced to work.

So during the 2019 government shutdown, predictably it was a white congressman who said, "Never in the history of this country has it been legal to make people work for free but that's what's happening to federal employees." Um, *there was this one time.*

Slavery was just swapped for the judicial system. Like

John Legend pointed out in his Oscar speech in 2015: "We live in the most incarcerated country in the world. There are more black men under correctional control today than there were under slavery in 1850." After slavery ended, black men were targeted by their former masters, arrested for vagrancy, loitering, and other concocted offenses. Once in custody, they were leased as laborers to farms and businesses. How wrong is that? But it ain't over. It's still happening.

Prisoners are used as cheap or free labor, making less than a dollar an hour to do work for corporations and the government. Major corporations like Victoria's Secret and Starbucks have used that labor. Hundreds of thousands of prisoners work making furniture, in call centers—even fighting fires.

Originally this prison labor was supposed to be rehabilitative—you learn a skill that you can apply when you get on the outside. Like a shittier DeVry. But a lot of these jobs aren't available to inmates after they leave. In California, prisoners are fighting wildfires for between $2.90 and $5.12 a day, putting their lives at risk. But when they come out after they got real-life experience, guess who they don't get to be? Firefighters.

Free black labor is part of an economic model. There's no incentive to stop it. People don't usually come out and say it like that, but sometimes they let an "oopsie" loose, like when the sheriff of Louisiana's Caddo Parish criticized a prison reform bill by saying, "They're releasing some good ones that we use every day to wash cars, to change oil in the cars, to cook in the kitchen, to do all that where we save money." So you're keeping people in jail because you need people to wash your cars or cook in your kitchen? What would you do without the prisoners? I don't know. Hire people?

Can't hire people? Listen, I'm not against interns. Maybe work for college credit or something.

And it's not enough that your labor's being exploited; in forty-nine states, they also bill you for prison. In Florida, they can charge you fifty dollars a day, payable upon your release. After one former inmate, Jeremy Barrett, was assaulted in prison, he sued the Florida Department of Corrections for negligence, only to get a counterclaim of $54,750. In some parts of the country, you can be charged all sorts of fees: for incarceration, DNA tests, use of a public defender, court costs, and more. It's to always keep you chained to the system.

HIGH CRIMES

A lot of black men are in prison just for selling weed. And we know now that this is a failed policy because eleven states and D.C. have already legalized it. Between 2001 and 2010, there were 8.2 million arrests for marijuana. And even though blacks and whites use weed at about the same rate, blacks are four times more likely to be arrested for it. All of these useless arrests and all of these wasted lives.

And while black dudes are in prison, white dudes like Kevin Murphy, the CEO of the marijuana company Acreage Holdings, get rich. In the first quarter of 2019, Acreage reported revenue of $12.9 million. From Kevin Murphy's bio:

> Prior to his role at Acreage Holdings, Kevin was most recently a Founding Member and Managing Partner of Tandem Global Partners, a boutique investment firm focused on the emerging markets. Previously, he was Managing Partner at Stanfield Capital Partners, where he served as a member of the Operating and Management team that oversaw all aspects of Stanfield's business, including risk management, sales and distribution, client services, legal, compliance and operations.

You know, he learned his trade on the mean streets of Tandem Global Partners. Normally, when a drug dealer talks about "risk management" and "sales and distribution," they're being euphemistic for taking out their enemies and slinging dope—but this guy really means risk management and sales and distribution.

Every single member of Acreage's executive team and board of directors is a white dude. Oh, sorry, all except Larissa Herda, who is a white lady. The drug trade can attract some rough characters, but this has gotta be the first crew to include a former prime minister of Canada (Brian Mulroney), a Republican presidential candidate (William F. Weld), and former Republican Speaker of the House John Boehner.

This is a newly chilled-out Boehner we got here. Back when he was opposing everything Obama tried to do, he didn't seem that into weed. He still doesn't see how his previous leadership in the Republican House helped to put black people in prison. "I don't have any regrets at all," Boehner said recently. "I was opposed to the use of it. The whole criminal justice part of this, frankly, it never crossed my mind."

Overall, decriminalization is good, but I don't think it's enough. I think that you should also give convicts jobs.

Because who knows the weed business better than them? Right? You know how there are certain business schools that the headhunters come and scout you from? Prison should be like that. Why are you going to hire a bunch of white guys for a weed business? Take a look at some of our prisoners: they've already shown proficiency. Prison should be like Wharton for weed.

Reparations Article 51. Weed Wharton

Upon ratification of this treaty, marijuana companies (weed businesses, marijuana holding companies, etc.) shall recruit their executives exclusively from the ranks of those incarcerated for doing an excellent job selling weed previously. This shall be the primary consideration for employment, not being in a hedge fund, investment partnership, management trust, or any other bullshit.

And meanwhile, look at what happens when you have white people like the Sackler family in charge of drug distribution: you get the opioid crisis. So we know that white people in charge of drugs does not work.

WE WANT A JURY OF *OUR* PEERS

White and black people are treated differently by the justice system. Justice is not color blind. Policing is different, sentencing is different, everything's different. But even if cops and prosecutors are biased, juries are supposed to be the people who decide. So here's the thing, because it's really not that complicated: When we have a trial by a jury of our peers, they should actually be our peers. There have to be black people on the jury.

Of course, I'm not saying I want y'all to call me up for jury duty. Last time I got called up, they asked me what justice looked like and I said, "Unfamiliar." They all laughed and then I was off the jury. I can't stop being funny just to help out the justice system, come on now.

When you want to frame up a black guy, you work hard to not have any black people on the jury. In Mississippi, Curtis Flowers, a black man, has been put on trial *six times* for the same crime by the same white prosecutor for a murder in 1996. He's been kept in prison for twenty-two years without a fair conviction.

Theoretically, you're allowed to exclude potential jurors for all sorts of reasons, as long as it's not based on race, sex, or ethnicity. Of course, these "peremptory challenges" are still about race, but the lawyers come up with some other bullshit reason to say why they are striking someone from the jury.

Doug Evans, the prosecutor on this case, has quite a track record:

In the first trial, in 1997, he struck all five black prospective jurors, and then an all-white jury convicted Curtis Flowers and gave him a death sentence. That first trial was overturned because of prosecutorial misconduct.

Nearly the same thing happened at the second trial: Doug Evans tried to strike all the black jurors, but he was only allowed to strike four of the five. So eleven white jurors and one black juror convicted again and again sentenced Curtis to death. Again, the Mississippi Supreme Court reversed it because of prosecutorial misconduct.

It happened again in the third trial! Only one black juror, a conviction, and then the Mississippi Supreme Court overturning the verdict, this time specifically for eliminating jurors based on race.

Fuck, do I have to list the rest of these trials? At the fourth trial, Evans struck as many black jurors as he could, but still had seven white and five black jurors. This jury deadlocked, black versus white, and a mistrial was declared.

The fifth trial also deadlocked, with nine white and three black people.

In the sixth trial, he got a jury of eleven white people and one black person. He did this by asking the black prospective jurors an average of twenty-nine questions each. The white jurors got one question each. This trial led to conviction. In the six trials, sixty-one of the seventy-two jurors were white.

In June 2019, the U.S. Supreme Court ruled that Doug Evans had violated the Constitution. Only two of the justices dissented: Neil Gorsuch and Clarence Thomas, proving once again that he's the worst. Clarence Thomas wrote: "If the court's opinion today has a redeeming quality, it is this: The State is perfectly free to convict Curtis Flowers again."

Curtis was just freed on bail. We'll have to see if Doug Evans tries to convict him again.

When you have black people on a jury, you can even convict cops. It's amazing. Nobody disputes the relevant facts of the Botham Jean murder. Amber Guyger, a white Dallas police officer, shot Botham Jean in his own apartment. She claimed that she was confused and thought she was entering her apartment. Most of the time, juries love to take cops at their word, even if their word makes no sense.

But justice looks different when there are people of color

in the jury box. Juries with black folks have empathy and offer different perspectives than juries without them. In Amber Guyger's trial, there were seven black jurors or alternates, five nonblack people of color, and only four white people. That mix is incredibly rare. In Texas, blacks are only 12 percent of the population, so finding seven black people to serve on a jury doesn't happen a lot.

This jury convicted her of murder and sentenced her to ten years in prison. Ten years for murder is a pretty good deal, especially when you consider the average murderer in America serves seven years. Then again, the average murdered person serves a lifetime.

In one way, I was surprised about the verdict, because usually when white women cry, it has a devastating effect on society. A blond white woman crying is more than people can usually bear. But then I wasn't surprised when I saw who was on the jury, because if there's one group of people who are impervious to white women's tears, it's black women. They're like, "Bitch, come on. Stop with that bullshit."

THE FIGHT FOR CUSTODY

White people: Admit that you don't know how the police treat people different than you. If you're going to put your "Blue Lives Matter" bumper sticker on your car, at least look at the facts about how police act toward black folks. Does it seem like they think black lives matter?

How do you explain how the cops killed Botham Jean, Atatiana Jefferson, and Stephon Clark because they thought they had guns, but took Dylann Roof, Gregory Bush, and Patrick Crusius into custody alive?

Ain't it weird how cops take you alive when they *know* you have a gun, but shoot you dead when they *think* you do? What can explain it?

That's basically how you can tell when the media is talking about a white person. When they say "apprehended" or "in custody," it ain't us.

So, for the purposes of the treaty, we're asking to be taken into custody. We're not saying that black people will never do anything wrong. We're just saying when we do, take us into custody. Don't shoot us.

Reparations Article 5j. Take Us into Custody

Although black people shall endeavor to be blameless in all respects, on the occasion of a dispute wherein the police or other law enforcement shall be called to mediate, we require an expansion of our options. No longer shall police shoot first, having been "scared" or having "perceived a threat." Police shall be required to treat white and black suspects the same, with the option to "apprehend" or "take into custody."

Shootings show what people value. I think it's interesting that right after Dylann Roof murdered nine people in an African American Charleston church, Cecil the lion was also killed. Remember Cecil? He was shot in Zimbabwe by a white dentist out on a trophy hunt. One of those shootings caused people all around the country and the world to send money; Jimmy Kimmel raised $150,000 in donations in less than twenty-four hours. One of those killings caused so much grief that people advocated and made sure that the shooting would never happen again. Not one other lion from that pride has been hunted. Not one other.

So you tell me: What do white people value?

BLACK LIVES MATTER, BUT NOT AS MUCH

Again and again, you prove that black lives don't matter. BLM activism has really irritated white people. It's so in-your-face, so aggressive. Why can't it be more convenient?

You like driving on highways? Sure you do! You got

places to be. I know you don't want some Black Lives Matters activists shutting down the highway when you're trying to get to Target.

And when you watch the big game, do you want more commentary on offensive plays or offensive knee-taking players?

Let me ask you: What's the most convenient protest you've encountered? What's the most memorable *convenient* protest you can think of? Exactly. They're supposed to be inconvenient. The Boston Tea Party was pretty fucked up for the British. I mean, I'm just saying they needed that tea, right? Nobody was like, "Oh, that's okay, I didn't need my teatime today." No. I'm sure people were like, "Where's my fucking tea?" They didn't hold a Boston Baked Beans Party because people would be like, "Eh, I got plenty of beans." But I digress.

This taking-a-knee thing has really gotten to you. Why? Colin Kaepernick is more upsetting than Robert Kraft? Robert Kraft got busted soliciting prostitutes during a sex slavery and human trafficking investigation. So apparently a black man on one knee is too much, but a ho on two is all right.

The point is, we've been trying to get your attention. And the only time white people ever listen to black people is when they're singing, dancing, or running a ball. But what if I promised you that we'd stop all these protests?

The Black Lives Matter movement started to protest police shootings, racism, and white supremacy within the ranks of law enforcement. I hope I don't have to go through all the examples of cops shooting black people for no reason. Didn't you all buy my other book? Come on. It's in paperback now; don't be cheap.

KKKOPS

The Blue Lives Matter crowd wants to pretend that racist cops are hard to find. But there's a million examples of racist behavior from law enforcement when they don't think anyone is listening. Behind closed doors, at home and in private chat rooms and Facebook groups, the thin blue line show their true colors.

Recently a couple was house shopping in Muskegon, Michigan, and they looked at a cop's house, a two-bedroom, one-bath ranch-style. When the couple, both people of color, toured the house with their kids and a Realtor, they came across numerous Confederate flags. They tried to ignore those, because you know—you probably won't keep those if you buy the place. A little paint and wallpaper, maybe. But then they saw the framed KKK application on the wall amid police paraphernalia. So they reported it to the city and the cop was suspended. Now—big surprise—this same cop killed a black man in 2009 "in self-defense." At the time he was cleared of any wrongdoing.

After it was reported, the Muskegon city government opened an investigation into the 2009 shooting as well as other incidents. So it takes the Property Brothers to get people to look into police shootings.

My real estate broker told me to put my family photos away, and this guy thought it was okay to have his KKK shit out? I mean, you gotta really think the Klan's okay if you're gonna let people see it on your house tour. That's some next-level racist shit. All you gotta do is watch a little HGTV to know that you don't stage your house for sale with KKK memorabilia. That's House-Selling 101. Put out some fresh-baked cookies, repaint a bit, and clear out the clutter. Replace that old couch. Maybe buy a new slipcover, or better yet just use one of your robes.

Even when they aren't KKK-Kard Karrying members, too many police and law enforcement officers are at least KKK-Kurious. They may not be members of white nationalist groups, but they agree with them. When's the last time a white nationalist did something and you saw policemen outraged? Yet you've seen them have to be restrained because a black motorist asked them what they'd been pulled over for. Have you ever seen them having to be restrained that way after a guy just slaughtered twenty people?

The way I see it, there's a symbiotic relationship between white supremacists and law enforcement. They have some of the same interests and the same views—i.e., protecting the powers that be. They're cozy. It's not hard to imagine that a lot of police officers have more in common with white nationalists than with a black dude who lives in the city, right?

And when we get a peek at their private conversations, that's borne out. In 2016, San Francisco PD officers got caught texting each other racist messages. One text message featured the image of a badly burned turkey and the words "Is that a Ferguson turkey?" One of those cops went on to rob a couple of banks, so you know he might have also had money problems.

In Philadelphia, seventy-two officers were reassigned after a reporting database, the Plain View Project, published some of their racist posts. The same project published a post from a Phoenix officer: "It's a good day for a chokehold." More than fifty police departments opened investigations of officers after Reveal from the Center for Investigative Reporting reported on racist, Islamophobic, and violent posts.

When Eric Garner was choked to death by an officer for selling "loosies," the officers on the scene texted their commander that "He's most likely DOA." The commander's reply? "Not a big deal."

When that detail was read aloud at a police disciplinary hearing for Officer Daniel Pantaleo, there was an audible gasp in the courtroom. And I don't think that gasp was from shock. I think that gasp was from realizing, "Oh shit, they have our text messages!" *Can they do that?*

And it's not just police. A Facebook group for Border Protection agents was found to be full of racist memes and violent imagery. The chief of Customs and Border Protection was herself a member of the group.

But do police departments really have a white supremacy problem? The FBI thought so. The FBI investigated the infiltration of police departments by white supremacy groups and issued a report in 2006, finding that "white supremacist leaders and groups have historically shown an interest in infiltrating law enforcement communities or recruiting law enforcement personnel." And again in 2015, the FBI reported that "domestic terrorism investigations focused on militia extremists, white supremacist extremists, and sovereign citizen extremists often have identified active links to law enforcement officers."

Despite this report, nobody's done much to address this threat.

And even though the presence of white supremacists in law enforcement has been exposed as being very active in the Trump era, the FBI has instead focused its sights on different threats: "Black Identity Extremists," basically a made-up idea.

As detailed in an FBI Intelligence Assessment Report, "The FBI assesses it is very likely Black Identity Extremist (BIE) perceptions of police brutality against African Americans spurred an increase in premeditated, retaliatory lethal violence against law enforcement and will very likely serve as justification for such violence." This came out around the same time that white supremacists were gathering in Charlottesville. And the FBI's 2018–19 "Threat Guidance" documents describe BIEs as those who "use force or violence in violation of criminal law in response to perceived racism and injustice in American society." These BIEs were perceived to be a major threat, higher than Al Qaeda or white supremacists.

So it's black extremists, then Al Qaeda, then white supremacists? I guess dudes in dashikis are scarier than dudes with torches? It's a weird world.

By 2019, the FBI decided to scrap the term "Black Identity Extremist" and fold it into a "Racially Motivated Extremism" category that includes both "White Racially Motivated Extremism, previously referred to as White Supremacy Extremism, and Black Racially Motivated Extremism, previously referred to as Black Identity Extremism." But here we go again, pretending that the threat from white supremacists must also have a black counterpart, when in reality there is no organized "Black Identity Extremist" movement. The few isolated examples of violence against cops don't make it a movement.

Inconvenient protests against police brutality don't constitute a "War on Cops." Protests *against* racism aren't a racist movement for *black* supremacy. That's more "both sides are to blame" nonsense.

This is another example of where helping us helps you. You don't want the FBI wasting money and resources on made-up threats. You want them to be stopping the next mass shooter, not the guys at the drum circle in the park.

All we're asking is, how is it okay for cops to say shit on Facebook that would get you fired anywhere? If you worked at White Castle and said, "Fuck the niggers," you'd at least be put on fry duty. Where's the HR department at the PD? And you don't get to carry a gun at White Castle, though too many sliders can be deadly.

In fact, that's a good way to judge it. I have more faith in the White Castle HR department than the police department. So we're gonna let White Castle decide. We'll call it the White Castle Doctrine. We'll run whatever you say by White Castle HR and see if they have a problem with it. "Go back to Africa," or "Why are we having all these people from shithole countries come here?"—we'll just check with WC HR, and if they say it's fine, then we're cool.

Reparations Article 5k. The White Castle Doctrine

Due to the historic infiltration of law enforcement by racists and white supremacists, and in consideration of the fact that White Castle serves up food without calling anyone the N-word, we now require personnel decisions to be made by the White Castle human resources department, until such a time as racists are rooted out of the police, border security, and so on. In the event of a dispute, White Castle HR can ask Taco Bell HR to arbitrate.

Once the last racist is purged from the PD, we'll stop making a fuss. You can watch the football players smash each other without ever having to think about violence. The only kneeling will be by the cooler in the parking lot. And you can enjoy your highways without any protesters getting in the way, as long as Trump passes that big infrastructure plan, that is.

In the meantime, how can we give the benefit of the doubt to police forces that harass us, lie to us, turn off their body cameras, text each other racist things, and then say they "felt threatened"? If feeling threatened were a reason you could kill someone, y'all'd be dead already.

We're supposed to believe Amber Guyger had no bias, and yet she'd been texting racist things to her boyfriend, a cop she was having an affair with, who had killed an unarmed black person in 2008?

In Fort Worth, the officer shot Atatiana Jefferson through the window after cops had been creeping around in her backyard without announcing themselves, but white people treat that like it's an aberration instead of a point on a continuum. Look at it in context. A year before, a black woman was with her kid and the kid dropped a raisin on the ground, and some white guy living there came and knocked her son over. When the cops arrived, they took the assailant's side, saying, "Why don't you teach him not to litter?" What explains an attitude like that, except bias?

A white woman at a Fort Worth city council meeting after the shooting told everyone about how the cops had been skulking around in her backyard on a different call. And all she was worried about was that they might hurt her dog. That's white privilege. That's the difference between worrying about your dog and worrying about your life.

The police are different in your neighborhoods. I can always tell how dark the neighborhood is by how long it takes the police to get there. Police precincts generally pride themselves on their response time, but in black neighborhoods there's no rush. And generally, in our neighborhoods, they're not coming to stop shit or arrest anybody. They're coming just to draw chalk or put up the yellow tape, so it doesn't really require a rapid response.

And any black person who calls the police knows that 911 is hairy. They know it's a dangerous situation—they need help, but they might not like the "help" they get. Black people who need help know that there's a certain protocol we have to have. So Atatiana Jefferson's neighbor, who was worried about her door being open, called a nonemergency line for a wellness check. The cops never identified themselves, walked right past the door and into the backyard. When Jefferson came to the window, one of the officers yelled, "Show me your hands!" and shot her in four seconds.

STAY PUT

Botham Jean got shot because Officer Amber Guyger went into *his* apartment. Atatiana Jefferson got shot because Officer Aaron Dean was creeping around *her* backyard. And it's always the same argument: they shot because they were *afraid*. How does the same excuse work for Eric Garner as works for Botham Jean? How does the same excuse work for Michael Brown and Atatiana Jefferson?

Because when you're black or brown, they don't just kill you. They kill your reputation. So you die more than one time. You know the old expression "a coward dies a thousand deaths"? So does a black man. They kill him, then they kill who he was, his reputation, the idea of him, his life's work.

How is it possible for *us* to die when white people are in the wrong place? It used to be we'd get killed when we were in the wrong place. Now, we get killed when white people are.

White people need to stop traveling so fucking much. When white people get lost and kill people of color, they get a holiday, like Columbus. White people in the wrong place cost black and brown people their lives, and always have.

Why don't you slow down? Settle down somewhere. Horace Greeley said, "Go west, young man." You've gone far enough! Plant some roots. Stay put.

Whenever Trump is accused by somebody of something, the first thing that he does is see what their affiliations are. "Oh, they voted for Hillary," or "They're part of the Deep State," or "They're a Democrat." As if someone who's not like him or who dislikes him must be unbiased. And his base buys it. He's convinced people that others lack the impartiality to be fair based on who they vote for or what they believe or who they like and dislike.

So I agree with him for once. I agree that it is impossible for somebody who doesn't like you to be fair. I agree. The problem is that the real Deep State is the deep state of racism in the police departments in America. One man's rogue cop is another man's Robert Mueller.

But I think racists gotta eat too, right? I think you can be a racist cop. I just don't think you should ever be a racist cop in our neighborhoods. Like, if you're a racist in your neighborhoods but don't ever leave there, I don't care. But don't come on over into anywhere black people live or work.

So I think racist cops should have a monitoring bracelet. You know, maybe an ankle bracelet that alerts black people if you go past the perimeter. That way you get to keep your job and you don't get sacked. It's like those dogs with invisible fences: you see them bark and bark, but they never cross the line, or they get a little shock. Racist cops get a little charge and that way black people don't get falsely charged.

Because we can't root out all the racist cops. What we can do is stop them from shitting in other people's yards.

Look at it this way: Wherever you white folks go, you get fucking scared. You overreact. Stay at home! You know how when there's an active shooter incident they tell you to "shelter in place"? Well, we're asking you to "shelter in place" so you don't become an active shooter of us.

You've got nice houses; you live in nice neighborhoods. Enjoy those homes you paid for. Stay in tonight. "Netflix and chill" means no niggas die.

Reparations Article 51. Stay Put

Whenever white people wander around, black and brown people die. Now that there are multiple streaming platforms, there's no need to go out quite so much. Stay home, enjoy a night in so that we may also enjoy a night in or out. White people, especially cops, are hereby ordered to stay in and binge-watch some of the new offerings on Apple TV+ or Hulu before they start going around exploring, and possibly killing.

WE ARE PART OF AMERICA

We're not going anywhere. As such, we demand full access to America, with full rights and privileges thereof.

WE'RE PART OF AMERICA

Come to think of it, white people wandering all over has been a particular problem for black people since the beginning. White people brought us here to America in 1619, and yet you still treat us like we aren't a real part of America.

GO BACK TO WHERE YOU CAME FROM

Anytime a person of color raises an objection about this country, white people say, "Go back where you came from. Go back to Africa." But everybody knows you can't return stolen goods.

YOUR TIRED, YOUR POOR NEED NOT APPLY

The American Dream used to mean the opportunity to build yourself up from nothing into *something*. That was the promise and that's the story so many white conservatives like to tell themselves about their own families: *My ancestor came over with a nickel in his pocket and built himself into something*.

But now, white people are trying to close the door. And even people here *legally* are having their status revoked because of the discriminatory, white-supremacist policies of the Trump administration. One such rule takes away green cards or visas if Immigration Services feels a legal immigrant is likely to use government benefits.

Ken Cuccinelli, the acting director of U.S. Citizenship and Immigration Services, defended this change. He was asked how to reconcile this with the poem on the Statue of Liberty, "The New Colossus," which says, "Give me your tired, your poor, your huddled masses yearning to breathe free." He restated it as "Give me your tired and your poor who can stand on their own two feet and who will not become a public charge." You don't get to rewrite history like that—the poem says:

> "Keep, ancient lands, your storied pomp!" cries she
> With silent lips. "Give me your tired, your poor,
> Your huddled masses yearning to breathe free,
> The wretched refuse of your teeming shore.
> Send these, the homeless, tempest-tost to me,
> I lift my lamp beside the golden door!"

If you're poor, you're not standing on your own two feet. If you're "wretched refuse," you might need some help. If you're homeless and "tempest-tost," you might need a housing voucher. That's the promise of America: You can start from nothing and become something. Not start from something and become something.

And because this guy can't leave well enough alone, he claimed that the "wretched refuse" was referring to "people coming from Europe." Well, that's interesting, because the Statue of Liberty was actually a gift from France to celebrate the abolition of slavery. As a matter of fact, the original designs had her holding broken shackles in her left hand. In the final version, she has broken chains at her feet. When's the last time white people needed to break chains? I mean, *Cool Hand Luke* was the last time white people had chains on. "*I'm shaking that bush, boss! I'm shakin' it!*" That was the last time.

So that's another thing we want: Be honest about history. You can't rewrite history, just like you can't rewrite "The New Colossus." According to Cuccinelli and people like him, his family has an incredible, noble story of how they came to this country that's *totally different* from the stories of the black and brown immigrants coming over now. It's always this great tale about how their grandfather came over here with nothing to his name and pulled himself up by his bootstraps. I always feel like it's the same dude, because it's always the same story. It's like they all had the same grandfather. *He didn't speak a word of English, he had a single nickel in his pocket, and he opened up a salami shop.* It's the same story! Either they're lying or they've got the same grandfather.

Anyway, the point is that people coming here *now* with nothing aren't any different from people who came over *then* with nothing. The restrictions people like Cuccinelli are trying to put in place *now* would have excluded his own relatives *then*. Southern Italians without any money or education like Cuccinelli's great-grandparents were just the kind of parasites that people would have gladly sent home at the time. Ken's great-grandfather came through Ellis Island with $8.75 in 1901. He worked as a laborer and by 1905 was supporting a family of six. Ken's great-grandmother came through Ellis Island in 1903 and was detained there as an "L.P.C.": "Likely Public Charge." She was literally labeled as a likely public charge, just like the "public charges" Ken Cuccinelli hopes to ban *right now*.

Nobody ever tells a white person to go back to where they came from. "Go back to Canada. Go back to Ireland. Go back to Italy." It doesn't happen. We have to be able to call things racist when they are. Not everything, but certain things we all agree are racist, like when Donald Trump said, "Go back where you came from." Why don't you go back to Germany? Or was it Sweden, like he said in *The Art of the Deal*? That's where Donald used to say his grandfather Frederick, originally Friedrich, was from. Huh. And why would Trump's father, Fred Trump, not own up to that? Why would a guy want to say his family was from Sweden, not Germany, when he was trying to sell real estate to Jews in New York?

Weirdly, Friedrich Trump *did* try to "go back where he came from" a couple of times. Germany wouldn't take him back because they thought he had tried to avoid military service by moving to America. Friedrich wanted to return, saying, "We are loyal Germans and stand behind the high Kaiser and the mighty German Reich." But the Germans wouldn't restore his citizenship. Donald's father, Fred, might have grown up in Germany instead of in Queens, if only Germany hadn't been so picky. Can you blame them?

So it takes some fucking nerve to tell black people to "go back to where they came from" when their families have been here a lot longer than Trump's. Black people loved America when America didn't love us.

The reason white people now have a problem with America is because it looks different than they thought it did. They're just now really getting to know America, and they don't like her. We've always known her.

WE'RE NOT REALLY PART OF AMERICA

Right now, we're not really part of America. We've got a holiday and some streets named after Martin Luther King Jr. That's it. They ran out of famous white people to name shit after, so they started in on unknown white dudes. I went to Robert E. Peary High. Nobody knew who the fuck he was. It turns out that his claim to fame is that he *almost* made it to the North Pole. He gets a school before a black dude who actually *did* something? (Or how about at least showing love to Peary's African American partner on the North Pole expedition, Matthew Henson?)

And all the schools and buildings and parks are named after white people who didn't like us. All over America, we go to schools named after people who hated us and barbecue in parks with statues of people who hated us. Why do we still have to deal with it? How many elementary schools are named for black people? How many high schools? We want to share America.

Even in the 2020 primaries, the Democrats ignored black people until we showed up in South Carolina and made them listen. Black people did not get their say until the nearly all-white voters of Iowa and New Hampshire had set the narrative. But South Carolina is basically Black Iowa. And black people said: We don't want Bernie Sanders, we want Joe Biden. We want the guy we know, who had our dude's back.

We want our share. We're not visitors. We're ingrained in America. White people do as little as they can to make us feel really a part of America. We've been here four hundred years. We have been here longer than the people telling us to go back.

FASHION VICTIMS

Here's what happens when you don't include black people: you get fuckups like Gucci putting out an $800 turtleneck sweater with blackface-style lips on it, then Katy Perry putting out shoes with big red Sambo-style lips, only a few months after Prada attached little golliwog-style dolls to its bags.

When Burberry sends a model down the runway with a noose around her neck, it doesn't mean that the KKK has an inside man with fashion sense. I mean, take one look at the Charlottesville dudes in their Trump khakis and polo shirts and you know there's no fashion sense in white supremacy. So I don't think the people at Burberry or Prada are inherently racist, I just think no black people are in the fucking room to say, "Hey, that's a bad idea."

Burberry defended itself by saying the rope was part of a nautical theme, and okay, sure, if you had a bowline or a clove hitch on a model, maybe that's fine. Bowlines are as nautical as a motherfucking sailor's cap. But you wouldn't look at that noose and think, *Oh, sure, it's just some Jacques Cousteau shit.* An upside-down loop hanging around someone's neck? That's a noose. And a noose is a no-no knot. A knot-knot no? You know what I mean.

Whenever white people get together in private, it's never good for black people. I don't care if it's a jury, I don't care if it's an Oscar nomination. Whenever white people get to close a curtain, it never goes good for anybody. The best thing would be to make sure that there are people of color in the room. That's the main thing. But until that time, we've gotta get rid of America's curtains.

Reparations Article 6a. It's Curtains for Curtains

White people can have sheer curtains only. Full transparency means full transparency. Maybe you can have those beaded curtains. But no drapes. Venetian blinds are okay, as long as they are partway open. You can use shutters the same way, because we know you all love those. Wiping out prejudice and bias will take time, and until then we want to keep an eye on you all. Justice is blind. Justice has blinds.

Fashion's always pushing the edge, but it shouldn't take 50 Cent burning his Gucci to get people to put some black folks in the room. And still, the fashion people fucked up. Chanel's first head of diversity is Fiona Pargeter, a white woman. Why the hell would you hire a white woman to be the head of diversity?

And maybe you can chalk up some of this to the fact that some of these brands are Italian or French and don't totally understand the nuances of racist imagery in America. But still, you're gonna let some old Italian guy decide what is okay to put out in America?

A lot of these brands don't really advertise as much as they rely on dope black celebrities to wear their clothes, showcasing them on TV, Instagram, and so on. Gucci ain't Aflac; they don't do commercials. What they do is LeBron. And still a lot of black people can't afford the things they see, so they go to get the closest approximation: it ain't Prada, but it's Zara. Regardless, I think that the fashion industry should give us black people a discount for acting as models and for making even cheap knockoffs look dope. So, since black people were considered three-fifths human, we should only have to pay three-fifths the price. That's like $2,000 Prada or $12.50 Zara. You're welcome.

Racist imagery isn't something we made up. It's baked into the bread in America. Aunt Jemima traded her "mammy" bandanna for a headband in 1968 and got a perm in the '80s, but she's still an old stereotype. Uncle Ben and "Rastus," the Cream of Wheat chef, are still on boxes at the supermarket, even if you can't buy Darkie toothpaste anymore. Why do black people still gotta look at the same motherfucker who said, "Maybe Cream of Wheat ain't got no vitamines. I don't know what them things is. If they's bugs they aint none in Cream of Wheat." I'm just waking up; I don't need to think about this shit so early.

So, okay, you still want to eat fucking pancakes, right? Fine. But we gotta set some rules. No more bullshit.

FIT THE BILL

So we can be a cook in the kitchen, but there's not one single black person on money.

Just before Obama left office, they were going to put Harriet Tubman on the twenty-dollar bill, replacing Andrew Jackson. Then it was announced that she'd be put on the back, but Andrew Jackson would stay on the front. It was too much to get rid of Andrew Jackson. Never mind how weird it is that a woman who helped hundreds of people escape slavery would be sharing a bill with a man who owned hundreds of slaves. I've shared some weird bills while touring on the road, but damn.

A slave on one side, a slave owner on the other. So even

when black people make it to money, we've still got a supervisor. *All right, Harriet, break's over. Time to get back to work.*

Predictably, the Trump administration "delayed" her twenty-dollar bill until at least 2026, after Trump is out of office. Or maybe never. Trump loves Jackson: "Andrew Jackson had a great history, and I think it's very rough when you take somebody off the bill." Rednecks don't want a black woman on their money.

But we're part of America, so we want more split bills.

- **ONE-DOLLAR BILL:** George Washington / George Washington Carver
- **FIVE-DOLLAR BILL:** Abe Lincoln / maybe no one; it feels rude to have someone come up behind Abe, given his history.
- **TEN-DOLLAR BILL:** Alexander Hamilton / Lin-Manuel Miranda

And Harriet gets her own bill.

IMAGINARY PEOPLE CAN BE BLACK

I always say that the most dangerous place for black people to live is in white people's imaginations. But damn, we're not even *allowed* to live in white people's imaginations.

Disney announced that Halle Bailey was gonna be Ariel

in a new live-action remake of *The Little Mermaid,* and of course everybody got mad because *how could the Little Mermaid be black?* Which is weird because she's an imaginary character. She's not real, there was no real Ariel. It's imaginary. You can't even let us be an imaginary character? Black people didn't get mad when they made that crab Jamaican. That shit is not real.

Or Santa. Kids, close your eyes—don't read this next part . . . We good?

Santa is not *real.* There is no Santa. But tell that to the people who got all agitated over the Mall of America having a black Santa in 2016. What is it about a black Santa that freaks you out? Yeah, normally he looks like a white guy, but we can't have *any* black Santas? You don't think a black dude can have a little round belly that shakes like a bowlful of jelly? Al Roker slimmed down, but I still know some heavy dudes. You don't need to see white skin to know it's Santa. If you see *any* guy in a red suit, you're probably looking at a Santa. It's not hard to figure it out. As the Mall of America's Santa Larry himself said, "It's no big deal, I'm still Santa, I just happen to be a Santa of Color." No big deal, but then again, a black Santa's gonna have to be a lot more careful breaking into people's houses with a sack of gifts.

Or 007—*Bond, James Bond*—is not real. Idris Elba would

be a kickass Bond, a natural choice. But some people can't handle a black Bond. The writer of the newest Bond novel said Idris Elba is "too street" to be Bond. A black dude in a dope car? That's our brand. You believe that Bond can shoot a rocket out of a boom box or have X-ray sunglasses, but being a black guy is too incredible? In *Goldfinger,* Bond put a duck on his head so he could swim into an enemy base. And yet a duck hat is more believable than a black Bond.

And you know, it's fucked up that you want to keep imaginary characters white when you've already made black imaginary characters white, like Jesus.

Reparations Article 6b. Invisible Men

Henceforth there shall be inclusion and diversity in the realm of the imaginary, the made-up, and the fantastical. There are real black people and there shall thus be unreal black people. The world of make-believe, science fiction, fantasy, and any other genre of fancy, reverie, or invention shall be open to black imaginary people. This shall include but not be limited to imaginary friends, fictional characters, spies, phantoms, and ghosts.

DON'T WRITE US OUT OF THE FUTURE

Unlike a lot of white people who blame brown people, I know that it's robots that are taking white people's jobs.

Robots and computers can do almost anything that a person can do, only quicker and with less complaining. Lucky for me, robots are horrible at telling jokes: *Why was the robot mad? Because people kept pushing his buttons.* See? That shit is terrible. I ain't worried until they get down comedy's *nuts and bolts.* But I digress.

Robots aren't going anywhere, so we gotta make sure they're programmed right, because people's biases are being built into technology. Y'all shut us out of the past; we gotta make sure we're not written out of the future. It's bad enough dealing with racist people, but robots? I just saw *Child's Play 2* and that serial killer dude input his personality into that Chucky doll, and before you know it, he's beating some teacher to death with a yardstick. Robots could be even worse.

Maybe you've seen the viral videos of "racist automatic soap dispensers" that dish out soap to white hands but not black or brown hands? The sensor on the dispensers isn't detecting the light bouncing off of black skin, so *NO SOAP FOR YOU.* I usually have to wait for a white guy to start washing his hands and then I'll stick my hands under. Used to be you'd have a black bathroom attendant to hand you a towel, but now we need a white guy just to get the soap started.

Now, nobody's gonna die from not washing their hands. Oh shit, actually . . . Personally, I'm not worried about the coronavirus because there's never been an epidemic so bad that everyone was okay with a bunch of niggas wearing masks. If it gets to that point, they will find a cure. But the people who programmed this thing: probably not a bunch of black dudes. That's 'cause there aren't that many black people working in tech. In 2018, Facebook was only 3 percent black, Google only 2 percent. That's typical and it causes errors like this.

And the same thing happens with facial recognition cameras: a study by MIT and Stanford found an error rate of less than 1 percent for light-skinned men and almost 35 percent for dark-skinned women. Because we all look alike? According to the robots, yes. That discrepancy affects all sorts of systems, from security cameras to image-sorting applications. In Brooklyn, a facial recognition program was introduced in a housing complex to use instead of keys. A robot that doesn't recognize you can lock you out of your home: "Open the doors, HAL." *I'm sorry, Dave. I'm afraid I can't do that.*

And in Detroit, real-time police cameras have been installed at two public housing projects. Isn't it weird that they put these cameras in black communities first? These systems are getting rolled out everywhere, but if the bias is built into them from the start, it's just another way for police to target people of color. Misidentified people end up in a system that can be checked by the police, searched, and scanned for people who "fit the description."

I don't trust the police and I don't trust robocops. People are getting arrested on the basis of facial recognition matching alone. In one example, the NYPD ran a picture of Woody Harrelson through a program after a victim said a suspect looked like him. "This celebrity 'match' was sent back to the investigating officers, and someone who was not Woody Harrelson was eventually arrested for petit larceny," the report said. Granted, Woody Harrelson is sketchy-looking as hell. But I don't want the cops using my headshot in a lineup. *Yes, officer, he looked just like my favorite comedian, D.L. Hughley.*

And once you get arrested, your sentence might get determined by an algorithm that's programmed against you.

ProPublica did a study of risk assessment programs that are used by judges to determine sentencing. In their study of these risk scores in Broward County, Florida, they found that the formula was likely to flag black defendants as "likely to repeat offend" at a much higher rate than white defendants. And it underestimated risk scores for white defendants. These sorts of biased systems are used all over the country, and nobody's accountable for their results or their accuracy—except the black people who get put in prison because of them. I didn't know *Minority Report* was just about reporting minorities.

It ain't all bad news for black people, though. Apparently, pretty soon you can have Samuel L. Jackson be the voice for your Alexa. Look how far we've come, right? Now we got black robots! But do you know how many people are gonna call the police when they hear "This nigga wants to play the Rolling Stones"—*Wait, wait it's just my Alexa, don't shoot!*

We've gone from whipping black people when they speak to making them our robot voices in a few generations. So it's great that Sam Jackson's the voice of Alexa, but that's not enough progress.

CONCLUSION

So that's really it. I know some past treaties you all have signed have gone bad, like:

1778—Treaty with the Delawares

1782—Chickasaw Peace Treaty Feeler

1784—Treaty with the Six Nations

1785—Treaty with the Wyandot, Etc.

1785—Treaty with the Cherokee

1786—Treaty with the Choctaw

17 . . . you get the idea.

But I feel like this one will stick. I got a good feeling about this one. Do these things and we'll shut the fuck up:

THE OFFICIAL TREATY ENDING THE 400-YEAR CONFLICT BETWEEN AMERICA AND PEOPLE OF COLOR

Preamble: A Peace Treaty Between
White America and Black Folks

The search for peace between races must be guided by the following:

Black folks ("African Americans," "people of color," "those people") have decided, after four hundred years of oppression and discrimination, to come to the table and issue demands for a lasting peace with their oppressors. That's mighty big of them.

White people ("America"), having determined to hold a conference with the black folks, for the purpose of removing from their minds all causes of complaint, making them stop grousing, posting annoying memes to social media, and otherwise throwing shade, and establishing a firm and permanent friendship with them, recognize D.L. Hughley as sole agent for that purpose and affirm their intent to come to terms.

Recognizing that it is in the interest of all that racial harmony be established and racial animus shall no longer be the default;

Acknowledging that cooperation in this goal is of the essence and necessary, that peace may prosper, even if that means talking about things that upset the apple cart;

Acknowledging also that everyone's been a little hot under the collar for a while about all this stuff;

Convinced that the establishment of a firm foundation for the continuation and development of such cooperation on the basis of mutual understanding accords with the interests of harmony and peace;

Convinced also that a treaty ensuring this peace, by nature, must be specific and must cut the treacle;

Now, in order to accomplish the good design of this conference, the parties have agreed on the following articles, which, when ratified, shall be fully binding.

ARTICLE I: WHITE PEOPLE SHALL CONSIDER REPARATIONS

Despite the protests of Mitch McConnell and other white conservatives, a good-faith effort shall be made to make amends to black people. Just like the Italians and Japanese, we want an apology, if not a little walking-around money. Furthermore:

REPARATIONS ARTICLE 1A. CHICKEN DISCOUNT

It is thus decided that due to the Popeyes chicken sandwich being much beloved in the black community, but in suspiciously short supply, all such sandwiches shall be offered to black folks at a three-fifths discount.

REPARATIONS ARTICLE 1B. NIPSEY HALL

In recognition of the fact that buildings are named after old white guys, some of whom were involved in the very systemic racism and oppression that have brought us to this fraught moment of racial tension, we hereby establish a new naming criterion for buildings in universities, cities, and other public institutions. Consideration shall be given to badass, dope niggas whose time passed too soon and who might not previously have been accepted as people to bear in tribute.

ARTICLE II: HISTORY BOOKS
SHALL BE ALIGNED

In order for black folks and white people to further understand one another, our history books must be aligned with the facts, agreed upon by both parties and taken into account.

ARTICLE III: WE SHALL ENDEAVOR
TO UNDERSTAND ONE ANOTHER

As we come to live together more and more, conflicts ensue and must be defused. We must attempt to understand each other and our motives. Furthermore:

REPARATIONS ARTICLE 3A.
STATUTE OF STATUE LIMITATIONS

White people having gotten overly attached to bronze statues of racists, and having erected statues anywhere they could in an effort to remind black people of who was in charge, now agree to end the practice of erecting new bronze statues. Bronze, a possibly racist alloy, will be replaced as a building material by plaster of Paris, Play-Doh, or some other temporary building material. New statues will be limited to a seven-year erection, which is more than you need anyway, in most instances.

REPARATIONS ARTICLE 3B.
BLACKFACE FOR WHITE FOLKS

White people, having embraced blackface as a fun dress-up tool, having enjoyed Halloween parties in the 1980s, having engaged in racist skits during fraternity parties of the 1990s, and having celebrated such problematic frivolity by documenting black-face in uncountable yearbook pages, shall henceforth be held blameless. Their love of Michael Jackson is hereby affirmed, and their right to wear blackface is retained. This privilege is restricted, however, to Election Day, bank loan interviews, and any other occasion where historical discrimination against people of color has been exhibited.

REPARATIONS ARTICLE 3C.
BLACK EYES FOR THE WHITE GUY

It is thus decided, Hollywood's top writers and producers must be brought together in pursuit of a relatable black comedy or makeover show for the masses. We need some of that creativity put in service of making people like us more. We want some shit on Netflix, on NBC, heck, even something that can run on CBS to catch some old white people after *NCIS*.

REPARATIONS ARTICLE 3D. DON'T CALL ME THE N-WORD WHILE I'M EATING

Racism has no place in America, and certainly not in a Buffalo Wild Wings or a Papa John's. Herewith, black people shall eat in peace, without having to deal with slurs and antagonism. Polite dinner conversation only, please.

REPARATIONS ARTICLE 3E. WE KEEP MAC AND CHEESE AND HALL AND OATES

Lest the foodstuffs and music much adored by all peoples become the subject of continuous wrangling and conflict, we heresoforwith declare cultural appropriation to be approved for use by all peoples. Just don't be a big jerk about it.

REPARATIONS ARTICLE 3F. BING ONLY

In consideration of Google's accurate search results, which serve only to dredge up true, horrible, unpleasant facts that make white people feel bad, all black people are hereby sentenced to use Bing only for searches, so that the information is less true, less accurate, and less painful.

Reparations Article 3G.
We Get to Be Average

Until such a time as the number of average black folks equals the number of average white folks in positions of power, acclaim, and wealth, black people shall herewith be allowed to be "normal," "average," and "unremarkable" without being deemed deficient. Until such a time as the amount of "remarkable" white people in charge of things, held up for praise, or otherwise regarded as successful increases, black people shall enjoy the same respect for being average as their white peers, suffering no penalty.

Reparations Article 3H. Take Kanye

Kanye is yours. He's an honorary white guy now. Since he likes to hang out with Trump so much and spout a bunch of crazy nonsense all the time, we trade him to you.

Reparations Article 3I.
White Black People

On the condition that you live like a black person but are in all other respects white, if you're forgotten, ignored, disrespected, economically disadvantaged, picked on, and stressed, you are henceforth, for all intents and purposes, a black person.

REPARATIONS ARTICLE 3J. IF YOU'RE BLACK, YOU'RE BLACK, UNLESS YOU'RE NOT

Excluding those already denoted by name (Kanye et al.), if you are black, you are black. No trading in your blackness until we've sorted this whole thing out.

REPARATIONS ARTICLE 3K. PERSONAL DAYS

All holidays must herewith be evaluated as a whole; i.e., all holidays will be put on a probationary period to ascertain their relevance and value to all Americans. Acknowledging that days off are nice and that mattress sales must occur, a number of holidays shall be continued, but no current holiday will by reason of tradition be kept without scrutiny. MLK Day excluded, because you already tried to take that shit away.

ARTICLE IV: WE SHALL DEAL WITH THE WHITE SUPREMACY PROBLEM

White supremacy, a loathsome American tradition, must be dealt with. Furthermore:

REPARATIONS ARTICLE 4A. FULL EMPLOYMENT FOR RACISTS

Acknowledging that "idle hands are the devil's playthings," and in consideration of the long history of idle racists stirring up trouble, ascribing their woes to the gainfully employed of other races, all efforts shall be made to keep racists employed, with job training to put their "skills" to good use.

REPARATIONS ARTICLE 4B. JESUS IN DA CLUB

To restore historical accuracy to the Jesus beloved by white nationalists and black folk alike, and to hopefully make Jesus a bit more accountable to everyone, regardless of the color of their skin, blond-haired, blue-eyed Jesuses shall henceforth be replaced with black Jesuses, modeled after 50 Cent. Jesus will still have abs, just black abs. Also, when there's a manger scene: let's get some black sheep up in that shit too.

ARTICLE V: WE SHALL BE UN-OPPRESSED

In America, we are still oppressed. In housing and wealth we are left behind. In health, we suffer. The South is still a big fucking problem. In justice and policing, we are discriminated against and abused. This oppression must be countered and lifted! Furthermore:

REPARATIONS ARTICLE 5A. SAILING SEASON-TICKET HOLDERS

All supporters of sports of dubious import, the sole purpose of which is admitting their children into college, shall be subject to season-pass requirements. Archery, rowing, fencing, jousting, dressage, or any other stupid sport shall be canceled if there are not enough white parents in attendance at the matches. In addition, every white season-ticket holder for an NCAA basketball or football team shall also be a season-ticket holder for the water polo team.

REPARATIONS ARTICLE 5B. PAY UP, OR RUGBY

The sport of rugby, being abhorrent in nature, undesirable to both black and white, who do both enjoy the Sundays spent watching "the Big Game," shall henceforth be set aside in favor of keeping black athletes playing ball. Black athletes will play ball if white supporters will likewise play ball, financing historically black colleges and universities, paying athletes their worth, and generally respecting the fact that nobody would give a fuck about Alabama without Tua Tagovailoa.

REPARATIONS ARTICLE 5C. TRUTH IN ADVERTISING

White people, being beneficiaries of racist housing policies, having written the rules to ensure all-white suburbs, and having extended opportunity to whites only, shall henceforth retain their cherished lies about the lack of privilege and opportunity that they had. Not having lacked for privilege and opportunity, they shall nonetheless henceforth have the privilege and opportunity of lack: that is, they shall retain the opportunity to say they did not have much, grew up in humble circumstances, are self-made in every way. However, if a place is named in such recollections, if an anecdote of their upbringing is in the offing, they must amend the place-name with the preface "All-White" to bring a bit of truth to the lie.

REPARATIONS ARTICLE 5D. TAKE IT EASY PASS

Until such a time as highways are put through white neighborhoods, and in consideration of the inequal use of eminent domain, the building of highway projects in black neighborhoods, and the drawbacks that accrue therefrom, black people shall be issued Easy Passes that provide discounted (free) tolls for all highways.

REPARATIONS ARTICLE 5E.
NEAR OUR HOUSES: ACTUAL FOOD

We need actual food in our neighborhoods: quality grocery stores with fresh fruit, vegetables, and meats. For the purposes of this agreement, neither a pile of bananas by the cash register nor any meat in a can shall constitute "fresh," regardless of the packaging's claims. We want real restaurants and coffee shops; the McCafé section of a McDonald's shall not count. We want environmental justice, so that we don't have to use Fabuloso to scrub out the pollutants in our homes. We want that fresh pine smell and that fresh clean air you all got.

REPARATIONS ARTICLE 5F.
BLACK NEIGHBORHOOD REHAB

It's makeover time for black neighborhoods, due to the lead pipes and paint. We hereby demand that the HGTV network send some of their experts in to get the lead out and spruce the place up, preferably that Chip and Joanna couple, as long as Chip keeps the corny jokes to a minimum. If they are busy, we'll take the Property Brothers.

REPARATIONS ARTICLE 5G.
STAY RACIST, MEDICALLY

White people, unable to eliminate racism and bias in all forms, are hereby allowed to remain racist in matters of prescribing medicine, especially opioids and pain medications. With expanded access to health care, we understand that risks to us increase, but we'll worry about that when y'all approve Obamacare's Medicaid expansion anywhere in the South at all. In the meantime, if a wealthy black person requires pain meds, please remember that he "Got the Look" of a black dude, so he ain't "Free Fallin'" into a coma.

REPARATIONS ARTICLE 5H.
REVERSE LOUISIANA PURCHASE

White people, having worked very hard to retain the South during the Civil War and having used voter suppression and other tactics to retain power, shall be given the South—just not all the good parts—to do with as they wish. No federal funds (handouts) nor voting powers beyond local control shall be retained, to make sure that the South can credibly claim the right to say they are self-sufficient. Let them build pride in their work, allow them the dignity of work.

REPARATIONS ARTICLE 5I. WEED WHARTON

Upon ratification of this treaty, marijuana companies (weed businesses, marijuana holding companies, etc.) shall recruit their executives exclusively from the ranks of those incarcerated for doing an excellent job selling weed previously. This shall be the primary consideration for employment, not being in a hedge fund, investment partnership, management trust, or any other bullshit.

REPARATIONS ARTICLE 5J.
TAKE US INTO CUSTODY

Although black people shall endeavor to be blameless in all respects, on the occasion of a dispute wherein the police or other law enforcement shall be called to mediate, we require an expansion of our options. No longer shall police shoot first, having been "scared" or having "perceived a threat." Police shall be required to treat white and black suspects the same, with the option to "apprehend" or "take into custody."

REPARATIONS ARTICLE 5K.
THE WHITE CASTLE DOCTRINE

Due to the historic infiltration of law enforcement by racists and white supremacists, and in consideration of the fact that White Castle serves up food without calling anyone the N-word, we now require personnel decisions to be made by the White Castle human resources department, until such a time as racists are rooted out of the police, border security, and so on.

In the event of a dispute, White Castle HR can ask Taco Bell HR to arbitrate.

REPARATIONS ARTICLE 5L. STAY PUT

Whenever white people wander around, black and brown people die. Now that there are multiple streaming platforms, there's no need to go out quite so much. Stay home, enjoy a night in so that we may also enjoy a night in or out. White people, especially cops, are hereby ordered to stay in and binge-watch some of the new offerings on Apple TV+ or Hulu before they start going around exploring, and possibly killing.

ARTICLE VI: WE ARE PART OF AMERICA

We're not going anywhere. As such, we demand full access to America, with full rights and privileges thereof. Furthermore:

REPARATIONS ARTICLE 6A.
IT'S CURTAINS FOR CURTAINS

White people can have sheer curtains only. Full transparency means full transparency. Maybe you can have those beaded curtains. But no drapes. Venetian blinds are okay, as long as they are partway open. You can use shutters the same way, because we know you all love those. Wiping out prejudice and bias will take time, and until then we want to keep an eye on you all. Justice is blind. Justice has blinds.

Reparations Article 6b. Invisible Men

Henceforth there shall be inclusion and diversity in the realm of the imaginary, the made-up, and the fantastical. There are real black people and there shall thus be unreal black people. The world of make-believe, science fiction, fantasy, and any other genre of fancy, reverie, or invention shall be open to black imaginary people. This shall include but not be limited to imaginary friends, fictional characters, spies, phantoms, and ghosts.

Huh. You know, I look at all the proposals and I worry that it's still not gonna work. So let's just put it this way:

We want to be part of America. Maybe you still won't agree to giving us money, but if you agree that you won't kill us without anybody being brought to account, if you agree that you're not going to discriminate against us in your laws and practices, if you agree to come to terms with the history of this country and our shared place in it, and if you agree that you're not going to deny us a fair and equitable opportunity to a reasonable life, that would be a start. *Life, Liberty and the pursuit of Happiness,* right?

SIGNATURE PAGE

NOTE: Must be signed by all white people. Please pass along to your white friends like a chain letter. Oh, wait . . . did I say "chain"? My bad. We probably shouldn't be talking about chains at this time, but I'm just saying make sure everybody gets this thing. There's less and less white folks, but there's still a lot, so don't skip nobody.

Please sign below to agree to the treaty. I already added my John Hancock:

If you are unable to make it to the signing of our treaty at the Magic Johnson Theatre on the date the treaty is ratified, don't worry. You can still be a part of history by signing on to the pledge below!

INSTRUCTIONS:

1. Fill out the form below.

2. If you're black, no postage necessary. Doesn't it feel good to be the winner?

3. If you're white: Come on, man; after all this, you still want us to pay for your postage? You have the fucking money. Consider your stamp a down payment on your reparations.

CUT HERE
··

☑YES, I SURRENDER! I want to agree to the above terms and take responsibility for making the world a better place by acknowledging the wisdom and truth contained in this peace treaty.

☐ No, I am still in denial and don't wish to be part of the solution. I'd rather keep the systemic oppression, aggravation, and fading social status of white supremacy. In supplying my contact information, I acknowledge that any information provided may be used in further enforcement actions.

Name: Address: City, State, Zip Code:	To: I Surrender! P.O. Box 555 New York, NY 11111

ACKNOWLEDGMENTS

I want to thank my literary crew: my editor Peter Hubbard, my collaborator Doug Moe, and my agent Richard Abate. I'm grateful for my radio family: David Kantor, Skip Cheatham, and Jasmine Sanders. Thanks to Leyna Santos; Yvette Shearer; my Comedy Get Down brothers, Eddie Griffin, Cedric "The Entertainer," and George Lopez; my road team, Gary Monroe, Lew Oliver, and Derek Robles! Thanks also to my managers Michael Rotenberg and Dave Becky, my agent Nick Nuciforo, my dude Kensation Johnson, and my right-hand Sonya Vaughn. Thank you, Molly Gendell, Anwesha Basu, and Kayleigh George. Love to my family: my children, Ryan, Kyle, and Tyler, and my sexy-ass wife, LaDonna Hughley.